GRAND CENTAUR STATION

ALSO BY LARRY FROLICK

Splitting Up: Divorce, Culture, and the Search for Real Life (1998)
Ten Thousand Scorpions: The Search for the Queen of Sheba's Gold (2002)

GRAND CENTAUR STATION

Unruly Living with the New Nomads of Central Asia

LARRY FROLICK

Maps and Illustrations by Steve Wilson

M&S

National Library of Canada Cataloguing in Publication

Frolick, Larry
Grand Centaur Station : unruly living with the new nomads of Central Asia /
Larry Frolick ; maps and illustrations by Steve Wilson.

Includes bibliographical references.
ISBN 0-7710-4782-7

1. Frolick, Larry – Travel – Asia, Central.   2. Asia, Central – Description and travel.   I. Wilson, Steve, 1972-   II. Title.

DS327.8.F76 2004   915.804'43   C2003-906680-0

We acknowledge the financial support of the Government of Canada through the Book Publishing Industry Development Program and that of the Government of Ontario through the Ontario Media Development Corporation's Ontario Book Initiative. We further acknowledge the support of the Canada Council for the Arts and the Ontario Arts Council for our publishing program.

Typeset in Minion by M&S, Toronto
Printed and bound in Canada

This book is printed on acid-free paper that is
100% ancient forest friendly (100% post-consumer recycled).

McClelland & Stewart Ltd.
The Canadian Publishers
481 University Avenue
Toronto, Ontario
M5G 2E9
www.mcclelland.com

1   2   3   4   5   08   07   06   05   04

To the memory of my parents,
Stanley Frolick and Gloria Kupchenko

"I'm the Devil, I have no home."
  – *The Tale of Savva Grudtsyn*,
  a seventeenth-century Russian folk tale

Contents

Author's Note   xi

Introduction: The Muzhik   1

PART ONE
Red
Circle Against the Square

1. Shadows of Forgotten Ancestors   9
2. Crime and Disorder (*Repeat*)   26
3. She Called Me a Romantic, the Bitch!   40
4. The Interpenetration of Light with Sorrow   50
5. Elektro-Shock Lady in La-La Land   64
6. To the Dacha with Two Monsters   74
7. Is This Yours?   85
8. Everyone's Dandy in Goon City   98
9. The Two-Centimetre Question   108
10. Spiritual Danger   120
11. The Styx Is a River That Runs from the Heart   130
12. Flatheads at Twelve O'Clock High   134
13. Crocodile *Shaslyk*, Anyone?   148
14. The Square Is the Icon of Our Age   157

PART TWO
Black
Beyond the Urals

15. The Choice Between Italian Shoes and the Exotic   165
16. Pahlavan Makhmud: Poet, Champion Wrestler,   176
    and Occasional Hat-Maker
17. Three Girls Named Star   186

18. At the Sign of the Blue Tongue   197
19. Who Was Natalie Wood?   211
20. Notes from the Underground   218
21. To the Summer Pastures   233
22. *Lonely Penitent's* Guide to the World's Worst Trips   248
23. Welcome to Kashgar City, Big Noses   257
24. The House of Stones and Earth   267
25. The Yellow King's Kids   276
26. Nocturnal Brightness: 283
    The Gods of Cloud, Rain, Wind, and Thunder

PART THREE
White
Life as a Horse

27. Midnight Border Crossing   291
28. The Bare Texts of Its Boundaries   296
29. Karakorum   303
30. So What Is Your National Pride?   315
31. Twenty-One Taras, *or*, I Married a Mongolian Train-Trader   323
32. Baikal   329
33. About the Dress They Sold the Cow For   335

    Epilogue: The Joke   346
    Acknowledgements   347
    Some Classic Works for Further Reading   348

Author's Note

The attentive reader will no doubt discover many flaming dysphasias, disgruntled participles, and cryptic solecisms running freely through these pages: the culprit stands before you, already bored with the subject, and looking elsewhere for his amusement. No attempt at a definitive account has been made. The transliteration of Cyrillic and other curious alphabets aims only for internal consistency, not the conquest of graduate school. Readers seeking an authoritative text are advised to consult Professor Nestor Malenky-Pupchyk's comprehensive ten-volume opus, *Ergodynamical Statistical Factors & Micro-Hagiographies of the Post-Soviet Regime*, a joint venture of Oxford, Harvard, and Duke of Earl University (Emerald City Campus) due for publication in May 2019.

Introduction: The Muzhik

It's late May, the summer of Central Asia is approaching fast, and the pasty-faced office manager of the Eastern European travel agency is telling me how to avoid getting robbed. In these brave new ex-Soviet democracies, he says the real trick these days is to dress down. Totally.

"When I go, I put on my oldest coat," Ihor, whose name would be Igor if he were of Russian descent, not Ukrainian, informs me with the air of an old hand. "And real crappy shoes. They never bother me. I pay the local rate for everything instead of the tourist rate. Which can be ten times higher, right?"

Judging from his proletarian attire, a shapeless dun jacket and baggy pants, all worn with an attitude of weary insouciance in a shabby office on the bleakest stretch of Bloor Street West, Ihor at the best of times wasn't exactly the Beau Brummell of Eastern European tourism. Dressing down obviously involved full-scale Shakespeare. Bit player, low theatre. The sort of mufti that celebrated hoodwinkers like Sir Richard Burton or Archie Grey Owl wore, when they passed themselves off as Malemuk atamans and Ojibwa shamans. My job was simpler: I merely wanted to look like an apparatchik who had blindly survived the Purges.

Winston Smith with a box camera.

"Here's the dough." I hand over a serious bank draft. Ihor doesn't even look at it.

"And watch out for the meat, huh?" he adds by way of afterthought.

"The meat?" I stare at my newly minted ticket. Was he talking about real meat or ...?

He gives me a significant look.

"Yeah, sausages, especially. You can never tell."

My excursion into Central Asia and its awful history began, as most bizarre excursions from ordinary life do, suddenly. In a flash of delirious insight. With a recovered memory . . .

My sister, Christine, was packing up her stuff, leaving the city for good. The Big Smoke had finally won, she couldn't stand it any more, she was headed off for a One-Horse Town. The city traffic, ruthless, the kids in her class swearing like bikers on crack. I'm helping with the cardboard boxes, listening, nodding agreeably at her brave assertions, how great Barrie is going to be, cheap tennis and neighbourly barbecues every Sunday. I'm also feeling monumentally defeated. Our parents ran like hell from a one-horse town, now their baby daughter is going back for the free parking. Potluck Fridays and snowmobiles, kiss the jazzy riffs farewell.

I'm brooding about her stuff too. It's depressing. Her house is a diorama of the family's karma in heavy furniture, a museum of parental endowments. The white five-ton piano, lumpy Persian carpets, tippy Chinese screens, chintz couches, a million vases – all the height of the Riverside Drive School of Decorating, *circa* 1965. Something slides out of the walnut sideboard.

"Hey, what's this?" A purple watercolour. I pick it up gingerly. "Jesus. Chris!"

She turns at the sharp spike in my voice. "What's wrong?"

"This! I remember this picture. Where's the *other* one?"

"The other one?"

A pause while the computer in her head whirs away. "Oh. It's there too."

I retrieve the other picture, the yellow one, and place them side by side.

Together again. The two pictures that gave me nightmares as a child.

When I was seven, my parents hung these two pictures on our plain, beige living-room walls. Two mesmerizing watercolours. The one over the sofa was a moody scene, two men on horseback, laughing as they galloped past a burning European village at night. The men had slanted eyes and hooded leather caps with jutting earflaps. Laughing *ha ha ha*. Even their shaggy steeds showed a vulpine joy in the havoc they had just wreaked on everything in sight. The turgid purple sky, the oppressive hinterland, the pall of unmoving smoke. These details spoke a grave warning about the long night of history past, a brutal past that remained unredeemed, sinful, and terrible.

Where was the justice in their savage laughter?

It was out of place, this watercolour, an alien presence in our mock-Tudor house in the Kingsway, sitting quietly on its tree-lined avenue. The familiar cycle of seasonal rites, the burning of oak leaves in fall, the shovelling of snow so pure it stayed blue into late winter, it all kept us safe and happy. Our neighbourhood was a cheerful haven, far removed from the conflagrations of the Old World. We were safe. But that picture, above the brocaded couch.

And those eyes, slits of flame.

Tartars, my mother called them, a daughter of Ukrainian-Canadian Alberta pioneers who had forgotten nothing from events eight hundred years ago. She repeated the word so that I would make no mistake about it. Tartars ... whose job it was to burn our cities and laugh about it. Tartars, a Greek word for men from hell, *Tartarus* – to be distinguished from the Tartars of modern history, an ethnic group in Crimea who told their own epic of ruin and close escape. Wasn't this the only lesson History gave us? That these rootless, shiftless hordes, the nomads of Asia, would come again one day and burn everything in sight for the hell of it? Wasn't "history" the last record of these ashes, the hasty notes scrawled by freaked-out scribes who couldn't believe what they had just seen, who had witnessed the collapse of their mother-nation, and who needed to commit the terrible sight to writing in a shuddering prayer of the highest order?

That was what this picture said to me, age seven. In the beige living room on White Oak Boulevard, with its rose bushes and weeping-willow tree. That history was a mere polygraph of an unending struggle between settled and nomadic states, between houses and horses, its valleys and crests marked in the deep violations of red and black. There was more import to this small watercolour than to a Byzantine icon or scientific journal, and heavy predictive power too:

It all disappears in a flash.

Was September 11 merely an echo of this past revelation, a foretaste of things to come? I had been to the Ma'rib desert in Yemen, the alleged training ground of the terrorists, only a few months before the attack on New York. Was the shocking raid the beginning of yet another long cycle of staccato violence, the uncanny attacks on the West coupled to our pre-emptive strikes in response, a deadly pas de deux that might easily abridge the centuries from one grand civilization to its mysterious and devastatingly powerful successor, as soon as the music died? Well, there was only one way to find out, wasn't there? To go there, straight into the rude, throbbing heart of the Asian steppe, and enter the infamous torch-city, which these civicidal passions claimed as their font, inspiration, and sanctuary from the beginning of recorded time. History's volcanic maw itself:

Outer Mongolia.

Across the room hung the *other* picture, the mailed warrior on his black stallion. The Avenging Prince, as I called him. Where the two marauders sprang like rabid wolves from the slurry East, the unprovidential left, our Prince boldly cantered in from the right, in the full flower of his manhood, peerless and self-assured. What was he doing here, alone in this sunlit grove of birch trees? Riding eastward, surely, to redress the scales of history. To assert (as I conceived it) the power of the noble and true, over the cunning, mindless horde.

Would he win his impending battle?

He had to, he must! For if he failed, all was lost. Here and everywhere. Yes here, in the defenceless world right outside my bedroom window. Our snug brick houses and carefully raked yards. Robins and roses, a white poodle barking. Pillage and ruin awaited us, no mercy after nightfall. The only question was, When? At what hour would they come, these wolf-men?

According to the logic of the first picture, when we least expected it.

Okay, now for the coup de grâce, I said to myself as I perused the smoke-stale inventory at Value Village, a second-hand thrift store whose financial success in this country demonstrated either the scandal of middle-class impoverishment or the triumph of renewable resources, depending on your thinking.

Eighteen bucks for the plaid wool topcoat or $21.95 for the poplin number with the coffee stain at the hem? Hmmm. I had already picked out my trousers, charcoal gabardine with hard pleats that would keep until Judgment Day. But the overcoat was important, the overcoat was the big gun of my apparatchik's wardrobe, my soon-to-be-adopted Eastern persona: the muzhik, the varlet who keeps a low profile, forever ducking the State's fatal clutches.

"Was this Raskolnikov?" I looked deep in the mirror for the sallow, God-fearing axe-murderer of *Crime and Punishment*. Or was it more your Chichikov, the clandestine creepy hero of *Dead Souls*? Could I skulk at will through the subterranean train stations of Kiev and Moscow, lose myself in an unkempt mass of unemployed office workers? Eat raw garlic and pick my teeth with the best of them? Sour cabbages and umbrellas; it was all coming back to me now. Russian Lit. 201. The famously unwashed characters, their shabby little rooms and candlelit frenzies. Big questions and hard drink, long past midnight. The whole arcana of metaphysical dissolution, numb pantomimes of besotted muzhiks and dispirited intelligentsia. Insane laughter and belligerent mummery, untranslatable epiphanies at page 934.

I practised my repertoire. The slight stoop, the dull, boiled gaze. The affronted glare. *Sche raz*, I muttered under my breath.

Gimme another one.

These were my tools, my strengths: a penchant for homemade method acting (Stanislavsky claimed you never created characters, you simply let them out of your brown paper bag), an avidity for vulgarisms, and this unshakeable interest in gruesome street-skits. Such appetites would undoubtedly stand me in good stead in the land of Ilya Kuryakin and Igor Kropotkin. I would study their Byzantine phrases, commit the ornate curlicues of Cyrillic to memory, no problem. *Bez problemy.*

Teeth-chattering, scurvy retorts to balky officialdom, merciless gold-toothed sub-lieutenants staring at my ticket. *Khto? Ya?* Who, me? Could I make it, twelve thousand kilometres or so, trudging over the toxic post-Chernobyl hinterlands, alone in cheap shoes? Pass myself off?

Ya ne znaiu.

Me-no-know.

The all-important overcoat taken care of, I needed only to choose my reading material. Careful now. Perhaps a meaty novel for the long and airless trans-Siberian train? Only please don't let me end like Dr. Zhivago, clutching at my ruptured heart as I topple over the edge of Platform 19. Was it now or never for *War and Peace*? Into the rucksack it went, a thirty-year-old student copy. Virginal, never cracked open. The rabid dreams came soon enough, the same evening. Zhivago and the Czarina's confessor, deranged Rasputin himself, plotting upstairs. Something unsightly rotting away in the dank cellar below. Reading doesn't help.

I turn on the lamp and open *Crime and Punishment* at random:

"Ha, ha! Clever, very clever! You notice everything at once, don't you? See the funny side of everything at once. Ha ha! They say of all our writers Gogol possessed this gift to the highest degree!"

Here it is, on page 346. The murderer Raskolnikov is discussing *prior* Russian literature, while playing cat and mouse with his bloody conscience, in the middle of his *own* novel. Ha ha! What was this? Talk about circular trajectories! It was mind-boggling. Self-consciousness was the great fiend of Slavic novels, and precious sentimentality, its little goblin-helper.

I shut off the light again and try to think of Lara. Fragrant Lara, lonely as an untended wood stove in her crystal ice palace. No Lara. Instead I get Lidia, the hollow-eyed young widow on the Web site Ukrainianwomenwanttomeetyou.com.ua, whose heartfelt personalized message in its entirety announced:

Two years my husband night kill, pistol.
Car robbers. I want meet good man, no drink.

I sink down on my bed like a spent cog. Exhausted by my prodigiously Slavic mental labours. Could I do this? Travel alone through the steppe lands that had killed generations before me, just for looking the wrong way? Who should I be? Ladies and gentlemen, meet Dr. Eugene Puriatkin, employee of the Institute of Advanced Borehole Studies. A statistician or perhaps assistant Bureau Chief, hale enough from a steady diet of his aged mother's potato dumplings, perhaps heaped with fresh sour cream bought with her dinky pension money. But a little distracted, shiftless you might say. An insincere fellow from whom I got the vaguest feelings that I would get to know him better. Indeed, far better than I ever cared to, in those long and meatless months, closing in like steel storm clouds on the coal-fired horizon just ahead.

PART ONE

Red

Circle Against the Square

Chapter 1

Shadows of Forgotten Ancestors

The story of the settled farmer and lawless nomad is ten thousand years old. It is cast in the paired figures of our daily bread and wild caprice, forever slipping away. Who can recall the Bible's hairy tattooed Esau, or imagine anything of his solitary hunter's life before he arrives at the ancestral table, rude with woodsmoke from his trackless forest, a triumph of natural odds? He doesn't want his fair share either. Deeming it worthless, he'll sell it back to us for a trifle. He looks at us with easy contempt, we hate his nonchalance and indifference to good chairs. He'll steal something before he leaves at dawn; yes, even a child if she's young enough and susceptible to the morning's new light. He always takes something far more valuable, however: our sense that we are complete.

In the myth-laden 1965 Ukrainian film, *Shadows of Forgotten Ancestors*, the hero loses his blonde, deerlike wife and must marry again, this time choosing a black-haired she-demon who practises Siberian witchcraft and brings down disaster from a livid sky. The film's intended audience understands that Tamara is the Mongol bride of berserker history, the usurper who will always come west when she needs fresh blood. They understand also that as a nation they have two mothers, and the dark one is to be resisted only on pain of death.

Historians of preliterate Europe have no problem dressing up this recurrent myth in the multiple effects of its archaeological remains, an abundant pottery that tends to show long periods of stasis, truncated by countless cultural irruptions from the south and east. It's a story of arrival and sudden disappearance, a clock with a thirteenth hour. It's a chronicle that takes place behind a murky curtain of smouldering ash, the frontier of Asia where former kings rot in wooden birdcages and Europe bleeds off into stinking river-mud. The name of this place is Ukraine, a condition of permanent extremes, which translated from Old Slavic means *borderless*. It's a reality that is always in flux, a heaving land of vast rivers and hidden dangers. I had visited it before, in history books.

It is easy to imagine the hazy wilderness of Eastern Europe before the arrival of the ancestral Slavs, six thousand years ago. The winding rivers of the Pripet Marshes straddling Ukraine and Russia rolled along much as they do now, effortlessly cutting their way through a black fundament laden with soft loess and stippled with sweet poplars, a pliant soil that could be worked with simple ashwood implements. The Vened waggoners, who had entered the river basin from an extended trek that began far to the south by the Caspian Sea, quickly spread themselves around the vast, swan-filled marshes, dividing themselves into eastern and western branches. Their astonished eyes feasted on these promises of plentitude, the myriad ponds and clear springs multiplied their reflections everywhere they cared to look. Beech trees grew straight and tall, free of the harsh gales of a distant homeland. Such green trees! Lovely as girls!

And beyond the wood's edge, knolled meadows beckoned; the immigrants did not need the anxious bellowing of their sharp-horned cattle to heed the new grass, for they had inhaled its sweetness for themselves. This was the place.

But they were not alone on this misty frontier. Red-painted bowmen hid themselves behind the larch groves, watching with curiosity and alarm. These were archaic Finn-speakers, distantly related to Turkic tribes living a full continent away. Their deceptively modest ochre intaglios marked the entrance to hidden caves and shrines of supernatural power. They had abided in these marshlands forever, wary deer hunters. According to their traditions, they had been slapped into existence out of red river clay, an afterthought by a forgetful Hunter – his familiar adventures made them laugh and cry with equal shudders of delight. For a hundred generations they had followed the Pleistocene big game, until the great beasts had disappeared with the onset of warmer climes; now they subsisted on lesser creatures that required more skill and less appetite. They knew these lands like the inside of their bellies. Empty or full, it was home. They were compelled to know everything; for it was all one, this World, the campfire of a roving trickster, who warmed himself on the fate of many. They knew the hidden copses and aimless ravines in a way these noisy invaders never would, collecting wild honey, trading furs and amber, trailing non-barking dogs, and moving silently from winter hut to summer camp, following the game, the red deer, wild boar, and brown bear; and coming together in fall to spear sturgeon in the pools from bobbing bark craft. Now things had changed. Now the insistent ringing of axes announced the plans of the sturdy Veneds. The farmers had come to stay.

The newcomers had arrived with their stock animals and rye and barley crops, moving slowly up along the shallow riverbanks, carefully choosing stable promontories for constructing palisaded longhouses, much like the native peoples of the Americas would build in a distant future. These habitations were more than sixty feet long and twenty feet deep, stripped cedar logs joined without nails or pegs. It was a lot of work, using only stone tools and the tricks of controlled fire, but work was what they were accustomed to, work made them who they were. They all joined in, sonorously chanting, men, women, and children, to get the complex of wooden fences and pens and lookouts finished by winter; their rhythmic worksongs ceased only at dusk. The dormitories were big enough to house the communal *vetch* or *rid*, the whole clan. Some of their dwellings were erected on pillars, allowing their half-wild animals to sleep on the sheltered ground below. The first time an ochre-painted hunter was tempted to shoot a wandering cow was his last; the Veneds immediately showed up in force, killed or wounded anyone who didn't flee, and deliberately burnt the tiny hamlet of rush huts to the ground.

These rye farmers worshipped their ancestors, propitiated them on feast days, greeting them with the formal compliments such ghostly apparitions demanded, feeding them choice ritual dishes at the communal table, and saying farewell in a singsong of tears and hoarse cries of passionate yearning. They burned abstract effigies of straw and twigs, and threw them into the river, watching them fizzle away downstream towards the great ancestral sea. The horse-headed inland sea, the heavenly Caspian. More astonishing, they replicated their entire world in miniature. They painstakingly constructed clay models of their dwellings and, after firing them in oak-fed kilns, lined them up on high rafters in perfect unanimity, to serve as sanctuaries for the Shadows until the height of summer, Midsummer's Eve.

Come Kupalo, the longest day of the year, when glorious Hors had risen high above the earth, as far as he could, and below him the whole universe came together – the past, the present, and the future, all temporarily visible as if seen from a high peak (the elders still remembered this mountain, a real crag in the Caucasus, Elbrus, whose snows had glittered since the beginning of Time, the crackling thunder-throne of Indra or Odin or Perun or Zeus, a peak their scattered children would soon forget) – come Kupalo, the feast day of Little-Man, and the clay houses would be washed meticulously with spring water and taken with great pomp and comic songs down to the river. They would be carefully passed through clouds of hemp and poppy smoke, commingling from two ritual fires, one male, one female. The villagers would break bread with salt, and sprinkle them both on the living waters for Marena, goddess of fertility. Maybe they would kill a slave, a prisoner, if they had one; but certainly a fat boar would meet its end by midday, for there would be no sleeping tonight, the guests would get hungry from the dancing and great gluts of freshly drawn barley beer and insidious hemp fumes. A child conceived tonight would inherit the whole power of the clan; he or she would be born at the auspicious vernal equinox and given a special name. Borys for boys, Bohuslava for girls. Heavensent.

The clan, the *rid*, was an indivisible whole, consisting of the living, the dead, and the yet unborn; there was protection in this arrangement, and a transcendent joy, a whole cloth in which the female was the warp, and the male, the woof. All things were sex-gendered, all things were roots and seeds of the Unseen, and everything contained the dormant power of pro-creation and life. Did not the whole world spring anew from the hardest things? The lifeless barley kernel and tiniest poppy seed? Even the wondrous visions that issued forth from the poppy smoke, this blood-stopping flower they had carried from their lost plateau, even this phantasmic dream-world grew from a black sprinkle of near-dust. The Vened maidens garlanded themselves with the voluptuous scarlet poppies, sang their lewd songs, and danced a saucy two-step clockwise around a *baba*, or grandmother pole, a stone idol whose ambivalent sexual features marked the exclamation point of Creation, where all things converged.

Six months to the hour later, on the shortest day of the year, when the thunder-god Perun endured his annual torments in the cold blasts of the underworld, or in another version of the myth, visited his Mother, *Tabitia* (She-Who-Holds-the-World-in-Her-Looking-Glass, dark queen of the Other Realm), they would take these same poppy seeds and, mixing them with boiled barley corn and wild honey, fling the sacred mixture up into the rafters. If the spurt of *kutia* stuck fast, a year of plenty would befall the clan. The rite fed the ancestors, invoked their aid in overcoming Stribog, the cannibal North Wind who waited without, screeching in the cold . . .

Three generations abided, and it was time to move again. After sixty years, on the first day of spring, the villagers all stripped off their tattered rags and tossed them into flames that spread quickly from lodge to lodge. They watched naked as the settlement burned to the ground, an offering to the sacred dead. Then they moved away to a new encampment in the forest valley beyond, to begin again. For forty days the spirits of the dead flitted over the smouldering ashes, unwilling to leave. Then they too departed.

This time, forever.

If this is how the ancestors of the Slavs came to their homeland, as some scholars claim, I wanted to know it. I wanted to know if the conventional account that begins most Eastern European schoolbook histories was true. Namely, that the original genesis of the Slavic people – the Russians, Ukrainians, Poles, Croats, and so forth, the people from whom the ugliest word in the world is derived, *slave* – was this historically documented throng of riverbank farmers who hid out for centuries in the forest wastes of the vast Pripet Marshes. Had they cowered in their village huts, while generations of horse-nomads, the Scythians, Sarmatians, Huns, and their ilk, raced about, hacking and slaying anyone who dared set foot on the Great Steppes that began nearby, on the shores of the Dnieper River, just south of Ukraine's present-day capital, Kiev? The Pripet was originally a

misty region of five thousand square kilometres northwest of Kiev, now considerably diminished as a result of continental desiccation and inten- sive land use. I would start my journey there, in the Pripet, the sacred genesis of a settled people who had confronted millennia of nomad attacks from the East.

In the days before I left for Central Asia, I e-mailed archaeologists and art historians, Slavic Studies specialists, telling them that I wanted the Big Picture, the overview. Maybe this was a mistake, like asking a professional football coach for a history of Spectacle. While not exactly indifferent to the issue of cultural origins and historical meaning, or the relationship of daily custom to Epic, some social scientists had their feet planted squarely inside a four-by-four-foot-square plot called "my speciality." What I needed was a nomad specialist – or was this an oxymoron?

Let's call this childhood intimation of mine the Prince and the Horde. It is an opposition that continues to haunt the imagination of the West today, a conflict I wanted to explore in many guises. It pits discipline against abandon, civilization to barbarian, the louche harem against the sanctity of true marriage. It lodges itself in loaded phrases like *oriental despot*, *satrap*, and *potentate*. It is most at home in the term *tribe*, a word first used to describe those horse-nations who appeared with the earliest historical records of the West, the nomadic Cimmerians of Central Asia, *circa* 700 B.C. They show up twice in Homer. The nomads' attacks made historical records in the first place, for it is always the chronicle-writing defenders who bestow them with names and dates. Nomads were other- wise engaged.

Are History and raging horsemen identical? Did their advent give rise to written history?

And what is this thing we call History, exactly? Certainly more than the written record, the debated consensus of academics whose accounts rely on contemporary chronicles, church and trade records, and archival flotsam. Writing is merely one effect among many that History generates, and produces almost sentiently. A perfect society has no need of history. Utopian works set in the distant future always figure such manifestly sage Councils that they have transcended history altogether, while anybody who has lived through what the Chinese call "interesting times" understands that History moves through ordinary time like a dark star, irresistible, invisible, and irradiated by a charged halo of spectacular secondary events. Did the great civilizations – Arab, Chinese, Persian, and European – succeed because they learned to contain the nomads' competing system within the Central Asian plains? Or was their civilization's growth and vigour dependent from the onset on the fertility of nomadic incursions? Who had considered such questions?

After false starts and haughty silences, the name Victor Ostapchuk came up, a University of Toronto expert on Tartars. Dr. Ostapchuk indeed proved helpful. He immediately e-mailed me his unpublished research paper on the long-range war campaigns of a nomad state, the Crimean Tartars, a clan of svelte killers who enjoyed their own little steppe-empire and the rowdy pleasures of overseeing same in what is now southern Ukraine, from the twelfth to the late-sixteenth centuries. Five hundred years. A good run for any empire, I thought – especially one based on rapine. Ostapchuk's paper served up a rich stew of exotic Turkic words. *Beg*, chief; *tug*, horsetail standards; *qilich*, swordfighting; *qish eyyamidur*, the winter campaign, when the rivers are frozen solid and the defenders huddle indoors, vulnerable to fire-arrows; *dil*, captured informants; and finally *jasyr*, fresh slaves, the whole point of the nomadic exercise, as his paper argued.

A scholarly gourmet, Ostapchuk offered up a buffet of delights. In the relative obscurity of its subject and the arcane terminology of an entire culture driven by pillage (the Khanate's Code, a series of edicts written on silk leaves and carried by royal geldings, even prescribes specific punishments for interference with another man's *jasyr*, his personal string of war-captured slaves), Ostapchuk's paper exhibited the high degree of connoisseurship that other writers might have shown for the golden peaches of Samarkand, the exquisite lapis lazuli of Khotan in present-day Uzbekistan, or the famed blood-sweating horses of Ferghana.

The East and its innumerable histories (burnt chronicles, half-lost, untranslatable) become a kind of catalogue of human excess in all its forms. The closeted mania of the collector, the secret thralldom of a total and wilful miscegenation. You can feel it, the fateful lure of the caravan. Ostapchuk concludes his research paper with an apologia:

> "This being said, it is hoped that today we can be even more open-minded about slavery ... as well as *jasyr* in the Crimean khanate."

To what end shall we become so open-minded? About *slavery*?
I had to meet Professor Ostapchuk.

"Revisionism has hit my speciality. The *right* answer, to the question of whether nomadic culture was a good or bad thing, these days, is now *good*. Not cruel or barbaric – just methodical."

I nod silently. We are strolling through a rabbit warren of dinky offices, the Eastern Studies Department of the University of Toronto. The professor's little den is on the third floor of a former dairy warehouse, hard by the smelly precincts of old Chinatown.

Victor Ostapchuk has just *shushed* me for talking too loudly in the concrete hall, disturbing the mental work being generated inside the open cubicles. My guide is a thirtyish boy-genius. Tinted aviator glasses, thick brown shoes, an adolescent's body lost to a fantastic inner life. Now he indicates the open cubby doors; the building's lack of ventilation has forced his antique colleagues to do their silent musings in public. A dozen elderly scholars sit frozen in deep contemplation, eyes fixed on their dropped ceilings. Some of them appear dead. Great walls of books every-where. Specialist texts in Sanskrit, Turkish, Chinese, Urdu, Russian.

And anxiously waiting outside Victor's locked office door, the requisite pimply faced undergraduate. No appointment. Ostapchuk tells her to wait, shuts the door on her, and immediately begins tossing books at me, offering to lend them "for the weekend," as if I were some grad-student polymath who will absorb three or four hundred pages of heavily annotated text over a cup of weak mint tea. In conversation he proves the keen collector, the sequestered fan of really good terror. Hundreds of rare volumes attest to his delight in nomads who never write history, who *make* it as a by-product of calculation and pluck. And his stuff is far better than *64,000 A.D.* or *Realms of the Haunting.* It's real.

Here's a photo of a human skull, rimmed in gold.

The caption says it all: *Penechang ritual drinking cup.*

Here are statistics estimating the Mongol carnage in North China, thirteenth century. One million up to ten million, killed in a single month. Mind-boggling, considering they employed hand-forged swords the size of gardening shears for the job. I love Victor's appetite for violent-luxe, his dreamy Peter Pan admiration for pirate civilizations like the Crimean Tartars. They're real to him, these blood-curdling khans. What's not to love from their side of the sword? These civilization killers go their merry way, slaughter a whole city nightly, and never admit a debt to anyone.

"Here, this one is really good."

Victor's eyes glint like steel as he tosses another text on the growing pile.

"Genghis's biography. He went into a shamanic trance before every battle." He picks out another volume with curious script. "You read Persian?"

"Is there an ecological basis to the expansion of the Mongols in the thirteenth century?" I ask, daunted by the homicidal largesse. He pushes the yellow aviator glasses up his nose.

"The ecological argument, yes. There's something to that. We see three environments, physical zones, in Ukraine. The name Ukraine means, of course, *frontier.* Real steppe in the south, forest steppe in the middle, and true forest in the north. Ukrainians are a people of the first two zones, and Russians of the third. These environments contributed to the culture in Eastern Europe in a fundamental way. The Ukrainians' farming culture, the good soil and so on, encouraged a high birthrate, and the upsurge of population density is visible in the census records of the sixteenth century. It's a strategy. They spread back to the true steppe again, partly because they have nowhere else to go, and they go as Cossack warriors, or as slaves, or as colonists – but they go. The Russians, on the other hand, are influenced by the neighbouring Finns, the tribes of the forests, their survival mechanism is a low birthrate. *They* expand by absorbing and ruling other people."

"Would you say the nomads' mindset is fundamentally different from other peoples'?"

I study a rare woodcut of European captives bound for the Sultan's harem in Turkey, far to the south. Big tree forks are stuck over their roped-off heads. "The Tartars seem to enjoy war for war's sake."

Victor nods soberly.

"Absolutely. I recently showed a friend some photos I took of a street scene in Crimea, and he assumed that, because the local Tartar people wore European-style clothes, they think like we do. They don't. In midsummer the Ukrainian Crimean steppe gets burnt off, completely, and you move or die. What happened in the Mongol period is that the Mongols adapted to the north forest steppe. In my opinion 50 per cent of culture depends on the physical geography, on our adaptions to it. And this culture, what's inside the head of the person, this can be very different."

"How different?" I asked, prodding as always for speculation. "As different as, say, Cameron, the author of *The Origin of the Bicameral Mind*, makes out when he insists that the Greeks invented the personality, the individual? Concepts we in the West take for granted, and assume are universal?"

"Absolutely." Victor now mounted a little ladder, in hot pursuit of another fat tome. "Take the Mongols. Fierce killers, but rational. A system based on terror, but a system. Strictly adhered to, the original fascists. Genocidal, for sure. The Ukrainians and Russians adapted to them, in a sense. Yes, it was dangerous to live too close to them, because they take slaves. Depopulation occurs. But still, it's better sometimes to have them as the local power. They have a system that's strictly obeyed by all. Whereas the local princes were like the mafia gangs in Ukraine today. Greedy, irrational, lawless."

"You find reasons to admire the nomads?"

"Yes, history books generally ignore them, ignore their contributions, you have to read between the lines. But their contribution to our culture is profound. The origin of the Polish nobility, the *szlachts*, were descendants of the Sarmatian cavalry of 300 A.D. The Sarmatians were Indo-Europeans, horsemen who ousted the Scythians. The Sarmatians in turn were forced to flee west too, yet they created the European knightly class. All their jousting, armour, helmets, had Sarmatian antecedents. The whole idea of personal nobility, honour itself . . ." He drifted off.

"The history books say that of King Arthur as well," I pointed out. "They say the knights of the Round Table were actually Sarmatians who emigrated to Roman Britannius from the Asian steppes around 300 A.D. Fleeing the Huns. So the nomads were sometimes welcomed by settled peoples?"

"Yes. My overall sense is, the princes of Ukraine and Russia *enjoyed* going to pay tribute to their Mongol overlords."

"Why? Wouldn't the Rus princes resent it?"

"Serai, the nomad camp-city on the Volga, was a holiday from grim reality. To hang out with them was great, the jet-set of the day. The best food, clothing, all you could drink. Great fun! All you did was party – and it was safe. Compare *that* to the princes' home cities like thirteenth-century Suzdal or Moscow. Dirty, dangerous, open sewers, they smelled bad. The nomads wore beautiful silk clothes, silk because, if they get hit by an arrow, twisting the silk allowed them to pull it out easily. Everything they did was smart, and beautiful!" Victor waxed enthusiastic; the world he studied was uncommonly beautiful. "They moved on whenever the accumulation of garbage required it. They looked down on the cities of the West and their dirty ways. And I can't help thinking that the princes of Muscovy came to share these same attitudes, over time."

"The sense that I have is they felt superior because they *were* superior."

"This is the great secret. This business of our invention of guns, and the supposed innate superiority of the technological West? It's wrong. Worse, it's anachronistic thinking."

Victor made a face like he'd swallowed a rotten potato. He shook his head and went on.

"I mean, we eventually overcame the nomad culture, but barely. It was never a given. Russia was almost wiped out in the Time of Troubles. And it's a miracle the Ukrainians survived at all. By 1300 A.D. Genghis Khan's hordes controlled their steppe empires in Astrakhan, Kazan, Crimea, and so on, a civilization that only ended in the eighteenth century, when Muscovy finally 'liberated' the Crimea. With the help of Cossacks who learned nomadic culture. On the rebound, as it were."

"And this European rebound? What is that? The result of material culture, or intellectual?"

This was the burning question. We were talking now about the big waves called the Renaissance and the Enlightenment. What was the impetus for recording history?

Was it the bow, or the idea of the bow?

"The rebound? I don't know. We don't talk, Europe and Asia, do we? Not then, not much now, as Christians to Muslims. With the nomads, not at all. But we admire and silently take from them – all the things we esteem about them – on another level entirely. They are always gathering intelligence about us too. Historians say, 'Oh, look, they weren't anything special, the nomads! A dead-end. Look at where are they now!' Not true! They lasted seven hundred years, their steppe empires. How long did the Soviet empire last? Seventy years? And *Pax Americana*? Hardly fifty to date! Yet these latter were more important?"

The long view: Victor shook his head over it. Other historians' lack of perspective was upsetting. Worse, it was biased.

"Are they a threat, today? To us in the West, I mean."

"Who?" He looked up over his glasses in surprise.

"Nomads. The horse-people of Central Asia."

"Oh, if you mean pastoral nomads. No. They are in decline everywhere today."

"And the new nomads? The people with cellphones, roaming the air-waves of the world. Looking for opportunity, for trouble."

"Ah yes, like the Ukrainian mafia. Cosmopolitans!" He shook his head. "I don't know, my field is the pastoral types."

Consciously or not, Victor had used a word that derived from the zenith of the Soviet regime. *Cosmopolitan* once meant Western lackeys, spies, for-eigners, Zionists, all conveniently lumped together in the newspeak of the command society. Now it would serve as a label for the new woes of Eastern Europe. The vagaries of the market economy, the International Monetary Fund, robber barons with beepers. New perils threatened a brutalized people who had overcome others through sheer fecundity and obduracy. How did he see himself in this great human flux?

"And your name, Ostapchuk? Is it derived from anything?"

"No, it's a real peasant Ukrainian name. I think the nobility is actually a different ethnic group, always. Different worlds. Inside the head, I mean."

"There's that famous ancient Kiev military saga about a battle with the steppe nomads, *The Tale of Ihor's Campaign*. Similar to the Viking sagas, and like them it also dates to the eleventh century A.D. Could this old chronicle have set a template for the nomadic element in Western culture?"

"No. In fact, it seems it was a nineteenth-century forgery. By Denhovski, to create a false provenance for Slavs. Edward Keenan of Harvard certainly thinks so!"

"Really?" I stared at him, flummoxed. Endless revisionism!

This was like claiming George Washington was really a Mississippi river pirate all along; or that the Hurons sailed up into the Bay of Naples first. How did you know what was real, from the hasty litter of potsherds and salty bones? It was too much. What else had the professor unearthed in his deep devotions? We headed out to lunch, skating on the images our dialogue conjured up a million miles from the concrete sidewalks of Spadina Road and College Street.

What was the impact of these long centuries of ferocity on the psychic life of a settled folk? Here, working on his hot-and-sour soup, was a scion of that race, a man whose career was spent scrutinizing an implacable enemy his own people were lucky to survive. I threw questions at him faster and more recklessly: Was his admiration for war-mad nomads a scholarly example of Stockholm Syndrome? Was race-war the deepest kind of black love? When the twin searchlights went up in the mute New York skyline of March 11, 2002, did he too see a phantasmagoric 1933 Berlin? The defiant city-spectacle that sought Heaven's sanction for all the revenge a newly militant State would exact from its treacherous enemies?

Oh, the burnt ozone of long memory!

"So is Fortress America just walled Byzantium, all over again?"

I signalled for more beer, enjoying our riff. I could ask Victor anything.

"Probably," he nodded, pleased with his deep-fried shrimps.

"Will we ever put the black towers of Metropolis behind us?" I needed to know.

"You have to stay open-minded about that too," he replied with a short bark-laugh.

We walked back to his office. I thanked him for his help, and left with my pile of books.

The pimply faced student rushed into his office before I was out the door.

My college textbooks in Russian history had always opened with *Ihor's Campaign*. That it might have been a nineteenth-century literary forgery only adds to its poignancy, for its elegiac tone suggests a deep-seated anguish over the terrible events from six hundred years earlier. Ihor, the Kiev prince, is the star of a doomed mission against Penechang nomads, recast as an epic. And with epic comes the fatal discovery that a whole society can be lost in an instant.

> Lances will be broken, swords will be dulled.
> O Russian land! You are already far beyond the hills.

Across Asia, the great historical writing of the last thousand years is always the work of witnesses to the inconceivable slaughters of Genghis Khan, his son Ogedei Bey, or their sadistic distant cousin, Tamerlane – and this, whether the writers are Persian, Arab, European, or Chinese. The Great Raids crash against the walled cities, and crash relentlessly. The human storms began with the Cimmerians, a horse-culture of 800 B.C. and rolled on with Crimean Tartars into the late 1700s, smack into the Age of Enlightenment. These lightning raids force reluctant historians to consider the possibility, the inevitable imminence, of culture as tragedy. The proposition, that Asiatic horse-nomads were instrumental in directly founding the original kingdoms of pre-Saxon Britain, is echoed in the folk memories of Russia, Greece, Spain, Italy, and the France of Clovis and Charles Martel, who both claimed descent from itinerant Frankish freebooters. For political philosophers of every stripe, from Plato to Rousseau, Nietzsche to Karl Popper, and modern historians whether Marxist or liberal-democratic, the issue remains starkly drawn: On what basis does the State claim its ultimate authority? Is the State merely a barbarian's fist, grabbing for a mace? Is all rule under heaven based on conquest?

Plato, David Hume, Friedrich Nietzsche, and Thomas Hobbes all argued that the origin of the State lies in the subjugation of a settled people by a nomadic elite. They denied that citizens can band together through delegation and voluntary committee. The opposing theory is the famous social contract of Jean-Jacques Rousseau, scornfully criticized by David Hume in his *Essays, Moral, Political and Literary*: "An artful and bold man, by employing sometimes violence, sometimes false pretences, establish(es) his dominion – this is all the original contract they have to boast about." The polemic is nowhere more fiercely debated than in Ukraine and Russia, where it has raged for three hundred years. The contest is between Normanist and anti-Normanist schools, the former crediting Viking river pirates (or Norsemen) with developing centralized Muscovite rule, the latter contending that the *idea* of Rus began spontaneously as an autonomous confederation of farming tribes in the Pripet River basin. Was "Russia" an inherently Slavic invention, or a foreign imposition? It was always a sensitive topic for rye farmers with an array of eye colours, unsure of their lineage and using the Tartar as their bogeyman.

Who's your father, anyway?

We in the West simply adore the tribalism of our presumed ancestors, and we love to imagine we are descended from robust Aryan charioteers who torched the moribund civilizations of the early Iron Age. Sure, we're the spawn of bare-assed Celts or Norse berserkers and head-lopping Goths! Conan the Barbarian! Xena the Warrior Princess! Krull the Conqueror! Our atavism shows. No shame for us bored commuters, we love our heavy-metal ancestry. The difference is, we've overcome it.

The past, I mean. We've learned its lessons, and the number-one lesson is to hold fast to our civic virtue, to stick to our *civitas*. To sublimate our lust for revenge and mass destruction in the trivial tasks of modern life, sublimate with all our might. There's lonely honour in paying off the house mortgage, isn't there? Of staying loyal to one spouse? Of course! Let's be honest about our attainments: orderly queuing, paying income taxes, hybridizing tulips, and raising Olympic hopefuls. No mean feats when you consider the alternatives. Political philosopher Taras Kuzio of Yale University even goes further, arguing in his essay "The Myth of the Civic State" that there is no functional difference between the political institutions of the West and the East, despite what Western academics of a certain mindset might otherwise claim. It was all a mindless bloodbath, History, whatever you call it before our time, this safety-net era of after-dinner speeches and annual golf awards. We've put out the flames of History with easy-credit shopping and religiously applied cultural relativism, inviting the rest of the world to do the same.

Oh, the possibilities of social control through mass consumer debt! What art! Inertia imposes its own order. Forget the past, the past is dangerous. Perhaps our bourgeois rectitude is even based on forgetting it all, on forgetting who we are at root. Or on mocking it with World Wrestling burlesques.

Still, it was all very good, Ostapchuk's written material. Gentlemen killers who watch jealously from river fords to see which rival *beg* will go first. Silk-clad paladins whose kingdoms are a fluid river of terror, with backwashes of lopped heads. I can also spot the loaded catch-phrases in the obscure texts he so kindly lent me. These phrases reveal a deep split between the ecumenical impulse and *realpolitik*. Above all stands the Western host, with its associations of divine armies and the dependencies of the guest to his gracious landlord. Eternally opposed to it is the Eastern *horde* – a cacophonous cavalry that blows its trumpets and bangs its brass gongs, taking what it wants from a trembling world.

I went home and pulled out my dog-eared copy of Machiavelli's book *The Prince*. The Italian author clearly had the great Khans and the Turkish Sultan in the back of his mind when he wrote his famous treatise in 1513. His version of *realpolitik* made arguments for the open uses of power to replace the failed philosophy of Christian Statism. It was written in the same era that saw Sahib Gerey Khan herd thousands of newly captured European captives to the Black Sea slave markets every winter, the seaports where Italian traders could pinch their buttocks at will.

Machiavelli espoused flexibility, ruthlessness. The Prince recommends that the ruler move against his enemies without hesitation, as soon as he recognizes them; that he punish swiftly, without hesitation; that he hand out rewards slowly, to make a lasting impression. But never touch the women; leave the women alone. Even Machiavelli believed in a Wheel of Justice. – Did the nomads? Perhaps Ostapchuk's approach was right; perhaps our task was simply to stare unflinchingly at the worst excesses of the age, to stay open-minded and free of preconception. So the old sagas were lies, pretty stories. So what? What is important is to know what happened, what really happened. To know what was real. But how to achieve that?

I was obliged to go there, into that Asian cauldron, if I wanted answers to the question: Who – or what – gives birth to this thing we call History? This silent power that seems to enjoy playing with us, a billion chess pieces that scream and howl back. I resolved my plans. I would start in Ukraine, the battered flank of Eastern Europe, visit the cities that had been crushed by these attacks, and make my way eastward over the steppes, heading always against the current, against the human tides that had swept out of Central Asia, and march straight into the ground zero of history, the horse-plains of Kyrgyzstan and Mongolia.

No time for more questions, enough book reading.

Now it was time to go . . .

Chapter 2

Crime and Disorder (Repeat)

Kiev is a fine place in early June, the city's parks are lush with chestnut trees and its manicured lawns are splashed with gold reflected from its Byzantine church domes. My translator, Dana, is an expatriate Canadian in her late thirties, married to a local doctor, Arkadi, and hip to the scene. The scene is rougher than the weeping pastel saints on the church frescos suggest. Today she is taking me to meet a member of the new capitalist class, post-Soviet style. A Ukrainian tough guy.

To make our meeting with Yasha the Enforcer, we are obliged to drive the dented Lada around the block twice, then park it away from the other cars. This is a precaution. One of Yasha's close associates went outside to start up his vehicle this past winter, and it is only because the windshield was covered with snow that Big Dmitry is still alive, for when he stepped out to scrape it off, the bomb just took off his heel, and left him standing there quite surprised, balanced for a full second on one foot.

I do not know who this Yasha is, exactly. My translator will only say that she has succeeded in securing his consent for our interview, but now that we are closing in on his headquarters, her heightened attentiveness and exaggerated manner suggest I should stay on my toes. The restaurant is empty, except for four or five young men who do not look as if they are customers of this or any other restaurant. They glance at me, and nod slowly. We are expected. A sub-audible intake of breath from Dana announces the arrival of our host through an unmarked side door. Yasha: medium height, early forties, in a banana-yellow Italian suit and black silk shirt. He approaches and looks me over with the quick nervous eyes of a fox-cat, or maybe a rising New York stage actor from the highstrung days of Sal Mineo and *West Side Story*. The boys pretend not to watch us. They don't walk, they pace, in the shadows by the front curtains. Back and forth. Keep cool, boys, real cool.

Yasha offers his hand, the overly soft clasp of the boxer, a street fighter who is afraid to hurt you with his pro's strength, and except for the scar that runs in a red crescent from lip to earlobe, as if someone wanted to give him a second smile above the first, he reminds one of an early Tony Curtis, recast with magnetic, yellow Asiatic eyes. A hit of garlic and Turkish tobacco.

"So." I look to my translator, who has forgotten to breathe. Dana is devouring him with her eyes. Yasha motions us to sit down at a corner table, where our lunch places are already set; we are separated from the main dining room by blue glassine half-walls. Every boite café in Kiev has one of these: the VIP lounge. The boys in the outer room begin to relax as a slim Botticelli blonde in boots and miniskirt, barely twenty, materializes and turns her baby-face to the boss, and waits.

"What would you like to order? Meat, fish, something else?" Yasha beckons; one of the hard boys comes over and wordlessly hands him a cigarette. His fingers strum the table with nervous energy. He's thinking of other things, now that he's decided I'm harmless. The girl murmurs something. "Yes, drink. Would you like beer, juice?"

We say yes to the beer, the Ukrainian beer we've had so far is excellent, as good as German beer but less bitter. Dana blinks rapidly. I find myself getting excited too, despite the persistent jet-lag that threatens to topple me into untimely paralysis. Yasha looks to me, anxious to proceed; he's coming into focus now.

"Yes, soup," I say quickly. "And mushrooms? Something with mushrooms."

"With eggs, is okay." He looks to the translator for confirmation. She nods, all sleepy-eyed and dreamy. Boiled eggs, sure. What is it with the girls and gangsters? The tragedy of a love that will never make it to that pent-house condo in Miami?

"How did you get that scar?" I venture, taking hold of the frosty Pilsner glass. No slow service in this joint.

"This?" He gives a short nod. His partner, Miki, a chubby dark man who has joined us from another doorway, snorts a gleeful little laugh. Yasha's purple tongue makes a brief appearance at the bottom of his lip, then disappears. An old joke, the five-inch scar.

"It has nothing to do with this story," he declares. "Something from my youth."

"Where were you born?"

"In Siberia. We moved to the Crimea when I was in school. My mother came for her health. I graduated —" A discussion ensues between him and the translator over the exact pedagogical course of his youth. "Oh, yes, engineering. State College, Institute of Construction, fully graduated."

"So did you work as an engineer?" I hope his answers will take a bit longer, because the food has started arriving: a plate of ripe tomatoes with dill and bitter tiny cucumbers, precisely carved into rosettes; cold devilled eggs mixed with wild mushrooms; a cold soup with a pretty mosaic of green onions, chopped ham, and sour cream floating on top; and chunks of fresh light-rye bread to wipe it all up. The food is dainty enough to be distracting.

"A little," he answers perfunctorily. "But I went into business soon after."

"And what year did you graduate?"

"1988."

"That was before the end of Communism. Was it hard to do business then?"

"Well, we had foreign contacts. Export/import, different products. It was difficult, yes, but it is always necessary to get capital. We went to Poland, Yugoslavia. Lots of different papers needed then, and travel was very restricted."

"And now, with the end of the Soviet era, do you find more competition? More rivalry?"

"It's not a matter of competition, but of the laws we have now. By the time this happened, of course, we had amassed the necessary capital and it became possible to set up some businesses officially, which I have. And I continue to look for more opportunity."

His eyes brushed my face in an unspoken query. Of course it's all allusive, coded, ripe with subtext. These ordinary words hide, not reveal. I don't dare a look at our intermediary. I went on, the foreigner with the deep interest in foreign business.

"What about rivals? Do you have to pay tribute like the princes of old times?"

He looked to the translator at this; I meant of course the Slavic princes of ancient Kiev, who had been forced to kneel to their Mongol overlords, while surrendering bales of martin and squirrel skins and old jewellery, gouged from the local trading class.

Yasha shook his head.

"No, I am left alone, because of my position. I have never had territorial restrictions. I have never had to pay tribute. This comes from my position in sports, as a semi-professional player. Here the sports people, football and so on, look after each other, so nobody bothers me."

Miki the partner says something at this point and laughs.

"Yes," Miki repeats in English. "Except for the government."

"That is true."

"So you have a lot of friends, it seems. A position is something."

"I do what I can, to help people. We have six restaurants. We give work to people. And I have a school for children, for sports training."

The translator asks Yasha a question in Russian and he shakes his head.

"What was that?" I say, taking the opportunity to dig into my devilled eggs.

"I wanted to know if they taught girls at the sports school yet," she replies evenly.

"Thinking of joining?" I raise my eyebrow. "Okay, what about the government then?"

"They don't allow stability," he answers instantly in passable English, and lights another cigarette from the old one. He wears a beautiful, fat gold ring with a precious red stone set in the centre, a ruby or something. Maybe carmelite, the old Kievan gemstone I'd seen in the Museum of Ukrainian History earlier that day. "You have to acquire the capital to keep going with your activities."

This is code; the translator's semi-frozen glaze reveals as much.

"You mean they try to take away your profits, so you must hide them somehow?"

"Miki?" Yasha turns. "How much?"

I understand what he's asking. *Taxes.*

"Yes, I ask my associate how much the taxes are now, he says they take 30 per cent. This is not so much. It used to be 60, 70 per cent."

"I see. So you must reinvest the capital?"

"To keep up, yes. Once, I used to seek opportunity throughout Ukraine, but it became too hard to keep control of your partners, so I restricted the business just to Kiev."

"And the government is the problem, now?" I chew delicately on a cucumber rosette.

"It is like this: you start a new business, coffee say. You make the calculation, how much you can get the green beans for, everything is fine. Then all of a sudden, they impose an excise tax on green beans, although we don't grow coffee beans here in Ukraine, so I have worked for nothing. The fixed taxes are higher than any possible profit."

"But you have other businesses that work okay."

"We have six restaurants, fifteen retail stores, a book-making business on sports with a foreign investor." He looks meaningfully at me, here. "A car business . . . The way it works is, when they decide to privatize something, like a government café, by law they must first give the employees' collective an opportunity to buy the business. But of course they offer it to them on impossible terms, so they can't buy. Then they have auction. I know ahead of time, having made all the necessary inquiries to the right people, that my bid will be successful. That is how we buy up the businesses here."

Another meaningful look.

"So you could do the same thing with industrial plants? What about the stock market?"

"We don't do the stock market, but it would be the same. I would go and find someone who knows the business, and make him a partner." Now a hopeful look. Yearning, almost. "Why do you ask me about the stock market?"

"I wanted to know how easy it is to raise money – capital – here."

"I can tell you a story about the stock market and the government. One of my businesses was security. This man, he worked in the government offices. Cabinet of Ministers, twenty-nine years old. He played the stock market, and one day he appealed to me to recover $100,000 he had been cheated of. So you must ask yourself, How does a thirty-year-old working in the Cabinet of Ministers get hold of $100,000?"

"Were you able to help him?" I really wanted to know how.

He took a long and satisfied pull on his cigarette.

"Yes, I got him back $70,000," he said coolly.

A commission of thirty grand, a nice fee for a couple of days' work, I figured. "So how much money does it take to reach the point where you will be happy? You seem tired. I think you must work very hard?"

"This is pleasant tired," he admitted. "When I was working hard, looking for opportunities. The other kind, when I get irritated that there is nothing to do, that's bad fatigue."

"And so, to be rich, what does this mean?"

"Rich?" He looked puzzled. Another quick exchange with the translator. "Ah, normalno!"

He comprehended. Normal. What does it take to be normal.

"Yes, yes, to have a normal life. I know that in the West it is normal to have two cars, three: a sedan, a Jeep, and a sports car. And the wife drives a car as well."

"Actually, she usually drives the Jeep," I interjected.

He went on with his evocation, turning his sulphuric eyes upwards.

"A nice apartment or house, living room/dining room, separate from the kitchen, two bathrooms at least, and to be able to pay for your children's education. To be able to take a vacation with your family twice a year. That's normalno. In the West."

"And you?" I prodded.

"I sold my Mercedes, I got a Camry, this year's model, $30,000. For me, I need between $3,000 and $5,000 per month, for me and my partner to live a normal life."

"And how do you split up the work, you and him?"

"We meet every day at six in the evening and decide what to do for the next day. Miki is forty-six, he's Jewish, older than me. He's more flexible, so he deals with the bureaucrats. Me, I can't stand them. They were interbreeding for seventy years altogether, and only the worst kind of people go into it. The government." It comes out like spit. He shakes his head with soul-deep distaste.

Yasha might have to kill people, and he is always worried that he will be a target like his friend Roman the Wrestler, who was killed last year despite being "strong, very strong," but he believes himself moral at bottom. I throw out a wild, shot-in-the dark question, not daring to ask him directly about his mother's influence, making my approach from an oblique angle.

"Did you ever think what it would be like to forget this business and become a priest?"

He takes this far-fetched request seriously. I see at once I have engaged him, his expression softens. It is a human, a real, question to him.

"We help people, we give them jobs, we help them raise children. A priest helps people in different ways, both are good . . . They shouldn't be compared," he concludes with a sigh of honesty.

"And if you had children – I don't know if you *do* or don't," I add hastily, "what would you want for them?"

"I do have children," he looks at me with amazement. It was normalno, and his life was based on being normalno. "My younger daughter just finished high school, the other one is training to be a psychoanalyst."

"A psychoanalyst?" I repeat stupidly. I can't think of anything else to say. He looks to his watch, a Swiss model I know to be worth twelve thousand dollars retail.

"If you are ever looking for investments here, please call me."

He abruptly got up and left the restaurant. The translator and I finished our lunch in a sustained, guilty silence. Dana giggled to herself, happy about something.

"You know what's amazing?" she said as soon as we had nodded to all the boys in the white designer T's and made our way out to the car.

"That you were able to keep your hands off him for a whole hour?" I responded, slightly jealous. Yasha was a self-made hero of the new demi-mode, one step ahead of everyone else.

"No, *these* guys like Yasha? Their suits, the way they walk and talk? You sort of think that they get it from TV, that mob look of theirs, but I think it's totally spontaneous!" She was gleeful, a sociological insight along with all that probing, bright-eyed sexuality. All in one free lunch, mere inches away from the justifications of my scribbly little notebook.

"Hmmph," I sniffed. "I know lots of guys like him, back home."

"Come on," she said, trying to make it up to me. "Let's go to the Kiev Museum of Contemporary Art. I want you to meet the director."

"Oh, like that's all I'm good for, eh? To jaw about abstract stuff that doesn't matter?"

"You'll like her."

"Mm." I was peevish. Scribe to the Mob. Talk about emasculation. Why not become a hairdresser, at least make some money at it?

I got in the red Lada as she instructed, and watched carefully as she turned the key. The old clunker's chipmunk engine sputtered and caught. A dull throb, nothing else. Normalno. We drove off in the insane traffic to our next meeting.

See that pretty girl across Kerchevsky Street, in the short skirt? She's looking at me. They all look at me; they know I'm a foreigner – and it's not my clothes, or my haircut. It's my outsider's stance, which I can't disguise as easily. I'm walking so buoyantly, still fresh from the Western sunshine of a million shopping malls and the anticipation of hot new films at the Cinemega. She knows to the dollar what I've got crammed in my neck-wallet too. U.S. cash, they take nothing else here, no credit cards, no traveller's cheques, nothing. Just cash. And she wants some of it.

Even though she already has a job in a trading office, she will sleep with me for fifty bucks. That banknote with squinty-eyed Andrew Jackson, or whatever his name is, on it. Old Jack. He's the bottom line here in Kiev, today, this year. We're in a land like postwar Germany, about 1946 or maybe 1947. People here aren't starving, they're not selling themselves for a pack of Marlboros exactly, but the bad times are not over yet. Shoes must be bought. Steps taken into the bright future.

The twentieth century was not good to the Ukrainian nation. First a Civil War in Russia that swept through Ukraine, immediately after the Great War, cropping more millions the Kaiser missed; then Stalin's Famine of the early 1930s, in which ten million steady farmers were deliberately starved to death; then the purges and show trials of the late 1930s, in which teachers, journalists, and many of those same ravenous, secret police grain-collectors and the other Party apparati themselves got bullets in their necks, or new jobs in Siberia. Fifteen million. A Ukrainian folk-saying quoted in the harrowing book *One of Fifteen Million* by camp-survivor Nicholas Prychodko: "Remember your neighbour and do not harm him, for shoes can switch feet in the night." Then, of course, the Great Patriotic War, when the German High Command kept its headquarters in Kiev and the other unused half of the city was deliberately incinerated. And then Baby Yar, a ravine just outside the city, where they heaped the Jews and many others who fell into their hands. How many died in total?

The numbers refuse to add up after a while. They're meaningless.

Peace finally, but the end? No. The Russification of Ukraine, a land the Soviets now call "South Russia," began in 1945, and the postwar years brought widespread school and church closings, local intellectuals were imprisoned, and thousands of Russians were sent to live in Ukraine and bury its identity under their hard g's and grumpy Soviet *davay*'s, their stone-faced *gimmes*. Their rudeness is institutional, calculated. The disastrous Five-Year Plans of the 1950s Command Economy followed; then Chernobyl; then a species of destitute autonomy in 1991; then an entirely predictable collapse of the banking system in 1998.

What shall we call this protracted nightmare? The Century of Shit? (Or, in Ukrainian baby-talk, *kaka* time?) And what shall we call the present, the post-Chernobyl era, with its hundred thousand Ukrainian women hustling nightly in foreign brothels; mobsters driving up on the sidewalks; World Bank loans disappearing like smoke. The Kiev tourist maps are so quick off the mark to tell the casual reader about the above calamities, and about other fine points of its murderous history (*Kiev Guide*: "The former church on this site was ruthlessly destroyed by Soviet atheists in 1934–1936"). This same and righteously indignant and self-proclaimed *free* guide prominently displays a full-colour ad:

> The American Introduction Agency invites all foreign men to meet beautiful Ukrainian women. *Your choice!*
> *OVER 14,000 WOMAN AT LOVEME.COM*

The photo shows a smiling blonde, stroking her hair in a gesture loaded with submissive eagerness and tabloid-style abasement. Yes, it really takes an American to set up this trade; it's that good old Yankee yellow-journal know-how and its world-famous dedication to the Bottom Line, the sworn enemy and conqueror of the Command Economy. Capital has replaced the Kremlin, but the same warriors trudge on with their new banners. What shall we call this latest program of defeat and destruction? The Big Slut Plan? Why not? Even in far-away America, in that distant galaxy where the phones don't cut out from under you, mid-sentence, and there are no sharp stones in your store-bought bread, the cheap availability of pretty young Ukrainian women presents something of a moral dilemma for TV shows like *Third Watch*. Shall we buy them or not? The dense but lovable New York cop, John Malloy, actually goes ahead and marries one, only to discover he's way out of his depth (read, his purely American innocence) in his Ukrainian bride's shadowy world, among too many ugly guys with gold teeth named Sasha.

So let's call it that. Let's call it Ukraine's latest ordeal, the country's belated entry into the era of fast-food 'n' sex franchises, Trick 'o' Rama. Shall I not write about the hookers on the street corners of Kiev? Or about the women here who are less than hookers but more professional than me, when it comes to getting exactly what they want? What am I supposed to write about, then? Condemning no one, least of all the girls, I feel like some foreign-born Thai who visits Bangkok for the first time in his life, only to find it has become a giant brothel heaving with smarmy Germans and ham-fisted Americans, all congratulating themselves on their good fortune at haggling five bucks off the price of a massage and lay? Maybe I should do what Professor Ostapchuk advised me to do, *ex* Socrates: Confront the issue.

But what would I like to do? Save four or five of these unhappily madeup women, picked at random? Give them all a sort of marriage and maybe a low-limit credit card each, and all live together in a big house in suburbia like some Latter-Day Saint?

How's that for a series pitch? *My Five Natashas.*

"Is that the best you can do?" Dana says after hearing out my rant.

"Well, they're all so pretty," I hasten to assure her of my objectivity. "It's heartbreaking, but it's not about the sex. In fact, to be honest . . ."

She's watching me carefully now, as we approach the downtown Kiev Art Museum. The word *honest* is a huge tipoff to women to expect anything but from the mouth of a man stupid enough to use the term.

"To be honest," I take a deep breath, "I don't really find them all that sexy."

There. I've said it.

"What?" Dana turns to watch a speeding *biznessman* (as they call themselves here) in a black Mercedes cut her off. A twisted smile on her face. Is she amused, outraged, or what?

Her sisters! What kind of game do I think I'm playing?

Me, the just-landed foreigner with his two-cent opinions!

"Well of course they're really pretty," I backtrack. "Those tiny wasp waists, nice long legs, pretty smiles. Engaging, in fact. And their complexions! Milk and honey!"

Am I laying it on too thick? I'm only trying to cover the whole list, in case Dana thinks I'm shortchanging anyone. She mulls this over, bent across her warped steering wheel.

"You really don't find them sexy?"

She says it in an arch tone of disbelief, sitcom-style.

"Not the bulk of them, no. It's that short-skirt, too-much-makeup thing. They're trying so hard, *too* hard. It's forced, not natural. Like they're selling this fake idea of themselves. Know what I mean?"

"You're absolutely right," she replies, biting her lip. "They are very insecure. They do exactly what the media ads tell them to do, what they think is supposed to be cool. They have no thought about anything else. I find it very pathetic."

"Well, there were a few." I try to quantify my short experience; it's a delicate topic. "On the plane, for example, there were these three women? Tall, no makeup at all, straight Greek noses, know what I'm talking about? Like they just stepped out of a Byzantine fresco, very . . . classic." I take a breath and go on; she is listening intently. "I thought I'd see more like them here, their type. But what you've got in the capital city is your dimpled little Natashas. Perky. Oh so perky and cute. In their pointy shoes, with the straps that lace up to their knees."

Dana coloured, rolling her eyes at my mention of this fashion catastrophe. It seems that really bad style was more of a sin here than doing tricks to pay for it.

We entered the grounds of the Contemporary Art Museum, a low-vaulted building with whitewashed walls and scoured wood floors. It

displayed indigenous avant-garde art, courtesy of the philanthropic bil-
lionaire and stockmarket guru Andrew Soros, a Hungarian-born U.S.
businessman who had set up similar institutions throughout Eastern
Europe in an attempt to kick-start the local intelligentsia into producing
new culture, thus leading the way to social renewal. His art theory, anyway.

"Only Soros is pulling out now," Dana nodded. "This year, next year,
then it's all over. So take a good look around, and then meet me at the director's office."

"Right."

I strolled across the uneven floors, smiling at the trendy new things who
sat in chairs like their old-lady counterparts, except that the chairs were
Mies knockoffs and their bare legs were ten miles long and they
were reading *Counter/Text* and other serious bilingual monographs on
video art. Dense technical criticism, voluptuous youth. The juxtaposition
of the obscure commentary with the comic porn splashed on the walls was
a thing to behold, and I beheld it. Here was Rabbitman humping Bunnygirl
in all his priapic glory, his previous climax still dripping slowly down the
canvas. The artist had sprayed his large-scale work with fat drops of pearly
shellac, or so one hoped. Here was a Barbie stretched out in bed, an
exploratory finger at the ready between her jointed thighs, watching a
tongue-kiss TV show labelled *Not Suitable for Children*. And my favourite,
a lascivious late-Victorian doll, propped up by a rushing waterfall with a
classic mountain panorama in the background, inviting the viewer to
choose between Nature and Her, whatever the hell she was. It was no
contest. The sex-toys were winning this ideological war with their eager,
probing little fingers, hands down.

Satisfactorily excited, I made my way past the three or four junior cura-
tors whose tight black skirts barely restrained their innate carnality and
found Dana sitting at a table, set primly for a formal tea. China cups,
spoons, and everything.

"I'd like you to meet the director," Dana said, pointing to a tall woman
with waves of dark hair cascading down her exposed back. Creamy skin,
the wide-open-sky eyes of a seafaring Celt. "Alyssa."

"Hello. Nice to meet you," Alyssa said in perfectly idiomatic English.

"Nice to meet you," I said cautiously. Dana was watching us from the
corner, reviewing some translation work, spreading it out carefully, page

by page, on the table. We talked about her work. Alyssa was twenty-four, turning twenty-five. She did not look twenty-four, she looked like a full-grown woman without a full-grown man in her life. Vibrating, barely contained. She said she had graduated last year from Kiev University right next door.

"You must have done very well in school, to get such a job, so young," I began. "When Dana said we were meeting the director, I thought —" I shot a glance at my translator. Was she smiling at my discomfiture?

"Yes, I did well in university," Alyssa nodded with a modest under-statement that probably meant she stood first, and won half-a-dozen scholarships to boot.

"And this was, what, a master's?" I guessed. "What was your thesis?"

"'The Systems of Art Values in the Ukraine Today,'" she replied.

"Systems, the plural."

"Yes, everything is much in flux. The conflict between traditional criticism and the new. There is more ambiguity, disconnection."

"It all comes down to that 's.'"

"Yes," she laughed. "The 's' – that was my whole thesis!"

She had nice white, even teeth, pearly. I was still inflamed by the pictures I had perused in the complicit dim rooms behind us. Now I turned and tried to break the attraction of her deep blue doll-eyes. Breathe a bit.

"Oh, look at the red, there!" I pointed to a crimson oval hanging on the office wall. It had a slit cut down the middle, running from top to bottom.

The nation was fast returning to basic urges.

"Really red." I swallowed, trying to ignore the frank message of the open slit. Was she five-ten or five-eleven, this bosomy demi-goddess whom all my spectral ancestors were suddenly wild about, screaming at me to get on with it, take her right there on the floor, and have three, four, *ten* children with her! *Immediately*, keep going at it like the erectile hare in the next room. Who cares what Dana the translator thinks? Forget Soros and his damnable art-capital millions! This was blood talking here! Red blood singing, hot and ready.

No, this was blood howling!

"What was I saying . . . ? Oh, yes, red. The pure element, the purest, ochre of the caveman." I blathered on, wondering if it would be okay to at least neck with her a little, in the interests of cultural exchange. Dana already had her gangster-idyll, it was my turn now.

"Well, that's a very romantic notion," Alyssa said, regarding me with a smile of unwilling approval.

"Oh, is that a bad word?" It sounded more defensive than I intended.

"Not necessarily," she smiled even more.

A pause. It stretched between us.

The brain ticked away, left to its own devices.

She had wavy dark hair. Creamy white, clear skin.

"You're very pretty," I gulped. Truth will out.

"I can live on that compliment for at least a month," she responded gaily.

We talked some more; she said the main problem with the men here in Kiev was that they were useless, whiners. Her last boyfriend had only called her to cry about how hard up he was, how sick he was of everything.

"It's the social conditions," she said. "In the war, all the men were killed. There were four women to every man, so they treated them like kings, spoiled their boy babies too. And they don't respect women. We are – how do you say it, Dana?"

"Undervalued," she replied, not looking up.

"Yes, undervalued."

"No one could ever undervalue you, Alyssa." I said, trying to escape her Circe eyes in the refuge of objectivity. "You're far too attractive."

"That's good, that's two months now." She laughed. "So tell me," she went on without warning, "are you married?"

A long pause. It might have lasted only half a second, before I finally croaked, craven worm that I was, "Sort of."

I gave her my best, a weak sick smile, as Dana smirked again in the corner, and the sweat dripped down my temple like a little pearl of pure shellac.

And stayed there, frozen. For all to see.

Chapter 3

She Called Me a Romantic, the Bitch!

We were a hundred kilometres north of central Kiev, sitting on a vacant road, staring at the nothingness that had overwhelmed Eastern Europe for over a decade now.

Giant horseflies roared around the parked car, pursued by legions of droning dragonflies so loud they made the ground shudder in their passage. The throbbing of fast wings hurt my ears; I could barely think. At the side of the deserted highway, a stork, a hawk, and a white-winged crow conducted a deadly standoff, blustering over a piece of offal hidden by tall weeds. Dropping from the sky, squadrons of swallows tilted at the earth like insanely committed dive-bombers, crashing again and again, freeing themselves for another loop at the last second before something lying in the grasses leaped up to swallow them whole.

It was feverish, violently green, uncanny: the Ukrainian countryside in June. The seen and the unseen, birds hectoring from clawlike shrubs, amorous bullfrogs moaning in delight, a delirious homage rising up from the muddy sloughs and lily-studded ponds; while the timorous sky kept to itself, the skirts of its diaphanous clouds played gently in the breeze, a little wistful, at far remove from the savage garden party below. So much life, so much distance. We were in the middle of a vast vernal plain, italicized here and there with great strutting stands of red pine and mature forests of oak, poplar, and birch; and we were all alone in this archaic splendour, because we were here illegally, at the edge of the Chernobyl Exclusion Zone, only fifty kilometres or so northeast of Kiev's last grotty suburb.

Yes, the dragonflies were radioactive, the frogs were burning with invisible fire, and the water lilies were cooking their genes in the agitated subsoil; life seethed in revolt, despite the morning dew and the promise of a cool rain later that afternoon. Everything was being consumed, its inner essence exposed. The excitement of the swallows was nuclear, the storks glowed with apparent good health, and it was all mirage, an illusion, a sparkly diorama illuminated by strontium 90 or maybe only strontium 89, maybe the reactor coughed before it sneezed, and these crusty lumps clinging to my boots were less than atomically perfect.

Who knew?

Who knew anything? Certainly not Arkadi, my muscleman driver and Dana's husband. He was a fiftyish doctor, who had worked here in the zone, right after the thing went off April 26, 1986.

"It was for the Ministry of Health, my job." He kept looking over at the deserted dairy farm nearby, a broken complex of red-brick walls abandoned to the elements, these newly created, high-number elements. "They were all so tired, from the radiation. It just made them tired. They wanted to lie down and sleep."

Don't we all, I thought. Want to sleep. Arkadi shook his cropped head, rubbing it with his strong knuckles. His tanned brow glowed with plain human sweat. He was examining things I couldn't see; he wanted me to take more pictures, pictures of all the abandoned houses and their primitive reverted yards, bursting with toothy thistles. He was urging me to document everything, shoot this huge absence that had chased us everywhere, this imitation of nature in all its latent and risky entirety, as if we could somehow capture a trace of meaning from those activities stewing away on the other side of reality. Or at least honour the dead, those men and women lost to the sudden rift, gone strangely into the night, and the dying who were still following them, every month. The local cemeteries were overflowing, blue paper flowers blew in the wind, but only the crows watched us. The outlying villages half-functioned, wooden shutters creaked on their hinges. People went on with their half-lives, hidden from the road. Old people from another time, slowly coming unhinged themselves.

"Still," I said. "It's nice out here. You can see the sky and everything. So green."

I needed to make up for the city, the city and its own dark, reversing charges.

"You should pick some leaves from these trees and take them home, compare them to the leaves there. See if they are greener, or if it is just the light." Arkadi restarted the car. His good blue office shirt was now sticky with sweat.

"I already know the answer," I said, sucking in my breath as we approached the big steel electrical towers, which greeted us like brother trolls, marching off across the plain to make war with the gods. "It's always the light. Only the light."

"You know," he mused, watching a frisky colt toss about a roped mare, "this is how we were supposed to live, inside nature. We are part of it. Not outside."

"Yes, it's true," I agreed. I got out slowly and took a picture of the demonic power lines.

Not a soul for miles.

"I think we have already destroyed nature. It's finished." Arkadi shook his head. "Now it's our turn to be destroyed."

I said I agreed; and a big part of me did, but the rest was urging the bugs and birds and weeds to get on with it, to rise up in the light and procreate, to multiply and fill the sky to the height of God's silent aerie. Remind Him of our existence. This vast, shuttered marshy emptiness (miles back Arkadi had driven right by the new blue signs, warning off those who did not have the special entry permits, without saying anything), this zone, for which ecological tours could be arranged back in Kiev – at two hundred dollars the half-day – this was my vaunted Pripet Marshes.

I had asked the doctor to drive me here a few days before, without comprehending that it was now and forever synonymous with a place called Desolation; and more, I had stupidly kept asking him, at every river we crossed this morning, whether this one was the Pripet River, finally, the original homeland of the Slavs. He would reply, yes, it's like the Pripet, this

one is called the Pri*pan*; and the slick meander filled with water lilies would eventually meet another, and I'd ask him the same question all over again, confused by this sparkling largesse that came and went, this criss-cross of cow-brooks and muddy gulleys that erupted and just as quickly disappeared underground with no resolution. He kept his eyes fixed on the road, for it did not matter to him if this was the Pripet or the Don. It was finished, over. The whole thing. Gone like the fart of a snail, as the folk-saying foretold.

Still, here was a mop-haired boy sitting alone in the waterweeds by a splendid pond, a scene taken from a nineteenth-century painting by Ilya Repin. His enormous fishing-pole scored across the duck weed, a horizontal slash of great natural intensity. So what if his catch was irreversibly tainted? Earlier, by the side of a forestry road, some kerchiefed farm women had stood linked in a chatty group, holding out artful paper cones of wild strawberries, offering them to the infrequent motorists who happened by, creating an impromptu market even more picturesque.

"How much are they?" I had asked my guide hopefully.

"No good." Arkadi forced himself to reply. The offence was deeper than wild strawberries could cure. Now we came to a deserted sandy plain; wind erosion had bared its basement rock and laid it open, a series of flat, scoured boulders on which shaggy brown moss found anxious purchase. Granite outcrops glinted like broken molars. Scrubby pines clutched at the thin topsoil in dry competition with each other.

"I want to take a picture," I said. "This looks exactly like the countryside around Vegreville, Alberta, where my Uncle Oleh goes camping."

I got out of the Lada, happy to feel the breeze suddenly pick up and cool my cheek, bringing with it pine-scented memories of my own still-pristine northern dominion.

"It's odd that my mother's relatives ended up in a landscape exactly like this one," I went on, turning to Arkadi, forcing my familiarity on him. He nodded, preoccupied with his two maps, comparing their respective versions of Soviet cartographic truth. He chewed at his lip.

"Lots of villages not on map."

"Really? That's odd."

What was odd was that, of all the people I met in my travels across the globe, these people (and this was true of recent Slavic immigrants to my city, as well as of the locals here) expressed not a whit of interest in my own country, nor in my experience of it. My opening gambits were always met by such perfunctory nods as Arkadi's. Were they being self-importantly dismissive in the superiority of their famous suffering? Or was this the natural diffidence of a people who avoided all unnecessary personal contacts, from a lifetime under pasty bureaucrats administering the harshest of expurgated regimes?

We were back on the road, and Arkadi slowed again.

"We are close to the Belarus boundary now," he murmured, dropping the Lada to a faint crawl as he reconnoitred. An old man puffing along on a wonky bicycle popped into sight around the next road-bend. My driver got out, to ask how far the next checkpoint was.

"Don't speak," Arkadi whispered to me. "Maybe they report to the authorities that a foreigner is here."

"Five kilometres," the old man replied in a high-pitched voice, scarcely looking at me, the foreigner with the baseball cap, two cameras, and the breathlessly impatient silence.

"Okay, we go." Arkadi hopped back in the car with renewed determination. "One more kilometre. Then, we turn around. If they catch us, maybe they take all your film away. Very unpleasant."

He was testing his limits, his own determination. Not mine. When we were almost at the location of the serious fallout, I began hiding my films. I did not want to lose my shot of the boy fishing. It was all I had of a morning that wasn't marred by this unspeakable confrontation with history. Arkadi hung over the wheel of the car, his ex-wrestler hands shifting gears expertly over the ruts, as he pulled us around a heap of fallen truck-debris, loose planks and plastic barrels that no one had cared to remove, although they had to be worth something. How far was he going to take us? Now I too was getting infected with his low-level anxiety, a background din of seamy expectation and a dire need for completion, for approbation. Where was the end to this road? The meltdown had happened fast, a thin plume of negative time-dust, an alternate ending that had blanketed Belarus, that dire half-country right over there behind that range of low hills. It made nonsense of our legal fictions of liability, accountability, and compensation. What was the damage claim worth? A trillion? Ten trillion? And what of the generations yet unborn? What currency would satisfy them in their netherworld of nonexistence?

What were the checkpoints protecting? The roads had been maintained. Arkadi's final and inevitable failure of nerve, a few hundred metres into the forbidden area, suggested it was the concept of authority that was being defended. What else? Surely not the land. It was no longer there, it had gone out of time, replaced in a flash by its simulacrum. We slowed at the bottom of a steep hill, and strolled a bit. The uneaten grass was improbably tender, fragrant. *Foompf!*

A grasshopper dashed against the windshield, then another and another.

Foompf! Foompf! Foompf!

Not with a whimper either, but with a *foompf*. Arkadi turned the Lada around, a clumsy four-point turn, as the engine kept stalling out. Guttural self-reproach. I struggled not to look at him. If we were going to switch shoes with the dead, it would not be on this trip. They stayed as silent as crickets shushed by hikers. The wind pushed us through the tall grasses on either side.

We drove back exactly the way we came, repeating our roundabout route over the blind corners, across the sloppy village squares, hazarding the cretinously steep grades. It all looked so different now. Arkadi visibly relaxed. He pointed out the greasy riverbank where the Russians made their final advance against the Germans in 1944 to recover the blackened city of Kiev. Here was the comfort of ordinary history. A swath of routine death and destruction that did not extend into the nameless future. The safety of the past, war museums and everything.

I concentrated on the ratty architecture of the villages, but something bothered me.

"Arkadi. When did it rain here? Last night?"

He withdrew from his inner battles to stare at me. "Maybe two, three days ago."

"Why are there so many puddles in these villages?"

"Situation in villages, bad. Worse, close to Kiev. They don't have time to work in village, they work in factory, so leave houses like this."

We passed a semi-derelict dwelling. The characteristic olive slat fences, carved wooden window frames, grotesque thistles the height of barns. A mongrel barking at the end of his tether. But the mud. The few villagers about were pushing their bikes around sour pools that effectively blocked them from free passage along the roadside. Black water lay everywhere.

"Arkadi! There are no drainage ditches!"

"You are right, I think."

"How can they be such sturdy farmers and not put in simple drainage ditches? These roads are ridiculous!" In the distance a shirtless man was scything grass, handbuilt wooden wagons bumped their way down the country lane, kerchiefed women sat under limed trees and gossiped, while their hands kept busy, plucking, weeding, knitting, something. An economy mired in pure muscle-power.

"Road is public. To make a ditch you need permission."

"So, no permission? All these villages? They must walk in mud?"

"Maybe yes."

Why did gross social ineptitude like this offend me more than the atomic blowout? Because I could relate to it more easily? Or because I was coming to respect these village women even more, these village women in their bright flowered scarves and sunburned hands, whose patient toil and limitless strength made light of all possible stupidities performed under this endless horizon of idle clouds? I was drawn to them, their mystery. I couldn't take my eyes from them, my camera finger itched. It was midday and they were suddenly everywhere, under the stork-nest tree, waiting for the bus, walking to an open farmers' market a dozen kilometres away. There she was, proud as the earth, sitting in a horse-cart, her red-and-yellow-and-blue outfit freshly pressed, accompanying her husband and her grandchild to a clinic in the next town.

They were ageless, perfect. The world revolved around them, and them alone. We stopped the car to visit a new Orthodox church under construction, with piles of fresh lumber in the rectory; and despite seventy years of militant atheism, and another decade of rabid secular consumerism, the kerchiefed women now filled the gloomy, candle-lit interior. The middle of a Wednesday morning, just before noon, and here they were, musing, aglow in prayer. Singing a mass a thousand years old.

Around them raw lumber sat in careful stacks, the pine resin mixed with pungent incense and melting beeswax. The middle-aged priest conducting the service was the only other male there, apart from the conjured dead rising in their hearts. They had proved themselves equal to all calamity, they were the indomitable, collective will of this country. Here's your book, I thought, searching among the knobby fingers and incandescent eyes. Forget the nomads, the arcane histories of disappeared dreamworlds. Just look at these women in their kerchiefs, who scarcely look back at you, because you are so out of focus. While they are crystal-hard, pure as flames.

That night, back in Kiev, I went to the Lesia Ukrainka Russia Drama Theatre to see a performance of Stravinsky's ballet *The Rite of Spring*, performed by a French troupe. It was a contemporary ensemble, meaning that it featured explicit references to homosexuality, frontal nudity, and electronic house music. Lots of sub-audible moaning. The audience loved it.

The nudity, I mean. They applauded when the Chinese principal dancer was stripped of her panties, and stood naked and pink under the throbbing house lights. You could not help noticing that her pubic hair had been artfully coiffed, and I found myself imagining the scene at the hairdresser's, when they discussed the finer points of her styling with Monsieur le Director.

"Round, or like zees? Triangular, Renee?"

"Triangular, *je pense*, Roche. But round zee edges! *Comme ça*, if you please."

What I had been hoping for did not happen; namely, for the power of art to transport me and cure my increasingly glum, post-Chernobyl psyche. The performance left me cold. It did not help that Stravinsky's music was accompanied at every turn by chirping digital medleys of Beethoven's *Fifth*, the *William Tell Overture*, or Bach's preludes, courtesy of a hundred cell-phones that went off all night in the audience; or that the people around me were particularly keen on getting a good flash-shot with their cameras of the naked sacrifice whenever she stood on the bright-green mound at centre stage, giving us a good look at her dark brown one.

We were back with Huck Finn, watching the Duke and the King enter-tain the good people of Squat Corners, Mississippi, as they pranced around the stage as naked as jays, but then what? What happens when we go outside? Everybody reached for their smokes except me and the old ladies.

She'd called me a romantic, the bitch. I remembered that now, as I filed out of the theatre with everyone else, trying to keep a lid on my growing claustrophobia as I began to notice the horribly unsafe details of the creaky old premises: the tiny exits, the bone-dry wood, the gross overcrowding (the high prices had really packed them in tonight, I'd been told. A *French* troupe). But who was she?

I don't mean Alyssa, of course, the woman who had actually uttered these words to me yesterday in a cleverly ironic art-joke, but that nude dancer on stage. A symbol marking the crest of the great human diaspora in its long flight from nature, she had to be sacrificed again and again, didn't she? Would her latest incarnation dare an approach to Modernism on her own terms, one hard, little neurotic pointe at a time? Would the locus of woman's collective strength regroup itself around another form in these fear-some post-Chernobyl days to come? Or was I making too much of a slutty burlesque? I wanted the dancer to tell me something; she remained mute.

Emancipation, exploitation, who was I afraid of more? The dozing village women in their floral kerchiefs? Or the naked girl who clutched and beat at the invisible wasps buzzing around her head?

As it turned out, Alyssa was at the same show, I saw her bussing cheeks with the other coolsters in the crowd outside the theatre. She spotted me and introduced me to her friends, asking my opinion in front of them as we strolled along. My thoughts on the production were too complex to be rendered in the noisy bar down the road, so I just said it was okay. Careful not to rain on anyone's parade. The bar owner was a pleasant young guy, celebrating his twenty-ninth birthday to a folk-rock recital performed in Ukrainian by two guitarists. One guy began dancing with him in a hot Latin lover's parody that brought the house down. The crowd sang along with gusto, drinking beer from quart tankards and chewing fried cheese and cute meat treats. Happy as clams, all of them. The table next to us was filled with staffers of the *Kiev Post*, an English-language weekly owned by American expats. I made the acquaintance of Scott Lewis, the business editor, who, judging from his pronounced cheekbones and reckless Slavic manner, appeared to be of Ukrainian extraction.

"No, I'm not, but I've been living here for two years. It's my home. I love it. I went to England last month and I couldn't wait to get back here. This is my home now, not Portland."

I found this incredible. But it was true. I watched Lewis laugh himself under the table, singing along with the hirsute, crazed band. Sometimes you find your place in life, and sometimes it's just another city with good beer and a few interesting examples of late-Baroque architecture.

Chapter 4

The Interpenetration of Light with Sorrow

In Kiev my practice has become to get up at dawn, just before 4 a.m. in my small rented apartment, shake the alien phlegm out of my chest as best I can, make myself a strong cup of coffee from the tiny reserve supply, and write as quickly as possible before the city stirs outside, before the bleeting car alarms announce a frantic new workday outside the vine-covered window.

I am having trouble sleeping. Last night, in a psychic pique from our journey into Minus-land, I dreamed of carnivorous ladybugs. They were everywhere, exploding underfoot as I crunched over them. Wherever I stepped, I created another miniature maelstrom of red, angry insects, fiercer than the first. In my dream, there was no escaping them, their wrath was omnivorous. A fellow named Jorge was taking his sailboat out into the water to flee them, and he ignored my pleas to save my family and take them along.

It was only in the coolness of the morning that I realized how this vision arose. It was a combination of the unnatural and still-unexplained epidemic of scarlet ladybugs we had endured back home last summer, artistically combined with my distaste for the odd cockroach to be found in the nuclear scientist's apartment I was renting here in Kiev. All this followed the central theme of the current epochal drama, as succinctly presented to me on the way home last night by a twelve-year-old street beggar:

"Please, mister, give me money. I am one of ten children, all poor. See? I have a certificate!" The *lopchy* held up an official form, wrapped in dirty plastic film. Unwillingly, I glanced at it, dubious. Cyrillic type. It could be anything, an expired truck-driver's licence for nuclear-waste disposal. An army conscription notice. He tried to take my sleeve.

"Please, sir! Why do you not help us? You are American and rich. We are Ukrainian and poor. You are lucky! You have money!"

He put his paper away, and pressed closer, making his final offer.

"If you do not help us, God will punish you. He will not love you if you do not help us, please!"

It was a strong pitch, straight out of the communal preachments of Tolstoy and Taras Shevchenko, Ukraine's chief bard and conscience. And if he had simply asked me, this jug-eared kid with the homespun wool sweater and no socks, rotten old shoes, I might have given him some hryvnia. Five to the dollar, pesos of the East, what did I care? But he didn't, he told me. He made his pitch based on humanity, yet I was an American, not a human being walking the same streets he was, and if we were ever going to fix this country, we would have to start with this huge chip on its shoulder. Even the street beggars are incompetent in their righteous self-regard. (Although I thought his costume rather fetching.)

See? That's why I am not sleeping well.

It takes me hours to work out these unsettled issues from the night before. And Jorge? That's me, George, my middle name. I'm the one getting on the boat, leaving my family alone on the deserted shore with these biting, fissioning insects of a globally warming summer . . . Only I'm not sure what the *sail*boat represents. Sale? Intellectual compromise?

Yes, God will surely punish me, as he has punished all my friends' parents, doling out Alzheimer's, breast and prostate cancer, coronaries, and all the other diseases with equal dispatch, these middle-aged plagues for which we need a new Bible, a new Exodus. But not today.

Today my plucky translator, Dana, and I are traipsing off to see her church, one of the oldest in Kiev, the tenth-century St. Michael's, located on a suburban hilltop close to a natural spring that once provided sweet water for its earlier pagan worshippers, as well their Orthodox successors. It was here that Vladimir the Great, (900–983 A.D.) ordered his Earth-worshipping subjects to abandon polymorphous nature in the form of Perun, Marena, and the other old gods, and plunge themselves headfirst into the freezing river where the old idols were also dumped. Today St. Michael's is the scene of an absorbing political intrigue that pits the powerful Russian Orthodox Church, with its new government funding and its control of 45 per cent of Ukraine's dioceses, against the renascent native Ukrainian Orthodox Church, which struggles to assert itself against this still-formidable foe. Few tourists who visit the more famous St. Sophia Cathedral complex on the hill in the old city know that the church, which was half-razed in the Mongol attack of 1240, is actually controlled by the distant Moscow hierarchy, or that its local officiants are generally opposed to Ukrainian nationalist aspirations, and make their case for faith in Mother Russia in their weekly sermons.

Inside the St. Michael's edifice, the icon-painters have touched up an angelic fraternity of blue Last Judgments, crowned by a curious fresco of St. Michael himself – not the human saint but the Archangel. He's got a smiley face inscribed on his brawny, dragon-smiting right arm. It isn't a tattoo, but something symbolic, perhaps denoting The Spirit of Righteousness That Guides the Smiter of Sin. There is a lot to smite, for I can hear an *al fresco* confession taking place right beside me, in the foyer of the newer main church next door. Judging from the priest's raised eyebrows, this fortyish woman with the hennaed hair has committed much odium since she was last at confession.

That's how it is in an Orthodox Church, very relaxed. You wander around during mass at will. No chairs or benches. Everyone stands around as if they're at an especially intense cocktail party, listening open-mouthed while someone tells a particulary juicy story. Instead of a light jazz trio playing Cole Porter, you have five or six women and a couple of older men chanting polytonic rhapsodies composed by cave-dwelling hermits eight hundred years ago. This church, St. Michael's, is built in the style of seventeenth-century "Cossack Baroque," an architectural movement the art publisher Praeger apparently missed. It's an arched fantasy, with white-washed walls and a big, acoustically perfect dome. The rounded space takes the priests' voices and doubles and triples them, producing a vibrato that overlays the chorus's pitch-perfect keening. Behind an elaborate gilt screen, the *iconostasis*, the priests intone their sonorous diphthongs as if they're going on that final trip, the one that ends in a gate guarded by fiery seraphs.

Altogether it is simple, sweet, hypnotic. After yesterday's forced march to the borders of the Strontium Empire, it feels calm and chaste. Dare I say it? Blissful.

I rock on my heels, remembering not to cross my hands behind my back (indicating a denial of the Creed) and watch carefully as the bearded Confessor beside me presses his penitent's head down on a Bible and speaks over her neck, intoning staccato prayers and urgent entreaties to act better next time. There are thirty people at this service, late on a Thursday morning, working-class women in tie-dyed jeans and skinny pencil pants, all wearing heavy polyester scarfs deliberately brought for the purpose. I am not sure what this modest ritual of covering the hair signifies, for these women are otherwise voluptuaries, bursting out everywhere in their womanliness and glamourized down to their toenails, painted in every colour from black to silver. The Confessor himself stands coolly off to one side, dressed in a black cassock and sporting a heavy gold belt and thick golden gauntlets like a rodeo division-champion. Bull-wrestling, maybe. With his grey ponytail and bushy, unkempt beard he might also be a member of the Grateful Dead, on the lam from the psychedelic-music business. It doesn't help that he is suddenly interested in the brassy-haired housewife, whose expansive contours show us she's got a few good miles left on her yet. Didn't he just smack his lips like a used-car salesman? Now he's patting her head, allowing his fingers to rest on the nape of her neck a trifle overlong. Is she oblivious to his carnal interest? Or does she take it in stride?

She's the one confessing; maybe she's calling the shots too.

Now he lets her get up off the Bible, and peppers her with questions, searching her dolled-up face for giveaway reactions.

So, Tamara. Did you enjoy it? Did you do it again?

I'm only guessing. They're a few paces away, and they ignore me, but the rising chorus fills every cranny in the church with heartfelt lament and reduces their soul-dialogue to a loud, mutual incomprehensibility. *Chto? Cchto tey cauzhe?*

What? What did you say? Come closer, my child!

She brushes her lips against his ear, getting it all out. The pink elocution fills the church, the eyes of the saints flicker and blink.

I take pains to meet this Father Peter, and wait by the lush rose garden outside the church. He emerges, and then struggles to tell me, in a mishmash patois of Ukrainian, Czech, and Russian, that he is a Greek, born near Mount Oros.

"Mount Oros? I know that place! It's the famous pagan site, home of the god Dionysus!"

"Yess, yess." The priest regards me with the quick brown eyes of the crafty-browed, hill-dwelling, goat-nimble, lofty Greek. "But iss also oldest church in Europe."

It transpires that Father Peter is also the local expert on exorcism, and that any persons who come to him to be exorcised must attend one regular mass here first. One would think that they would not be able to do this voluntarily, before attending to the real business if they *were* possessed, but that's a one-sided, logical track. This is the multidimensional, paradoxical problem of demonic toxicity, in which the goal and only measure of success is spiritual relief.

Uncanny efficacy. Spectral results.

"I've seen them come here too. Literally beside themselves," the ever-helpful Dana tells me in a quick aside. "Frantic and incoherent, out of their minds sometimes."

Father Peter smiles vacantly. He adjusts his thick gold armbands.

"So he has a lot of, uh, patients, or what?"

"No, he's not patient at all. He practically boxes their ears off. It can be quite disturbing to watch."

"You're there, watching?" I am too busy setting up a photo of the Exorcist to worry about our little communications glitch.

"Yes, we must sing throughout. The evil spirit hates our music."

"The Devil, or some personal demon?" Seeing the camera, the soul-fighter himself positions himself heroically against the black doorway of the chapel, the place of holy fire where he does his ten rounds with hell. Black on black, against the blackness.

"I really don't know," she shakes her head cheerlessly.

It's clear that even in this heady garden, filled with pink blooms and fantastic summer light, the interpenetration of dark cosmic sorrow continues to haunt each fragrant moment. After the pictures, the priest dismisses us with a curt nod. It's his lunchtime.

"That's interesting," I said to Dana as we drove back down the steeply pitched, sylvan avenue. "People back home wouldn't get it. This. The times. You coming to a tenth-century church once a week, to sing the devils away."

"No, you're right. It doesn't sound real, but ..."

"It feels real."

"It sure does."

"A bit spooky." It's not the right word, but she knows what I mean.

"There's a lot of magical healers and such-like, here. One fellow styles himself the Grand Sorcerer of Ukraine. They have degrees, certificates,

associations that they all belong to," Dana explains. "The local name generally for them is *kaldos.*"

"*Kaldos*? How would you translate that?"

"Sorcerer, in Russian, maybe. Do you want to visit one? It can be
arranged."

"Sure," I respond immediately, hoping all this does not turn into an
extended bout of psychosomatic self-obsession. "As long as I can get out of
it in one spiritual piece."

I look at her. She shrugs again. Placid green eyes study the narrowing
lanes for an opportunity to bolt through a fleeting hole. She slams down on
the gas pedal, and we shoot into the violent traffic of the lower city.

"Ask Larry what he thinks of Afghanistan," Dimi says to Arkadi.

The five naked men all turn as one and wait for my answer.

We are in the dilapidated anteroom of the sauna for the Construction
School of Kiev, seated around a homemade picnic table, six men ranging
in age from an eighty-year-old submarine captain who has mined off the
Baltic Sea in 1944 to Sasha, a youthful software entrepreneur whose two
cellphones provide us with nonstop musical interludes from the bottom
of his new Nike gym bag. I study the single piece of decoration on the
paint-peeling walls, an ad poster of a white-haired gent in a tuxedo, dancing
with a young woman whose skirt is slit up to her bare bum and beyond.
The caption under the champagne bottle (pointing into her crotch) reads:
Life *Counts*!

"The Americans are in trouble," I say deliberately, turning my mind
from the tricky semantics of post-Soviet advertising. "They think they
will get out of there in one piece, but we'll see . . . If they choose the
Pashtuns, then the Uzbeks and the Tajiks will get angry. There is no real
country there, only tribes who hate each other. So when they try to leave,
disaster follows."

This provokes grave nods and busy commentary. The men are all
heavily muscled, even the eighty-year-old submarine commander. What
strikes me is the surprising range of voices echoing through our sweat-
chamber. It runs from the deep basso profundo of the naval commander

(who explains he trained his voice to be heard over the roar of the high seas) to this pipsqueaky castrato of the man to my left, who appears to be a completely normal male otherwise.

This whispery-soprano vocalizing would be funny if it didn't sound like a film spider learning how to talk. I have found it emanating from many such apparently stolid he-men, something I've noticed on the public streets as well. At a demonstration of striking coal workers on Kruschvevksi Street the other day, the union leader spoke through the bullhorn in just such urgent Garboesque whispers, as if he were the recent victim of an unsuccessful strangling. Overall, I counted four distinct male vocal-styles in Kiev, all quite distinct, but none that came close to the rich middle-C tones we know as the American Business Class. These four styles begin with the low bullfrog registers of the Red Army Chorus, then rise to hit a dulcet neutral pitch, the carefully enunciated monotones of the quiet types like Arkadi and Yasha the Enforcer, and finally split off into two odd factions. On the right came the querulous whispers of Sasha, a creaky harpsichord verging on the hysterical, splintery shrieks that might easily end in the straitjacketed singsong of Gogol's manic novels; and on the left, the anti-social grunts of the real heavies, the dogged non-talkers, a sizable portion of the local population who merely point at what they want and usually get it.

Do they deliberately chose their styles at adolescence, the way we end up choosing our shoes for life, for the identity they stamp on our future courses? What is the cost? Do Sasha's voluble crescendos hurt or advance his career as a foreign-connected *bizinessman*?

I could see Arkadi's neck stiffen whenever I spoke to Sasha (the only other man who spoke good English). Arkadi plainly didn't like him, a fact I later confirmed. A few years ago, his attitude might have stemmed from political concerns. The KGB's stooges were everywhere, especially in the men's saunas such as this. Especially the saunas.

"Come. Let's go." Arkadi brusquely led me into the steam room.

I got the full treatment. First they beat me with swaths of fresh birch leaves, then they pressed the hot, sopping leaves hard against my internal organs, chasing my overheated blood up through the various chakras or whatever they called the major nerve centres there. I began feeling better, like the silver-haired Lothario on the fake-champagne poster. The exotic microbes of this country, hard by the outskirts of vile, pestilent Asia, had grown more lush and lively in my guts with each passing day. I felt worse and worse. Now my multiple reactions included coughing fits, swollen glands, headaches, fever, and sleeplessness. After the birch leaves, it all quieted down to a pleasant lassitude, disturbed only by a few minor exhibitions of frenzied midnight shudders. Maybe a dry heave or two. Nothing major.

Or so I told myself.

Forget art, forget music. Only life can cure life. I'm sick, I need life. More life, the real thing. Ukraine is getting to me, or maybe it's the threat of an evil end so visible everywhere, ranging from the mega-corruption of its seamy street-politics to its chaotic nuclear dis-industry. My childhood friend Myron Spolsky, an expat entrepreneur who moved here from Winnipeg eight years ago, tells me yet another unhappy fact over lunch in his latest café. There are mini-reactors everywhere, ensconced in all the cities of the former Soviet Union, including downtown Moscow, and so the idea of getting organic food here is total science fiction. Organic food will only be delivered after the Last Judgment is rendered. In writing.

"They hide the real statistics," he glowers. "Thyroid complaints are the tipoff to radioactive leaks." He calls the waitress over for more food, he's testing his restaurant's latest recipes on me, the discriminating consumer from back home.

Great, I say to myself, staring at my enormous platter of beef lasagna with alarm. Only another two thousand calories, hopefully. Maybe this is what Ihor the travel agent meant when he said, Watch out for the meat. Food was cheap enough here and there was lots of it, eating was the major outdoor sport here, in fact. What did they do with the glowing cows? Well, the lasagna was good, exactly like Myron's culinary-genius mother would have made. Probably the same recipe.

"So what's the medical situation here like?"

"Oh, I've got a good doctor," he says proprietarily. "He's a specialist, but his government paycheque is only a few hundred hyrvnia a month. And it never arrives."

"Meaning that he officially earns only a few hundred dollars?"

I want to be sure of this fact.

"If you want to see him, you pay him twenty, thirty hryvnia. He can't afford not to take it, and he knows what he's doing."

"Good to know. And what's doing business like here?"

"Well, I was selling commodities, bulk. Arbitraging too. One night a couple of burley guys come to my house and tell me I am out of the coal business."

"Just like that?"

"I'm lucky. They warned me. Often they don't."

"So it's tough here?"

Myron crinkles his eyes with pleasure. His restaurant is full, his factory designed for making wholesale food is finally in production. He tells me it's all good, and going up. "I was the first to introduce home delivery to this country. The first to do frozen pizzas. The first to do coupon advertising of any retailer. It helps when you're first, and there's a lot of firsts to go."

He is setting up a cheese factory next, using the McCain family's potato empire as his template. Creating his own dynasty.

"So what's the biggest problem then?"

"My wife. She doesn't like it here."

"Really? She's Canadian?"

"No, she's from here, in Kiev. She can't stand the bullying. The shaved-headed guys in the black Mercedeses have no qualms about running you off the road. It happens every day."

He referred to the endemic boorishness. "It gets to you after a while?"

"No, it happens instantly." Now his eyes became encased in concrete. "They're so stupid," he went on. "They come into my restaurant, barge around, loud voices, complaining. Shouting, 'What kind of a place is this? I could take it over, tonight!' It's the old Soviet mentality again, but with money now."

Outside the patio, two or three car alarms suddenly go off in unison. I wonder idly if the local mini-reactor just broke down, perhaps in that ruined office building across the street. Dangers lurking everywhere, but the biggest threat was the national style. Let's not talk about ideology and economics, they're irrelevant here. Let's talk about this ecosystem of bad attitude, those ignorantly square-toed shoes and gelled buzzcuts. The Dalai Lama wasn't kidding when he said he knew the Chinese were going to kill his people. He could tell from the black tappy-toed shoes their Interior Minister wore.

"I wouldn't say I am going to stay here forever." Myron signalled to our pretty waitress, a young Natalie Wood fresh from the countryside.

"What you want to do is take the good. Leave the crap. Dessert?"

The pretty girl stands smiling, all legs, awaiting my order.

My chest cold and earache get worse. There is an Institute of Alternative Healers only a few blocks from my apartment, and I welcome the opportunity to pay it a visit, even if it is simply to get away from the insidious dust of my Stalinist-era digs for a few hours. The fresh swarms of cockroaches hiding inside the garbage chute don't help either. They actually watch for me to finish eating.

Dana escorts me to the eighteenth-century building on Gorky Street, once a trading house for a sugar-beet baron. We pass through a honeycomb of offices on the second floor, and join a variety of women sitting abjectly in the unlit corridor. Old and young, poor and rich. Nothing is free any more, especially medical treatment. How are these wretches supposed to pay? Dana looks up. A florid lady with many good meals tucked inside strides quickly by, *clappety-clap*, in her new pointed shoes. The elektro-therapist. She is late, she has at least ten people waiting for her, and her consulting fee is seventy-five hyrvnia for the first visit, almost half a month's typical wages. With her dyed-blonde hair and ebullient self-importance, she reminds me of a residential real-estate agent on the hustle, smacking her lips over a particularly good month of open houses. Bustling, overdone. The smell of money cures much.

"She has this little electrical thingy that she waves over your body. To measure your flows," Dana explains as the lady slams the door behind her.

Bang! Nobody jumps.

"My flows?"

The young and real blonde lolling beside me catches on and comes to life. An Amerikanski! She crosses her legs and looks over with suddenly healthy interest.

"It measures the differential voltages or something. Like that."

"I see." We begin to sink into our seats like the others. Half an hour. The lady still hasn't seen one patient. She's re-emerged and now she's chatting with a smooth young male colleague across the hall. Does the comatose lineup make her feel important?

"Your point about the male voices at Arkadi's sauna?" Dana interrupts my musing.

"Yeah?"

"I think that's true. Once, in England, me and two other women drove this fellow from London into the countryside, and as we flattered him, his voice got deeper. He grew visibly taller and expanded the more we talked like that."

"There you go," I said wearily. The woman beside me ventured a smile. Bad teeth. Too bad.

"But then, when we came back to London, his voice weakened and he shrunk."

"His mother," I guessed carelessly.

"Yes. It was incredible. Man to worm in a few hours, a real transformation."

"Castration, you mean."

"I guess."

"There's too many people here, Dana. And we don't have an appointment even." It came out like whining.

"That's the trouble with productivity here. All these people have booked off work, claiming they're sick, now they sit and wait, and she has no receptionist, can't even organize a timetable. It's hopeless." Dana shakes her head as the blonde elektro-therapist quickly exits the colleague's office and just as quickly dashes into another, an elusive jackrabbit in a shooting gallery. Her dozen patients doze. More have begun to accumulate on the stairs, and another two hundred collective hyrvnias drop into a national void of billions. Still Gogol, two centuries later.

"Come on, let's go." I get up.

"Really?"

Dana wants me to recover, I know. I embarrassed her this morning by coming to the front door in my underwear, grotty, unshaven, wheezing and confused, when she showed up exactly on time for our scheduled meeting with a double professor. Both Philosophy and History.

"I'm okay," I reassure her. "Really. I feel better already."

Back down the sugar magnate's original parquet stairs. Oh, these cherrywood herringbone parquet stairs! The wealth, the lavish fortunes of those good old parquet days! We stop at a yellow tank parked at the sidewalk outside and order a cool cup of *kvass*, a peaty brew made from fermented black bread. It tastes like fizzy rootbeer, four cents a glass. An acidic, clean aftertaste. Not bad on a muggy summer's day.

"We had these other types of healers before." Dana examines her drink carefully before tasting it. "They were called extrasensi. They were psychic TV healers. They conducted their seances, mass seances, through the television sets at home."

"Maybe I should go to one of them instead," I responded gamely.

"Not possible. We don't have them any more."

"What happened? They all flew off to Mars on some Ukrainian rapture?"

"No, they disappeared around 1993. When we had 10,000 per cent inflation, and people started worrying about money instead."

"Ten thousand per cent? That'll do it." I watched a middle-aged woman bend over and smile at a white stray dog, studded with the massive multi-tits of the totemic Roman wolf that suckled Romulus and Remus (the dog, I mean). "Look at that woman," I pointed. "She seems to be actually talking to that white doggie. Is that some form of telepathy too, or what?"

Dana turned. "That? That's *dusha*. Kindness, soul. People have it here, but not as much as in the western part of the country."

"*Dusha?*"

We continued walking back to my apartment, making plans for the big trip to Dana's dacha in the country this coming weekend. *Dusha* and *dacha*. And *doozhe*, meaning *very*. When I got there on Saturday, I would say, "Doozhe dusha dacha, Panyi Dana!"

Very soulful cottage, ma'am.

I climbed the dark stair of the seedy apartment block and fumbled around with the intricately Byzantine key arrangement, a brass utensil as long and sharp as a jailhouse file. Something small and warm pressed gently against my calf.

A little black dog. No collar, another stray.

It had followed me up three flights of stairs. Now I knew why the lady in the adjoining apartment kept that plate of pork bones outside her door.

Dusha.

Chapter 5

Elektro-Shock Lady in La-La Land

Blood and dreams, you choose.

Me, I'm going to Friday's pub night at the Canadian Embassy. It's a Soviet-era Modernist bunker, the Albanians or somebody were here before, but they went broke. After the armed guard buzzed me through two electric doors, solely on my say-so ("Where's the party?"), I made my way upstairs to a wood-panelled reception hall, where I talked to the former ambassador Ken Lewis about the politico-economic situation for about three minutes, for icing.

"Ukraine is not going to jump over its own shadow overnight," he repeated two or three times, to make sure I got his point.

"I see," I said.

"It's not a Central European country, but an Eastern one. The first private company here was only begun in 1863, they never had a true plurality, only autocracy, here in the East. Look at Turkey! It's been eighty years since Attaturk! Give her time!"

I did. Fortified by two overpriced glasses of local plonk, I went over and sat down beside Julia, a svelte local attaché in a pink suede suit whom I had overheard speaking English and French with equal aplomb. In true patriotic fashion, I gave Julia everything I had.

"You're from Kiev?" I searched her face, her dark, yearning eyes, extra-sensorially, for key personal information. "So. You graduated from Kiev University in, uh, political science."

"Of course . . . you know me?"

She crossed her legs, and her nylons played the smoky zithers of paradise.

"No. I've just got my intuition on full blast right now."

"I see." She showed off a manifestly white set of even teeth.

"Nice outfit. What colour pink would you say that is?"

"Pink pink."

"Pink pink? I would say it's elektro-shock pink."

"So you *are* a writer."

"Yes, I are."

"And what kind of writer are you?" More slithery leg crossing.

"A very good one."

"Modest too."

She was right up there with me.

"So let's talk about love," I began.

"What kind of love?" she countered.

"Oh, the true kind."

"I *would* talk about that, if it were real conversation. But I think you are still writing. Not serious."

Yeoww. First bodycheck of the game.

"Ouch," I yelped, clutching at my heart.

"You're not so hurt." She watched me carefully, just to make sure.

"I may look tough on the outside, but . . ."

"What kind of work exactly is this writing you do?" she suddenly asked me, breaking the spell at once. Or maybe it was, "What exactly do you write about, work?" Something I didn't catch: Work? Exact change? Write off? It sounded like she was aiming directly at the size of my bank account; I was genuinely slammed by the remark, but she took it for more play-acting.

"You know, if you were a spy, I would tell you anything." I hung my head, duly vanquished, barely hanging on to the edge of my seat.

"Anything? Who cares about *any*thing!" Now she was being rhetorical.

There was another local woman working the bar, a cute blonde sporting a lot of gold rings and an easy smile. I took my leave of Julia and loped over.

"You're really pretty," I told the new woman, glad I managed to stop before adding the fateful word *too*. I was relieved at the prospect of another glass and more oxygen, it had grown awfully thin back there.

"She's married! Too late!" Her fellow bar attendant mockingly jeered at me in singsong.

"Oh, but thanks anyway." The blonde dimpled easily and handed me another sour chardonnay, poured to the brim. It slopped over my shirt.

"Didn't you see her wedding ring?" her friend continued, eagerly milking the moment for all it was worth. She took up her friend's hand and held it out for my inspection. I took it up and scrutinized her collection of jewellery carefully, pretending I had an eyepiece.

"I thought this ring cancelled that one out," I offered, holding tight to her long fingers. They laughed and laughed. I turned to see if the pink lady was watching, but she had already entered the end-of-the-week la-la land with her Embassy co-workers. They were hunched over a giant bowl of pretzels, eating them mechanically as they talked shop, the sure sign of a low-grade addiction to a well-paid and meaningless government job. I headed off to the opera without looking back.

If I were single and I lived in Ukraine and I had a real job, maybe as a government cultural attaché, with an official car, flashy red licence plates, those tan Hugo Boss summer-weight suits, maybe a soft leather floppy briefcase in nubuck caramel (the international NGO staffer's uniform, to be exact), and I learned to run these treacherous streets daily, and if the local mob didn't get me ("Get out, this now *our* bedroom!" "Can I at least take my latte?"), then I suppose I actually could marry a twenty-four-year-old ash-blonde named Larissa, from Donesk or maybe Donbass, a factory-worker's daughter, who wouldn't care that I was twice her age and sloppy, coughing and hacking at night, my lungs filled with strange Pripet Marsh fluid – at least, not the first year, as long as I didn't beat her, and succeeded in putting a selection of fine imported sausages on the table. But then what? What happens after pork chops and beef stroganoff? What does this hypothetical couple do, after their RDA of protein is secured? Go to the opera?

The opera was Borodin's *Prince Igor*. A late-Romantic pastiche of Western and Oriental and Slavonic choir music, bare-bellied dancers and avid gymnastics, fatalistically fiery sets, and thunderous climaxes from an exuberantly sweating orchestra. It featured an innovation too, in the duet between a tenor and a contralto that still sounded exotic a century after it was first performed. The libretto is based on the verse epic *The Tale of Ihor's Campaign*, which, as Professor Ostapachuk had pointed out, was quite possibly a nineteenth-century forgery. The stage work was set in the pre-Mongol tenth century, after the manner of the romantic tales of Sir Walter Scott and James Fenimore Cooper.

The central story revolves around the lascivious Prince Igor, who has been captured by the Polotvsian nomads and refuses to escape when he has the chance (pride of station, nobility in defeat), and I am struck, watching the performance, by all the archaeologically significant details of set and costume that together create a sovereign language, one that might easily escape the casual onlooker. I've spent months reading up on this stuff and, obviously, so have the set designers.

The Khan (hooked nose, black, snaky dreadlocks, the very image of Satan) clutches a horse whip, which was the pre-eminent close-order weapon of the nomads, for it was used to beat the armoured foe about his unprotected eyes until he fell from his horse. A large silver shield hangs from the blue tent, and nine horsetails hang from the shield, the classic Mongol standard, representing the nine realms of heaven and thus a sacrificial bargain made with their collective supernatural powers. Meanwhile the Khan's noble foe, Prince Igor, wears a red cape and red boots, a historically accurate depiction of the Rus leaders, the ancestral Slavs of the early medieval period. The name *Rus* almost certainly meant red, as *russo* still means *red* in Italian today. Igor's son is in green, the sapling, and the enemy camp is rendered in black and blue, the cardinal colours of the south, the steppe. The ancient Slavs had two main gods: Vales, the daily household god of fruitfulness, and Perun, the equivalent of Thor, god of storms, water, and festival. According to a novel written during the Ukrainian Famine of the 1930s, the rich land makes you soft and sweet, whereas life on Perun's open water makes you hard and watchful.

Remember this, the lesson of Prince Igor:

Water makes you hard.

Damned to another sleepless night. Some kind of shiny beetle wakes me up, crawling over my shoulder blade. A bright-red spot on his glittery carapace. Is he seeking simple companionship, or my blood? I don't care; I will smite him for waking me. After watching him a moment, I smash him with a mighty fist against the mattress, careful not to break my Walkman in my wrath.

He's crushed; it's very satisfying.

No, he stirs anew. Wriggles, flips over, and continues trudging across my bed, heading for the open window. The Rodon of the insect world, another nuclear creature that will not easily die. I must unleash the ultimate arsenal:

BLAMP!

A few more atomic wallops just to make sure.

Whamp! Whomp! Whamp!

My beating heart exults. Got him!

Great, now I'm really awake, thinking about Gregor Samsa between bouts of coughing. It's two-thirty in the morning. Only an hour or so before the holy light of another Orthodox dawn, a time when I can sleep again in relative psychic security. What was Kafka's cockroach about, really?

Not about the self-pity of being, the absurdity locked away within the family zoo, surely. Isn't that what I wrote in my first year of university? Something like that. But now that I am here, stuck alone in the murky depths of Eastern Europe, it seems too patent. No, it has to reflect the constant and indigestible intrusion of the irrational into daily life, more of that here in Eastern Europe, a huge mound of foreign matter that we must all circumnavigate in our busy thoughts, like so many ants. And where is this resistant pile of duff located?

Smack in the middle of the 2 a.m brain.

In the taxi on the way to the opera, I had asked the driver what they called the red ladybug that was crawling up the huge crack in his windshield.

"*Bohje carova*," he answered, after glancing at the insect.

"*Bohje*? God?" Had I heard him right?

He nodded vigorously.

"And *carova*, cow?"

"*Da, da.*"

God's cow? It didn't sound right, but he made a milking motion with his free hand.

"And how did you get this crack?" I pointed to the complicated frisson that was showing me downtown Kiev in the style of Picasso. "Bang, bang?" I made a pistol of my fingers.

"Bird."

"Big bird?"

"*Neh volecky*, 'not so big.' Autobahn." He made a smacking sound with his lips, making me wonder if he had ended up cooking it for dinner.

"And how much does it cost?" I rapped on the glass.

"*Scho*. A hundred dollars."

See? There's a story in everything; I was about to ask him about the one told by the aquiline crack on his side of the cab, but we had reached our destination.

"There's a persistent misconception in the West about this book," Professor Yuri Paulenko said, waving my unopened copy of *War and Peace* in the air. "*Voina i Mir*, we call it in Russian."

"Oh?" I replied rather defensively, my brain racing.

Professor Yuri, my breakfast companion today, with the foxy eyebrows and a thick head of auburn hair that traced his ancestry back to the eighteenth century and the Norseman Kievans, was, at age forty-five, a mere stripling by the standards of the Ukrainian Academy. However, he held not one but two doctorates, in ancient history and the philosophy of history. Besides being a member of the Institute of World Economy and International Relationships, he kept a full teaching schedule. We sat in the kitchen of my rented apartment, and he talked while I searched for a teaspoon that was not too corroded.

"*Mir*," he said, "has two meanings. Peace, yes, in the general sense. But more, the world, the home of mankind. It should be translated as War and the Universe."

He set my novel down with a *thunk*.

"I see." I wondered if he had noticed the book's spine was pristine. It was too early in the morning for facts, let's get away from facts and into speculation. "Do you think that Tolstoy was saying war is a permanent part of the human condition, like the Manichaeans claim?"

"Tolstoy was a pantheist. He was studying the effect of war *on* the society of the times. No, when you look at the time spent in war, it is only 7 per cent of history. The other 93 per cent is peace."

"But the nomad culture is based on war?"

"On trade." He watched me pour his coffee. I watched a cockroach reconnoitre the kitchen wall. Yuri continued: "On perfecting trade routes. They need settled civilizations to survive, for produce, for their implements. The only time they attack a settled state is when they are paid to, by another settled state, or when they make the calculation that the country is weak and they can take what they want without paying for it."

"In the opera *Prince Igor*, the colour red is associated with the Kievan Rus troops, and the nomads are all in blue. Is there a historical reason for this depiction?"

"It's a very interesting question." The professor settled back and sipped at his coffee (black, no sugar) and half-closed his sleepy-badger eyes. "*Chevrona*, Ukrainian for *red*, also means the heart, the source of life. Colours are directional in Eastern Orthodox culture. So, white is north, and you have Belarus, white Russia, and Moscow's Czar is the white czar. Black is south, *chorni*. And there you have many place names in the south, like the town Chernivetsy on the Romanian border, with this stem. But as for red, this is the colour of the centre of the Slavic world, of the simplest, most primitive colour, the hue of memory. The ancient Indo-Europeans used red ochre for their chiefly burials, just as the Cossacks used red on their war banners."

"So there is a continuing culture here, from ancient times?"

"Yes, by the sixth or seventh millennium, the people here all looked like you and me."

"What do I look like?"

"Average European type."

"I see." Was I disappointed?

"You find these ancient survivals everywhere here, particularly at the margins, like the Carpathians. In the sixth century A.D., a warlike tribe of cattle-herders called the Roxolani settled here in the west of Ukraine, and their name specifically gave rise to the Ruthenians of Austrian-Hapsburg times."

"Some of my ancestors," I nodded.

"Undoubtedly."

The professor went on. "Then you have the Veneds, who, in my opinion, spoke an Illyrian-Celtic-Italian tongue that had nothing to do with Slavic speakers, and they moved north from the area around Venice, hence the name."

"So the Veneds are not ancestral to the Slavs?" I was dismayed, thinking about my earlier, painstaking historical reconstruction.

"Absolutely not." Paulenko set his jaw, prepared to contest the point. "They did create the most common archaeological culture in our local pre-history, the Lausanne complex. But they were utterly destroyed by the Scythians in the sixth century B.C."

This gave me the opening I needed. "Dr. Paulenko, is it possible to find logic, meaning, in the flow of history? A structure, without the folly of egregious hindsight?"

"Of course. Several facts point to this. One, independently in the New World and the Old, you see the same invention of agriculture, metal work, writing, and statehood. Two, throughout the world since the Neolithic you see a rise in population density, and a rise in the mean density of commercial-information ties."

"Right." *Mean density*. I liked that phrase.

The Embassy cypher-clerk in the pink suit had dismissed me with a look of mean density.

"By the great discoveries of the sixteenth century, a worldwide trend commences, the sharing of information for reasons of commerce. Today we call it globalization. Now, in counterbalance to this progressivism, we have the clustering of distinct societies we call 'civilizations' – Hindu, the West, Muslim, China, and Eastern Orthodoxy. Five. These each have distinct values, and the important thing to recognize is that all five are self-sufficient – for human development, for self-actualization, for seeking answers to ultimate questions. They are existentially authentic. Each culture is absolutely rich and potent, yes?"

"And the dynamic that rules today?"

"Since five hundred years ago, their relations have grown more and more intense, and strained. The West began to achieve a higher level of technology, and slowly began to subordinate the others, striving to disseminate its values and worldview, leading by the nineteenth and twentieth centuries to a growing protest."

"And these controversial values? What would they be?"

"Individuality. Private ownership. Enterprise. Rationality. Democratic government."

"The whole nine yards, eh?"

"What?"

"Nothing . . . so what are the human values here, in Eastern Orthodoxy?"

"Ah!" The professor was happy to be at home again. "The collective will, equal distribution of property, authoritarianism. Mainly, the attitude that property is not the chief element of life, but that good public opinion, community, is. The revolts and revolutions we see in Russia, China, and the Islamic world are all related in this sense: they are reacting against the rapid changes to which their people can't adapt, these conflicting Western values. China has taken business practices from the West, India less successfully so. But the Muslim world is attempting to close itself off and fight globalization."

"And Ukraine?"

"The situation here is complicated, because the roots of Christian civilization are the same, but the basic tradition here is Orthodox, which is why all these Western values of private ownership, individual entrepreneurship, are completely distorted, exaggerated. Out of context."

"How, out of context? Aren't people the same everywhere?"

"For Westerners, private property conveys certain rights and carries certain obligations. But here in Ukraine, private property is used to exempt yourself from rights and obligations entirely. And here, too, individualism, which properly carries the duty to regard the individualism of others, degenerates into private aggrandizement."

"You're saying that the Mafiosi syndicates here, these guys that practically run you over on the sidewalks, these originate in the West? And not from the Tartar hordes and the bully-boys of Bolshevism?" I was incredulous. The professor almost had me, up to this point.

"Banditry, state banditry. We had it before, but never so bad. Our so-called democracy is reflected back to the West as a mirage, the mirage it wants to see. But it's really a means of manipulating us. We have the props – a president, parliament – but really our society lives by a different set of laws."

"Invisible laws?"

"Invisible to the West."

Chapter 6

To the Dacha with Two Monsters

My friend Myron, expatriate czar of the Kiev pizza empire and whole-sale food concern, is driving us out to the country on this lucid Saturday morning. We're going to a *shaslyk* barbecue, or pork-kebab cookout, at Dana and Arkadi's dacha on the western banks of the mighty Dnieper River.

To get there, we have to get there first.

"Look at this bastard, trying to sneak in," Myron growls as the road narrows and the traffic funnels into a knot. I turn to look; the guy beside us is unconcernedly holding a cigarette between his thumb and forefinger as his grey Volga slides forward, mere centimetres from our bumper.

"*Neh cohje*," Myron's wife, Rada, pleads from the back seat. "Don't argue."

"Gee, they sure drive funny here," I remark.

"I need gas." Myron spins the car around the offending driver and lurches the wrong way into a gas station, against a red hail of painted arrows shooting straight at us.

"*Voyjai, voyjai!*" His wife warns in a soft-but-emphatic voice, the trill of a woodland thrush. Watch out!

"It's okay." Myron stops the car and begins to do a three-point turn to get to the pump when a white Skoda, much like his except newer, pulls in tight behind and blocks us off.

"*Veen na delacko!*" Rada cries. He's right behind you!

"I know! Move, you idiot!"

I instinctively duck my head to avoid the blast of driver invective.

"Okay," Rada says. "He's moving."

Myron inches the car into the pump. Triumph.

He gets out and watches the attendant carefully. I am not sure why, for the petrol machine is fully automated. I turn and look at Rada, sitting quite regal in the back. Cool as a November morning, despite the boxes of emergency auto accessories piled beside her.

"So you help Myron drive like this."

"Of course. I must." A little smile on her rosebud lips.

"I think he is a good driver, no?"

"He's okay." She laughs.

Myron gets back in the car.

"That was quick. How much gas did you get?"

I am amazed at the efficiency of the new system, much faster than ours.

"None. They didn't have any."

"No gas?"

"Not the kind I need, ninety-five."

"Ninety-five? For a Skoda? I thought it takes eighty-nine, even less."

"The octane isn't the same here. They don't use metric, plus the gas is lousy to start with."

"They put in water," Rada explains.

We hasten down the highway again, heading due south, with the great blue river on our left. Myron points out a half-dozen sights along the Dnieper's banks, and today, because of the brilliant summer light, the whole city is awash in new colour, the stuccoed buildings of azure, cream, and mustard expand and embrace the midday sun, the drunken chestnut trees shake themselves out of their stupor and lavish their attention on the breeze coming sharp off the water. I love this place, even though it's intent on killing me. My strange malady has a thousand symptoms and no remedy in sight. Myron stops at another gas station and quickly changes lanes to exit, even as his wife tells him it's coming up fast.

"I know, I know," he says to the road, as if she were floating there like an angel in the middle of his vision, instead of sitting right behind him. Has Rada succeeded in immaterializing herself into his executive consciousness, Fellini-style? Beyond her other wifely domains?

"So, Rada. What do you think of your husband?" I turn around. "He's from Canada, maybe very different from the men here, yes? But he speaks Ukrainian and acts something like a Ukrainian man would act, I imagine. So do you think of him as some kind of monster, or what?"

"Yes, he's a monster." She laughs hard. Myron shrugs and gives me a look of spousal resignation, mixed with a bite of sexual tension.

"How long have you been married?" I ask him.

"Eleven years. We had two weddings, one in Canada and one here, later. I count from the first one."

"Eleven years!" I turn and take another look at her. "How old were you when you got married?"

"Seventeen," she says. "The first time. With Myron, I was twenty-five."

"Twenty-five? You don't look thirty-six, you look twenty-five!"

"I think I am monster too," she says reflectively.

I turn to examine her again, and it dawns on me for the first time how fascinated I am by these Ukrainian women, with their flashing black eyes and narrow waists, their perfect beestung lips. They aren't pretty, they aren't lovely, they aren't beautiful. Rada and her sisters are none of these things. What they are is *krasny* – their own word for what they are – spritelike, high-spirited, with the sexual magic of life-sized Tinkerbelles, and jet black hair instead of blonde.

Having the opportunity to study Myron's wife up close, I am forced to consider my own conditioning in North American standards of beauty. Here is a thirty-six-year-old woman of impetuous flammability, a woman who goes quickly from sullen unhappiness as we drive by a sulphur-belching coal-fired generator plant ("Great, huh?" Myron sarcastically remarks. "In the middle of the Trypilla district, the prehistoric foundation of the Ukrainian nation. And right beside the banks of the Dnieper, yet.") to breathless joy when we spot large fishhawks chasing each other across the horizon. She is mercurial, charged, stylish.

Today Rada is wearing a smart black suit, pencil pants and jacket with white counter-stitching, and up-to-date French sandals, and when Myron tells me that the women in Ukraine always buy the best outfits they can afford, I ask her how much money she spends on clothes.

"Nothing," she says in perfect English. "I get all my clothes from our store."

"You've got a clothes store here too?"

"Yeah, it's our outlet store," Myron explains. "We sell stuff from a factory in western Ukraine. They produce lines for Paris, where they sell for five hundred dollars apiece."

"What do you sell them for?" I want to know.

"Don't ask. Five bucks apiece, maybe even less."

We pass another accident in the middle of the highway. An old Zaporozhets sedan has come undone, flopped on its side like a snagged carp, while its antagonist, a bottle-green Pontiac Bonneville, sits unscathed.

"Broken ball-joint," Myron offers his diagnosis. "Happens all the time. I've just got mine replaced. It's the roads."

A white van with flashing blue lights and no other markings roars past.

"Security company," he explains. "They are picking up money from stores. They go faster than ambulances or the police. Shows you where our priorities are here. Stupid bastard, look at him go."

Now the van cuts across another car, almost colliding, and speeds off the ramp on two wheels.

"They're not the worst though."

"Yeah, what's the worst?"

"You'll see. The president's official country residence is coming up. There'll be lots of police and it's posted down to forty kilometres, but his guys will be doing a hundred or more without blinking."

"That must create accidents. Two sets of speed limits on the same stretch, forty and infinity?"

Myron nods vigorously. "Last year, just around here? Kuchma's aide comes whipping by, kills an old man on a bicycle, and the official investigation says it's the old man's fault."

"How old was he?"

"Seventy-two." Myron breathes invisible fire, his eyes narrow as we pass the presidential cottage. Elaborate, manicured grounds, wrought-iron gates, decorative gold-tipped spears, a villa for the new Byzantine prince.

"I can just imagine the inquiry," I respond, trying to cool him down. "He's seventy-two, they say, that's one more year than the national average. He's had a good life already, whereas our Pavlo here —" I pretend to cuff the bad-boy driver in the ear. "He won't do it again, will he?"

"I'm sure that's what happened," Myron bitterly agreed, and sighed.

"Turn off, next exit." Rada is reading from a detailed two-page typed set of instructions. "Turn left at the war monument past the school, and go left at the high hill."

"High hill?" Myron obeys, but scans the horizon anyway. "*What* high hill?"

"That one. Listen!" She repeats the directions carefully.

"That one's not very high."

We pass villages with huge, overgrown torrents of grass; wild winds, cascading freely off the river, engulf us from every direction. The grey slat fences divide the cottage yards of the neighbours haphazardly, but with morose purpose. There is a fractal village logic at work here, a blunt, severely wooden order, born of peasant necessity and grievous social history. The real story began, or ended, here, behind these shuttered windows, for this is the ground zero of modern history, the bull's eye of the twentieth century: a Ukrainian village on the long road of death between Berlin and Moscow.

Only the fields lie open and more; they are so open they stretch off without limit, the tiny, bent figures scything hay in the sunshine today are dwarfed by their unpossessed vastness. Here is the essential contradiction of the West's eastern frontier. To whom does Ukraine belong, in its inestimable devotion to a forsaken utopia of light? To these tight-fisted little communities themselves? Divided and subdivided into the tiniest meddlesome factors of the social calculus? Or to these green miasmas, to trackless Asia, steppelands unspooling indifferently, melting away into the haze of the south, leaving behind them no trace of order after centuries of human effort?

And here in the peasant villages the young girls continue to walk alone. Short skirts, new sandals, fashionable blouses, but going where? Where is there to go?

The rutted shoulders of the main road provide the only social space available; the old ladies sit in tight avian clusters, a single, pointless bucket of just-picked potatoes giving them necessary justification for their collaboration. A decaying bus stop stands empty, decorated with a brittle photogravure mosaic of frozen cosmonauts and kerchiefed handmaidens; a flock of white ducks scurries along as if they, too, seek the freedom of the open road, diesel-rank and polluted though it might be. Between the fences, dirt tracks ramble away at eccentric right angles to our passage, but the village itself has no inner streets as such, no direction, and I am reminded of the wall-sized map of eleventh-century Kiev in the hall of my rented apartment. Ancient Kiev had been laid out just like this. No grid, no parks, no real centre. No town. The only social spaces abutted its many churches, like little frozen afterthoughts, and a defiant wasteland lay beyond the gates, a barricaded reproof to civic aspiration.

"Sheet-metal roof, sheet-metal fence." Rada reads aloud. "That's the one."

She points off to our left. They all have sheet-metal roofs, I think.

"They all have sheet-metal roofs!" Myron insists. That's why I like him.

"This one. Go this way." Rada is getting impatient. She adjusts her smart little top, fiddles with her lipstick. Another important social occasion coming up. Myron and I exchange looks of the semi-defeated, gamely doing the Man's Right Thing.

The dacha owned by Dana and Arkadi was a two-storey concrete-block house, outfitted with a steel roof and shutters, and separated from its neighbours by the aforementioned steel fence. The door was open, a pair of elk antlers hung prominently in its whitewashed interior. The grass in the yard was knee-high, scratchy hard, ready to burst its seed; red poppies grew wild in clusters here and there, opium poppies, the real thing. There was a cherry tree, two tabby cats, one orange and one ginger. Three or four couples sat in the grass, their sunburned faces just visible over the flowering tufts. Arkadi greeted us in army shorts, giving us the happy smile of a lover of the countryside, frankly relaxed, in his home element at last.

"You find us okay?" Dana held her daughter up to the sun, as if seeking the healing powers of the Mighty Orb for her. Or a dose of Vitamin D, whatever.

"No problem," Myron snorted. "The directions were so detailed, it read like a novel."

"A good novel, I hope!" Dana looked to me.

"One can tell you're an editor." Another Myron spoke up. An engineer, he was bigger than the first Myron. "Footnotes on the footnotes!"

We introduced ourselves to the other guests; like Myron, they were mostly expats too. Peter and Lily were American and French, respectively; he worked for a cigarette company. Their two-year-old son, Nathan, had pulled off a wiry grass-head and invited each of us to sniff it. Oksana, who walked with a new cane, and Ihor, her husband, were from Edmonton, Alberta; they owned a factory in western Ukraine that made commercial neon signs for other businesses, having converted a local optical plant that had produced surveillance technology for the previous regime. Lidia published the *Eastern Economist* in Kiev, an English-language weekly featuring current economic affairs in Ukraine. Slava and Lubomyr, an international trade lawyer, were on holiday. Their stories were all fascinating. But Big Myron's were scary:

"Eighty thousand Ukrainian scientists engaged in theoretical weapons research – we're talking mass-destruction weapons here, stuff you wouldn't dream of – were suddenly made redundant. So, in an attempt at an incubator program, they were all given grants to branch out, and many wasted their money on such useless projects as earthquake prediction and human electromagnetism. But still the government pronounced the program a success. Only sixty thousand remained jobless, from the original eighty thousand."

"Only. So where had the twenty-thousand nuclear scientists gone?" I asked him.

Big Myron pulled at his moustache.

"Iran, Iraq. Turkey too, probably. Whoever offered them a job."

"Talk about nuclear fallout," I grimaced. "That's worse than Chernobyl!"

"Oh, yeah," Oksana the factory owner joined in, waving her cane. "This is one weird country."

"How did you hurt your back?" I asked her solicitously.

"Car accident, last year. I broke my spine."

"I'm sorry."

I shuddered, for we had driven here in the relative emptiness of Saturday traffic, and I was still terrified by my seatbelt, which kept popping off, and by the other drivers too. Drivers in bigger cars cared nothing for my life, judging from their profound interest in their own smokes. My friend Myron also said he had been struck down recently – by a serious illness – and he had pointed out his rehab clinic next to the president's country estate. Were the expats shocked by such terrible conditions, or was the problem here deeper than their comfort zone?

Deeper than that. Lidia told me she got sick all the time too, despite her lithe figure, good constitution, and sensible lifestyle.

"We get sick here all the time," she offered. "Bad health system."

"Terrible health system," someone countered.

Five or six of us decided to stroll down to the river. Arkadi brought out chunks of veal soaked in brine, mayonnaise, and dill, and waved his collection of wicked *shaslyk* skewers at us.

"Don't go far. This will all be ready in twenty minutes!"

The sudden view that emerged from behind the ridge of twisted bushes was completely unexpected, and profoundly disturbing. The Dnieper is a river, in the same way that Superior is a lake and January is a month. It is enormous, imperious, unrestrained, and unfulfilled. Great treed islands floated like specks in the middle of the main channel, and more green islands dotted its other channels, blue channels that raked the land eastward, cutting it a dozen times over, it seemed, as far we could see, a great, divided sea of surging, tumbling waters that swept quickly by the naked, sand-struck cliffs, bearing away with it all the desolations of millennia. Indifferent and sovereign, it rolled on in astounding silence. No human habitations marked its passage, no ships or boats traversed its calmer stretches. Glittery little rapids, broken pillows of scoured bedrock, fumbling heaps of sediment, these were what provided the scale and measure for its passage to the sea. These, and a few plumes of smoke, far in the south.

"Are these waters relatively clean?" I asked the lawyer, Lubomyr.

He squinted his blue eyes against the afternoon haze.

"You asked the right guy," he replied evenly. "I'm working for the UN right now, an attempt to set up a bilateral water commission for Russia and Ukraine. From the studies I've seen, these waters are loaded with radio-nucleotides."

"Radio-nucleotides? Is that a new word?" I stared at the blue immensity coursing below us; we simply never see colossal forces like this in the West. And it runs through the country.

"Yeah," he laughs. "It covers the radioactive sediments, strontium and so on. Our word. We measure them, and we keep getting further readings. They're still dumping, these countries."

The conversation now turns to what is safe to eat these days. Wild mushrooms are toxic, domestic are okay. Peter the American executive listens with a horrified expression that grows grimmer with each food category. All berries are suspect, the milk is dangerous, rumours persist about the boxed juices, soup can be deadly. Even the simple apple has an ugly reputation.

"Time to go, folks."

We head back to the dacha, hungry now.

"How long have you been out here, Peter?" I inquire.

He's about forty, a young marketing manager on the way up.

"Two weeks. We came here from Lausanne, Switzerland. It's been quite a transition."

He looks aghast as we are forced to step over broken bottles, sparkling in the tall grass. Dangers lurking everywhere, never mind the onion soup.

"How are you going to spend your weekends? Do you have friends here?"

"Just the guys at work. There's about fifteen of us," he says, meaning expats. The cigarette company he works for is one of the biggest in the world, and one of the biggest taxpayers in Ukraine. I asked about his job.

"I'm in strategic planning," he bit his lip. "It's a twelve-hour day."

"You're kidding! I thought the expat lifestyle was pretty loose."

"Not here. It's all about taxes. The total taxes are over 100 per cent. And they keep coming up with new ones. So you have to deal with that. That's my job, figuring out how to deal with their tax laws. And the tax guys."

"Two different things."

He nodded imperceptibly, then changed the subject, asking about my book. I told him my game plan, and he seemed happy that someone else thought he could bring mental order to this unruly land. His apartment was on the sixth floor. Already the elevator had broken down completely, while the hot water had disappeared inside the clinking of unseen plumbing.

"How's your wife with it?"

"Oh, her family was originally from Kiev, so it's interesting for her. She's okay, I guess."

His wife, Lily, told me her family was Jewish; her great-grandfather was a sculptor in Kiev, who had moved to Paris in 1905.

"Was he a great art celebrity?" I asked her.

She was a classic European beauty, bearing the chic style of the Parisian madeleine: doe eyes, expressive fingers, a temperamental eyebrow that did most of the talking.

"No, he was one of the great *inconnus*, the unknowns," Lily laughed. "I have one of his sculptures only. All the rest are gone, destroyed in the war."

She told me she lost family in Auschwitz; now she was here, in the sunshine of an effervescent garden patio, on a summer's day picnic with her American husband and blond son. Is life a kind of strange delirium? We watched little Nathan chase the ginger cat through the tall grass. Dana brought out the food: a salad of wild mushrooms and chopped onions, *borecki*; chopped beets mixed with pulped carrots; another salad of lettuce, parsley, and dill. *Shaslyk*, seared chunks of veal, with a violet sauce of chilies, tomatoes, and pomegranate juice. Potatoes, boiled, of course. And baskets of the famous black bread.

"I think I should mount this slice on my wall, as an icon," I said, holding my piece up, to general hilarity. Meanwhile the ginger cat had found a field mouse, a tiny pretty creature, caught it and let it go again.

"She's torturing it," Slava murmured knowingly. The mouse ran straight for us, and dived between our legs. The ladies duly lifted their feet, and shrieked a little, as they ate.

Little Nathan had discovered a set of red binoculars in the grass, and now he used them to study Rada, who stood tall and still like a supermodel, dreaming of the perfect red, perhaps.

You could tell from his childish squint, he found her as fascinating as I did.

Chapter 7

Is This Yours?

Back in Kiev, I barely the survive the night. My eyes water, my chest heaves. My lungs reject everything, I massively self-medicate at midnight, with antihistamines, cough syrup, Aspirin, and caffeine, the whole works, anything to get some badly needed sleep. I managed only two hours the night before. The next thing I know the phone is ringing and it's the landlord's wife, asking me when I'm leaving, and I still feel too sick to go anywhere. Too weak to go the bathroom, never mind Crimea.

I force myself to go down to the smart little corner café and order a cappuccino and a sweet crusty roll, still warm, and a cold grape juice in a foil packet. It revives me. Riffs of light, jazzy acid-house music too, from the silver mini-speakers. I order another of everything, stand over the polished marble counter out in the street, and turn to face the fresh breeze coming up Chervoniskarminska Street. I begin to feel better. I can breathe.

Maybe it's just that stale Stalinist dust in my lodgings.

Sunday morning, about ten, the sun is out but not blasting. Traffic is light. I walk back to my apartment block, slowly, admiring the pretty girls in their miniskirts, still so out-and-about, even at this early hour.

As I turn into the corroded tunnel-driveway that leads to my old building, a young guy in a track suit edges past me, close on the right, stops, bends over beside a parked car, gets up, and, with a look of deep shock on his wide, bland face, holds up a soiled cellophane package, a stack of U.S. cash clearly stuffed inside, and says to me,

"*Toh vash?*"

Is this yours?

With a look of great respect, he holds it out. To me, the rich foreigner.

Of course, the cash wad wasn't there before. It's a scam I recognize from the guidebooks, but they mentioned it as occurring only in dusty Uzbekistan, not here in civilized Ukraine. I walk away quickly, run up three flights of stairs, unlock the door with my hook-toothed key, lock it up again, double, triple lock it, and take a deep breath. I want to go to the window and look out, but I am afraid to: they might be watching.

The way it works is, you say, yes, it's mine, then the guy's friend comes over and they demand a reward for finding your money, which is worth more than the newspaper scraps folded inside the U.S. twenty-dollar bill. Or more likely they beat you up, which I think was the plan in this case, because he was so careful to do his number in the deserted lane, from which there was no chance of escape.

Violent hustles like this are a common part of daily existence in Kiev these days, Myron said, as we drove away later that morning to the tenth-century Cave Monastery to examine their famous collection of ancient nomad gold.

"Well, how many people do these guys get a week, and how much money do they earn?"

I was still unnerved by the experience, mainly because it happened only a few yards from my apartment, in the best part of town, and I felt that I had been under surveillance the whole time I was blissfully enjoying my little Euro-moment at the café. Was my mistake in taking that second cappuccino outside the little place, where they had ample opportunity to size me up? Undoubtedly. Now I was thinking like a local. Like Arkadi, who just the other day had been compelled to analyze exactly why a traffic cop stopped us, us of all the drivers flying by him. They were still here, this legion of dangerously unpredictable watchers.

"I don't know," Myron shrugged in reply to my question. "But it's really common here."

"Which way are you going?" Rada asked from the back seat.

"I'm just showing him some buildings . . ." Myron pointed out the stuccoed Ukrainian parliament buildings, and made me pay particular attention to the plaster-fretwork trizub, the ceremonial trident dating from medieval times, a symbol that had replaced the hammer and sickle. "The best estimate is that, between 1915 and the end of the Soviet occupation in 1991, fifty million Ukrainians were killed."

"Break that down for me?" I stared off into the middle distance of historical duty, the burden of the itinerant chronicler weighing heavier with each morning.

"Ten million in the Great Famine, twenty million in the Second War, and another fifteen in the First War and its aftermath, and then five million killed individually as members of the intelligentsia by the Soviets in 'peacetime.' Directly, from lists. Priests, teachers, lawyers, village elders, what have you. Anyone with brains."

We passed another monument, this a huge iron-and-bronze sculpture honouring the dead, the effigy of a pro-nationalist politician. Impressive in a whiz-by glance. But how many monuments would it take to satisfy my speeding friend? The city was already full of such statues and newly restored churches, gilded and festooned with garlands. And still the memories haunted and burned, and all the loot of the world wouldn't bring back the lost summers of the dead. So what would? What would answer all this blood, was there enough silence in the whole universe to frame that question in some final honour?

We entered the highly decorated archway of the Cave Monastery, a collection of white, Eastern-style churches with gold domes and delicious pink-and-powder-blue frescos, facing a cobblestone plaza shaded by more opulent chestnut trees. In the middle of the square, a rough chunk of the original church's masonry had been lovingly preserved, covered with a copper cupola and emblazoned with a large cross. People stood around, respectfully bowing to it.

The sacredness of history.

This artifact of the first millennium reminded me we were entering the third, and that we were now exactly where they were, a thousand years before: waiting for something big to happen. Inside the museum housing the gold collection, we were met by Professor Vital Zubar, an archaeologist specializing in the Classic Greek remains found in the Crimea along

Ukraine's Black Sea coastline. The most famous site was Chersonessus, a Greek settlement that had traded with the nomadic Scythians for hundreds of years, and whose continued existence as a solitary outpost of civilization, locked deep in the nomadic heartland, poses a puzzle about the true relationship of nomadic cultures to urban ones. Indeed, Chersonessus's long existence raises huge questions about the true nature of Greek civilization itself. It may be that the dynamism of Greek culture derived from its continued and long-term contacts with such "barbarian" cultures, and not from Plato's abstract "logos." It's a secret that the recurrent myth of the Centaur, who teaches the Greeks critical life lessons early in their mythic history, seems to imply, for Zeus himself must ally with the Centaurs to conquer the fearsome Titans. And, according to Robert Graves's book *The White Goddess*, the Titans were the pre-Greek, indigenous people of the mountains of Thessaly, and the war relates to a prehistoric struggle for the region about 1500 B.C.

Zubar is a young, robust man in his late thirties, with black stage-eyebrows like a front-row spear-holder in the *Prince Igor* opera. He leads us through rooms guarded by slouching sentries with well-oiled machine guns. The Scythian gold collection that gleams provocatively in these glass cases is the country's patrimony, and priceless. The Scythians swept through Central Asia around 600 B.C. and erected their *kurgans*, their royal burial tombs, everywhere in eastern Ukraine. They dug out a vast tomb only thirty kilometres from Kiev, near the present-day Bosporil International Airport, a fact I found both satisfying and mysterious. Had this location always held some special significance for transportation, I wondered? Zubar refused to be diverted by such questions from his intended program; he led us from room to room in sequence, explaining that there were essentially three zones of geology in Ukraine, the woodland in the north, the forest steppe in the middle, and the true dry steppe in the south, including Crimea.

"This is as far as the Royal Scythians go, in the West," he remarked airily. "From here into the West, you have only the *common* barrows, which are to be found all across Europe, to England."

I heard Rada swoon from the next room. She had found the central display case where the Great Scythian Necklace was kept, a fabulous masterwork of incredible complexity, illustrating the worldview of the Royal

Scythians the way Michelangelo's *Last Judgment* illustrated heaven for Renaissance Italians, except the former was portable, possibly worn by one noble woman and only in her lifetime, then buried below the steppes forever, in the dark "third" realm. Rada couldn't tear her eyes from it.

"The original is in the State Bank vault," Zubar whispered reverently. "Insured for seven million dollars."

I bent to take a closer look, after Dana recalled there was a tiny man sewing a tiny shirt in one corner of the necklace, but I couldn't find him. I did find the gold honeybees, and gold boars, gold panthers, gold horses, and gold gryphons in abundance. The necklace stretched eight inches at its widest point; it must have weighed a good five or six pounds. It clearly divided itself into three horizontal sections, and the professor confirmed the general consensus of his peers, which held that these three parts referred to the three zones of the nomad cosmos. The daily life of robust animal husbandry was at the top; then a geometrical frenzy, the fantasy world of dreams, lay in the middle. The mythical realm lay at the bottom, presided over by horse-killing gryphons.

"What's the gryphon mean?" I asked the professor.

"It's a Middle Eastern motif, from Babylon." Zubar shook his head. "The influence becomes less as time goes on, with the Scythians. Then, around 300 B.C., there is a catastrophe, a Big Season cycle of high heat and terrible drought begins, and it lasts for two hundred years. By the end, the Scythians are gone, replaced by a new people from the east, the Sarmatians, who arrive by 100 B.C. They are more primitive than the Scythians. But they have iron."

"So these cycles of wet and dry are natural?"

"There is nowhere for nomad people to go. It's a dead-end culture. A short cycle every fifteen years kills off half their herds, so they are not self-sufficient, they can't support themselves. Settled people can survive these natural cycles. Nomads die."

We came to a scale model of Kiev that filled one end of the room, a series of fenced log houses, carved wooden churches, and Viking-style dragon-ships that plied the Dnieper River.

"How big was Kiev at the time of the Tartar attack in 1240?"

"I do not know," Zubar shrugged, but the big blonde women sitting on the custodial chair behind us spoke up.

"Fifty thousand people," she said proudly. "When Paris had only ten thousand, and London, thirty. And four hundred churches too!"

I shook my head. "And after?" Meaning the Mongols.

They looked at each other and shook their heads. Zubar answered carefully, "Enough people survived that the Mongols kept coming back, for three hundred years."

He turned and led us deeper into the vault.

Much of the country's ancient past had been converted into loot, not information, by its previous societies. We saw fantastic pieces dating to the sixth and seventh centuries A.D., but the archaeologists couldn't say where they originally came from, not with certainty. A cache of gold crosses, presumably taken in raids from Constantinople in the seventh century A.D., had been found in a pagan burial mound.

"So what's the meaning of history?" I asked Zubar as we sat down to iced tea in the rain-swept courtyard outside. His answer surprised me.

"You see all this gold, all this effort? For the tombs of the dead? For me, it is the same today. Here, and now. The money is spent on monuments, and rebuilding churches, on memories of the dead. And not on the living, who need it more."

He gave me his card, and told me to use it when I got to Chersonessus in Crimea, suggesting hotels and restaurants on the way. I was reminded of those pilgrim maps that guided the faithful to the Holy Land, which consisted of a black squiggle scored by notes on the experiences one might expect, scaled to their anticipated intensity, and culminating in a mysterious black cross marking Jerusalem itself. Did he like Greek classicism? I asked him.

"Ancient Greece, yes. Modern . . ." He shook his head.

The rain had failed to clear the city's air, the humidity soon grew oppressive. Beside us at the next table, a little girl of three unaccountably began screaming her head off at us. Her hoodlum father had a shaved head and a pretty suit. Her mother was young and wisp-haired. They sat together in utter silence, ignoring her shrieks, as a pretty waitress brought them dish after dish, lavish food they barely touched.

◈

There is too much to see, too much to do. I did not attempt to see the famous monkish mummies in the caves below the monastery, or a hundred other curiosities either; and as we drove away I was already fending off future exclamations of surprise and disappointment ("You didn't see the mummies? Why not?"). I have nothing against unrotting old monks from the eighteenth century, believe me; it is just that the dialogue is so one-sided. They have Imperial Death on their side; and me, all I have is my rapidly dwindling supply of antihistamines and a bottle of suspect, thick-as-lard, brown Russian cough syrup. Yes, I am still indisposed, as an English travel writer, perhaps smitten with leprosy in Calcutta, might say. And more, I am disturbed, but strangely gratified, to read in my *Lonely Planet* guidebook that certain of my predecessors on this eastern literary circuit have also come to strange medical grief. The Central Asia edition of *Lonely Planet* unkindly scolds travel writer Brad Newshan for "toting a bale of misery" around with him, and so too Mary Morris, for "labouring under a cloud of self-created doom." The final thrust by the Aussie publication: "Both of [their] books will be of greater interest to psychoanalysts than to Trans-Siberian travellers." Well, pardon me. In the country where I come from, we stopped equating disease with moral lapse about forty years ago, but apparently that notion hasn't quite made it to the ruddy Island Continent yet. If what I've got is anything like what these two writers suffered, then this malady is a key part of the real story of Central Asia, whether its psycho-whinging or not; and it's making me look more closely at these guidebooks for real he-people, to see what else they might be omitting or suppressing in their campaign for branded virtue.

You need to have the hide of a drunken walrus not to feel the icy claws of death unsheathe themselves, each time you go out, here in Kiev. Day or night. The town fairly reeks of secret evil, and I've barely begun my trip. Are these thousands of churches and museums intended as a prophylaxis against the fatal black icicle? Does the limpid choir music provide a direct salutary shield against a legion of uncanny ills? As far as I can see, there is no intellectual content to the local religion. Orthodoxy was never a religion of speculation anyway, but a waterfall of sound and colour, bleeding beauty off into the wings, overwhelming its unhappy brood with its mystical cant, and sending its harmonious dirges down the soul river of time. By that, I mean both that real blue river outside the city's windows, the defiled aqueous life of the nation, and the river of images we call a person's inner life. Orthodoxy is not all that orthodox. It's held together by two or three key symbols, three great unsolvable koans: the Trinity, the Mother of God, and the Crucifixion. None make any a sense, they're not *supposed* to. Beeswax candles priced according to size, doe-eyed saints staring back at you from every dark corner, an intimation of Mercy, an absolute certainty in the existence of Evil, and there you have it. A Mystery Religion fit for the masses, complete with a few sparrow crumbs of hope. Just enough to be realistic. No promises. Who *cares* about doctrine? The need for pure faith and regular attendance is abundantly self-evident here, just look out the window. Horrors everywhere, ancient and digitalized. What else is going to restore us, when absolutely nothing works in this afflicted society? No, only these archetypal Absolutes can deliver clarity and purpose. What will it be? Divine Motherhood? Supreme Fatherhood? Transcendental Justice? Take me to the nearest eagle-winged angel. Please.

These icons arise straight from a collective imagination set at ground zero; or as one Father Olech, a radical Uniate priest, told me the other day, "There are three ways to approach God. First, prayer, directing yourself to God. Secondly, contemplation, and the imitation of saints. And finally, meditation, looking deep within yourself. Good works, yes, charity of course, but the final job, for the sinner, the big obstacle, the greatest setback, is to work on the miserable soul within you."

Do I miss my semi-Protestant homeland, yet? Do I miss my self-reliant Baptists, community-minded Catholics, and circumspect United Church neighbours? Not yet, not quite.

It's late afternoon, and Dana, my indefatigable translator, and I are standing in a parking lot, looking for an apartment number provided by Arsen Savadov. At age thirty-nine, Savadov is Ukraine's leading avant-garde artist, a man to whom all things have been given: boundless energy, the good looks of a younger John Travolta, huge talent – and the job of re-sacralizing the profaned wastelands of his nation through the fierce strategies of his radical-art projects.

Savadov bounds up the basement stairs – he's an underground artist, yes? – and leads us back down into his grotty New Yorkish studio. A large, bright room greets us, with two big oil paintings in progress at either end. One depicts a Messerschmitt fighter plane that has crash-landed on the moon. I ask him if it's Joseph Beuys crawling out of the cockpit, the German conceptual artist who was saved by Central Asian nomads in the Second World War when he crash-landed over the Urals in the dead of winter.

"Beuys? Boys on the Moon! Good title!" Arsen laughs out loud, and invites us to sit and take some fresh-picked cherries from a large bowl that is set in the middle of a battered 1950s coffee table. A pouty sixteen-year-old girl airily slides around the room, mumbling to herself, or maybe she's singing along to the tape in her Walkman. Someone's daughter, Arsen carefully explains. The phone rings, and Dana kindly gives me a running translation of Savadov's efforts to beg off a dinner date with a lady friend:

"Lola! *Lola!* Don't be offended! Look, I have guests from America! I had a terrible trip, I'm exhausted! Please, please. My dearest, I have guests, I'm exhausted. I kiss you, I kiss you again. Bye bye. Yes, yes! Tomorrow, of course."

He puts the telephone down and looks at me, sees that I am happy. I like it here. I like the music, ambient industrial house mix. The lofty art space.

I tell him I feel safe, the first time in Kiev.

"Yes, yes. It's the energy, the energy of art. People come here all the time, drop over. I am moving to a new studio down the street, so I can work. This place I will keep only for social gatherings."

"How important is this *tatsolka*, the obligatory art-gossip socializing, to you?"

I mean by this the worldwide trend to ephemeral art forms, the micro-shows by invitation only, intended to wholly bypass the traditional systems of commodification and mass media in favour of spontaneous communities. It was one of the few defences available to contemporary artists, permitting them to keep working without being labelled, and then disposed of, as "last-year's model."

"*Tatsolka!* I love *tatsolka*. Except that I am professional *tatsolka!*"

"You're more than that." I pointed out. "I saw your video on TV the other night. You staged a brilliant street-theatre event in 1999, May Day. Half-naked men in red tutus and red capes, standing silently in fashion-model poses, as the old Communist Party did its traditional march-past parade. This was deliberately provocative, yes?"

"Of course. That was part of my project entitled *Collective Red*. I began it in 1998. For that, I was arrested during the performance. I was taken to the police station, and they stopped the project."

"Who are the people in the projects? They seem to be real, ordinary people, many of them, if I can use that expression for such profound faces, such interesting bodies."

"It works like this: I begin a project, I get together the people to be in it, then we shoot photographs for maybe five hours, for two days or more. There is no 'audience.' Just the participants themselves, up to a hundred people, real coal miners like in my project called *Deepinsider*."

He handed me a large colour photograph, a high fashion shot taken in a cemetery, seemingly.

"I understand. And is this funeral real too?" An old baba was weeping, piles of raw yellow earth. The drugged mourners were slack with shock.

"Of course, real funerals," he said happily.

I thought of Tantric practices, meditating in the fresh graveyard, and I went there.

"It seems to me, your work is Romantic? Devotional? Is that how you would call it?"

"Yes, yes, yes." He was happy now, I understood him. Not like some critics, as he would tell me, pulling out his indifferent reviews from the *New York Times*:

> Evidence of the show's low budget is the untitled photographic installation by Arsen Savadov and Urii Senchenko from Kiev. Large photo murals are fixed to the walls and the floor with black electrician's tape, a humble counterpart to the high life depicted in the murals.
>
> > "Eastern Europeans Envision the Future"
> > by William Zimmer, *New York Times*,
> > February 1, 1998.

"I am romantic underground," he continued. "Real underground! For Donbass Chocolate we went deep underground, 1,500 metres into the famous Ukrainian coal mine."

He pulled out more colour photos, real miners, their naked torsos smeared with a dark syrup I *hoped* was chocolate, or maybe diesel oil, but it looked worse than that. Social protest, yes; but no derision. An almost-innocent playfulness shone through his photo tableaus, an attitude that managed to confer his participants with a childlike joy. It was as if Savadov had decided to dress real people up (and undress them) in the manner of a much-loved set of toy soldiers, whom he then played with, for hours on end.

"What is the effect on the participants of your exhibitions?"

"The performance is in real time, in real space. It is very difficult to get them to participate, so that is the first piece of work, and the second is to film it. And I suppose, the most important part of my work is the first thing, that something remains with them, something new arises. And changes with us also, that we move together."

It was his child-models who really got to me, these happy, innocent children, depicted nostalgically as the sunny flowers of a Soviet-promised *kinder*-paradise. And as I flipped through the box of photos, I found a real school class picture, dating from the late 1960s or early 1970s. Rows of seven-year-olds smile into the camera, with a tinsel-laden Christmas tree, a glittery full-scale snowman, and a portrait of Lenin looking on benignly from the corner. The kids are wearing white bunny ears for this festive season, a season dedicated to secular make-believe and childhood fantasy.

"Children take heart," begins the manifesto of a 1993 show that Savadov curated in Munich, "There is a life after this one!"

Savadov's art insisted on innocence, the primacy of first experience, the heroic acceptance of what is; coupled to a decorative delight in vast industrial-scale schemes, what one American critic calls "heroic simulation." I asked Savadov about Andy Warhol, whose parents immigrated from the nearby Carpathian Mountains, and his answer was instructive on what it means to be a permanent foreigner in this obtuse world:

"Warhol wasn't American, an American would never be so prolific. Warhol invented a meta-language, an American would have just spoken it. The distance of the immigrant? Maybe, but Warhol consumed with his intellect."

Because his artwork requires the collaboration of the most profane settings – Ukraine's one atomic battleship, leaky with pestilence, a filthy coal mine, or those relentless Communist Party marches – the experience Savadov seeks is only conceptually Romantic, and therefore of the highest moral purity, innocent of all agenda and earthly motive. His *Bloody Mary* show was filmed in a real abattoir: he shows off his photos of a strong man staggering around, wearing the tornoff head of a real bull, ankle-deep in slags of blood.

"The smell was so hard, so hard. Two days, five hours each. All the butchers were there, and participated in the performance."

I notice how he says hard, not bad. A tough butcher plays the matador for him, the whole thing, cape and sword and suit of lights, while his opponent the Minotaur shows off unrestrained musculature from decades on the killing floor.

"For me, this is a place of composition . . . Now, would you like hard or soft?"

Savadov eyes me speculatively as he takes the final box down from the high shelf.

"Either way, I'm okay."

I open the box, stare at the first photo, stupidly thinking that this naked man hosting a dinner party, with a weird suture running from his groin to his throat, has himself a good makeup job, and that the mortuary-tag on his big toe shows some really convincing, artistic workmanship. I flip to the next photo and see twenty dead people sitting on Victorian furniture, some staring into the camera, others with their dead arms embracing each other. The nude ones all have this same purple ripple of a recent autopsy disfiguring their bellies. Even a toddler, chubby arms locked around a plush toy, dead as flesh can be . . .

"This is *Book of the Dead*," he now explains, from far away. "This show set all of the country on its ear."

I gulp, there are at least twenty more photos to go.

More and more ghastly-true, large colour photos of dead people arranged in little scenes.

I am paralyzed by his deep artistic transgression. Then I notice something decidedly odd. In the corner of each tableau he's put a carved piece of traditional Soviet kitsch, a wooden "Carpathian" mountain eagle. It's exactly the same wing-spreading raptor my grandfather brought home from his visit to western Ukraine in 1967. Yes, it's there in every one – the flying eagle, presiding over every dead cocktail party, and each dead family reunion. Staring enigmatically at all the naked dead people from its perch in the darkened living rooms.

My throat runs dry, my pen runs out of ink at the same moment. I cough.

Dana turns to me, holding up another pen.

"Is this yours?"

Midnight, and again sleep evades me. Who is going to come for me out of that dark blot in the middle of the hall doorway tonight? The mugger from this morning? Or the dead toddler with her chubby arms around the little toy duckie? Neither. It's the bald gangster's daughter, the three-year-old with the mad, convulsive eyes and shuddery pale lips, a spirit of the gloomy courtyard of the Cave Monastery, shrieking over and over again, "Who took my chair? Who took my chair?"

And everyone there, too afraid to answer her.

Chapter 8

Everyone's Dandy in Goon City

It's the kids who spook me. For a city of this size (three million), there's not many of them in evidence, and the ones we see tend to be coddled out of authentic existence, with goofy ribboned clothes and fussy little patent shoes, so that they get to know early in life that they are lost freaks of nature. A boy about eight or nine goes by on Red Army Street with his older sister. He's got on a pair of plush cotton overalls with pink-and-blue polka dots, which hang just below his knees, bright red sandals, a Little Lord Fauntleroy straw hat, and, worse, an attitude of complete devotion to his own artifice.

Nothing speaks Eastern European more than the way they decorate their kids like cheap birthday cakes. Is this a class thing? No, they are all madly consumerist now. At the mafiosi's restaurant last week, one of the heavy guys was setting up for a dinner party, and his four-year-old daughter posed for a snap in front of the buffet table – a starchy white voile dress that stuck out from her little frame, almost perpendicular; blonde hair sprayed hard as ice; and little jangly earrings that set your teeth on edge. The parents sat off to the side in an indistinguishable lump and watched her tippy-tap back and forth across the empty floor, not so much proud of her as momentarily appeased. Their product.

She will, of course, Grow Up Alone, protected from the contagion of other kids by a jealous family that will not trust the collective society in any form, ever again. And why should they? Here's one way they grow up here.

Dana insists I meet a woman who "sometimes works" as a clothes designer. I don't want to go; I only like real people, maniacs, and artists, and I am definitely not crazy about a woman who keeps pointing to her heart, beating somewhere beneath a heavily sequined jean jacket, while proclaiming her resolve to give to charity, should she ever get rich. Too many silver rings for that to ever happen. Olga (of course I go, Dana is relentless) says that her main purpose in life is promoting the national interest, Ukraine's, yet she speaks only Russian; and that there are only two paths for a woman to follow in this country, "to find a broad pair of shoulders to hide behind" or "to learn to think for oneself." This last said proudly, as her blue eyeshadow falls off in flecks when she blinks. Now Sergei, her dentist-boyfriend, swaggers over. He's got a rank Turkish fag dangling from thick purple lips, a gold necklace, and he doesn't look anyone in the eye. A heedless scavenger. She leans against him coquettishly, burying her face in his over-cologned hairy chest, a schoolgirl necking in the park while her friends watch enviously from the bushes. Off they go into the night. Does she look back to see if I'm watching? You betchya.

"Okay, so what was that about?" I'm tired, and I didn't like the art at the opening we just left. Too much green, soulless acrylic.

"She's had a hard life," Dana says defensively.

"So what? That seems to justify all kinds of shit here."

"Sergei cheats on her."

"What a surprise."

"Plus he's married."

"That's her problem." My dislike is growing purer, an ingot of forged steel.

"She lost her baby to medical malpractice."

"Why are you telling me all this?" My translator's inflection makes her sound like a lecturing taxonomist, "She's what, a type?"

"Maybe," Dana shakes her head as she follows her friend's erratic departure down the cobbled market street. The woman has her arm stretched like an octopus all the way around Sergei's fat gut. "The point is, people here have to overcome *huge* obstacles. Especially the women."

"Number one being their choices."

"The *men*, yes. The women here are beautiful, smart, educated – and they can cook! When Olga said that the men in her office were dead, she meant useless, passive. Deadweight."

"Useless to her, maybe. That's another thing, Dana. She's a designer, but she works in an insurance office?"

"You have to support your own dreams, right?"

"I see," I say listlessly, exhausted by the frenzy of her friend's exit. "I'm feeling like deadweight myself."

Of course I'm tired. Once a day someone here screams at me for nothing, carries on like a banshee. Everyone who visits this country comments on it, these sudden choleric outbursts from ordinary people going about their daily business. It's the overwrought child coming to adulthood, let loose on the world with no more self-control than a gnat, and multiplied by the millions. A cashier at an exchange bureau shrieks at me because I ask her the name of the street outside, while I'm giving her regular business. A woman on the third floor of a second-rate museum screeches hoarsely for my ticket, for which I have already paid at ten times the local rate and surrendered, as requested, to the armed guard below. The clerk in a pharmacy loudly refuses to show me the package of antihistamines, sitting right at her elbow. Are they stretched to the limit? I ask people, and they admit it's cultural. The explanation always is, "It's from the Soviet times, this mentality," but the simple truth is the problem begins at birth, not at the office. The traditional defence for such widespread bad behaviour is as facile as Professor Paulenko's view that the West's alien values gave rise to the local mafiosi. Yes, it's always the outsiders. There's a universal refusal in Ukraine to take responsibility for anything, a condition in its extreme form we label sociopathic in the West. We're in a land suffering chronic mass-psychosis, pandemic depression, and it's not a question of lost cultural identity but of primitive mental health. Bad behaviour is accepted here as social theatre; I've noticed how the screamers are actually putting on a show for others in the same room. Yes, it works as low-grade entertainment; and more, it functions as a kind of a societal levelling device, in the short term reinforcing the collective identity. But it is ultimately self-defeating and socially destructive. We're far too busy with our screaming fits to build drainage ditches. The expats I talk to about it are generally of two views. Some say it was a lot worse only a few years ago, and it's getting better on its own. The weight of history is lifting. Others say that people here are so intelligent and educated, they will eventually solve their own problems. This last is the view of Lidia Wolanskyj, publisher of the *Eastern Economist*, a weekly English-language business journal in Kiev. I had met her at the expat barbecue in the country dacha. Over lunch, Lidia, who was born and raised in cosmopolitan Montreal and exhibits the worldliness of that city, told me she has seen momentous changes in the social landscape since Ukraine's belated independence in 1991.

"But I can still hitchhike at 2:00 a.m., and get a ride with a strange guy, even two men, and not worry about it. So some traditional things from the Soviet era are worth preserving."

"What about accidents?" I ask doubtfully. Meaning, of course, car accidents.

She looks at me puzzled, until Dana explains to her that I do mean *car* accidents. Lidia nods, and goes on to tell me about her own broken collarbone, from a terrific collision earlier this year. It's the first I've heard about it (Oksana the factory-owner had a cane and a big accident story too). I suddenly wonder if she's on medication.

"Well, that's nothing, what happened to me," Lidia says breathlessly, her blue eyes sparkling with pleasure at the cautionary tale she is about to relate. "My friend Wasyl? He was beaten up late at night by two guys, and so he called me from a payphone. I drove him to the military hospital. The chief surgeon met me at the door, and they performed the neurosurgery by noon!"

I waited patiently for the punchline, but there wasn't one. What happened to her broken collarbone? I looked to Dana, who merely shrugged. I decided my translator's new job was to render this random English into usable content. I ventured to declare that I was getting interesting material out of my trip, but I needed to take a break occasionally, and I couldn't find anywhere to cool off.

"You know what I mean, Lidia? The European experience? Café society, the theme from *A Man and a Woman* playing in the streets?" To make my point, I hummed a few bars, then stopped when it looked like the other restaurant patrons were going to join in for the chorus.

"Oh, you people from back home! You just love to complain!" She sounded pleased. I was another whinging tourist with a silly lack of perspective. We said goodbye over caramel ice cream with raisins, amid the green splendour of the chestnut trees of Shevchenko Park.

On my way home, in the middle of the sunny day on Red Army Street, a well-shod businessman passed by me on the right side, stooped and retrieved a dirty plastic bag filled with American cash from the busy sidewalk, and turned to me —

I fled before he had a chance to open his mouth.

Am I making myself clear, dear reader? This place is not Europe, despite the deliciously creamy raisin-and-pumpkin treats and the yummy, tummy-baring white-skinned girls, the sleek legions of roaming black Mercedeses, and the thick wafts of Obsession and Homme de Nuit. Oh, and the high-end stereo shops! No, this is Palermo, a brigand border-town set down in Asia's front yard, home to a primitive tribe of unknowable savages, to whom we foreigners must look like uncooked pork chops ready for the *shaslyk* skewer. If we look like anything at all. Not to say I don't get politeness, kindness, even humour from the locals, and I do; but I am talking about the masses here, about their insulated, bricked-in souls, something you can hardly call privacy, judging from the dented beef tins that pass for public conveyances here. The buses are Kiev's Purgatory and its subway system, the local Inferno. And there is nowhere else to go, they are already here: so they go inwards. Professor Yuri Paulenko cogently argued that there were only three directions for the settled Slavs. North, *belo*, as in the White Sea; south, black, *chorney*, as in the Black Sea; and finally red, *chervon*, the centre. The real world, by extension. But for nomads, for the Asiatic horseman of the steppes, and for us, too, we restless Westerners, heirs to the expansionist sixteenth century, there are four directions and *no* centre – as our own Yeats famously realized. If that makes us hollow men, so be it. It's our existential predicament, this moral relativity of ours. Not theirs.

As for these people, it comes down to the way they structure their living space. The tight little villages, clinging to a roadway or railway spur, palisaded behind slat fencing and jammed with shuttered cottages, are laid out in blind obedience to an unconscious discipline on the theme of *us* and *them*. That is how I read these fences and walls and enclosures and barricades and dour faces. It's a psychological vise-grip that wholly predates Christianity, with its Greek-based origins in open theatre and easy tricks of public illumination. Call it rural-stronghold, call it forest-keep, candle-lamp, or spiritual fastness. Call it what you like, but this hidden, defensive submergence in the unconscious black soil is duplicated on a larger and larger scale everywhere, right up to the president's latest, mysteriously financed, subterranean country abode, which the expatriate press sniffs and barks at, a strange beast found lurking in the woodshed. But it's *his* village, the president's, an architecture designed to keep the locals in, and outsiders, out. Rooted and stuck fast to its particular history. It's not going anywhere this year, or the next.

So why not try to make the best of it?

We decide to take the train to Crimea, the good doctor Arkadi and I. He understands that I must see for myself this summer-burnt grassland where the Crimean Tatars lived, and from which they pillaged Eastern Europe for six hundred years. Stalin expelled them, but they are now drifting back, setting up mosques and reclaiming their homes.

"Do you know," Arkadi says as the hilly countryside flashes by, "that in Ukraine the women's legs are two centimetres shorter than in the rest of Europe?"

"Two centimetres?" I turn from the window, exhausted by the decanting of too many nameless rural villages. More desolate villages than a thousand fat Russian novels could use. I hold out my thumb and forefinger to confirm this significant measurement. He nods.

"Yes, and it is very interesting why. It's genetic. From the Tartars, the intermixing. The Tartars ride these short little ponies, like this." He gets up to demonstrate. "So they have short little legs like this." He hobbles about the second-class compartment.

"Bowed legs."

"Yes."

I see what looks like a minaret in the distance. The countryside is hilly and cropped close, but there are no animal flocks. Just the odd tethered goat, and semi-abandoned factories of one demonic style or another. Sulphur, brimstone, black slag. Every twenty minutes, a choking breeze crosses the track like the yellow snake of hell.

"What do you feel about the Tartars?" I put my right hand on my heart to show what I mean. Arkadi doesn't hesitate.

"The last time I was here? I see an old Tartar woman, walking with crutches. So I step up and try to give her money, I feel sorry for her. She doesn't even look at me. She keeps walking. I think, in the end, they come back. And we go, finished."

"Why is that? So many ships on the Black Sea, so many Russians, came here already."

"You will see, when you got to Bakhchysaray, the Tartar's Khan's palace. They have a system, they collect water from the morning dew, in jars, to keep for drinking. Because of the mountains, there is shadow of no rain here, yes?"

"Rain shadow, yes."

"So when Russian people come, they break these jars and things, they make all the water dirty. Now they get water from canal, from the big river. But is big problem. Tartar people know how to live here, really. This is their home. And now they are coming back, from Central Asia."

By midday we reached Sevastopol, a former high-security naval port, on the Black Sea. On the west side of the train we could see rusted black submarines, black as midnight, lifeless, listing in the stupor of history, and then a big blonde woman cavorting in the green scum under a decaying pier. It was water in name only; I shuddered to think of how many pages it would take merely to list the ingredients of the port's strange brew.

"Look, spy submarine!" Arkadi delightedly pointed at a baby sub, less than twelve feet long, a part (a key part?) of that great modern conceptual work, the Third World War. Now the show was being disbanded, wrapped up after its long and successful run, the giant props sold off; and for every odd-looking blue uniform we passed, Arkadi's answer was always the same:

Merchant sailor.

Yes, a lot of merchants around, but no money. It took us about forty-five

minutes to check into the Crim Hotel, a decrepit Soviet-era hostelry, despite the fact that there was no one else in the lobby. A sign taped to the front desk said there was no hot water because of renovations, but the only evidence of any work was the two old women dragging their twig brooms along the gritty terrazzo floor. From our eighth-floor balcony we had a magnificent view of more high-rise encrustations exactly like ours. Soviet concrete does not age well.

"Let's go have some lunch," I suggested cheerfully, feeling restless despite the thirty-hour train trip. We walked down to the cobblestone harbour, past beggars and small sellers offering tiny bags of black sunflower seeds or wildflowers, wilted daisies, and purple-tufted grass. Two teenaged girls in matching red satin pants caught my eye. They were taking photos of each other holding Ronald's red plaster hand outside the busy McDonald's. The restaurant offered ice-cream cones for ninety-nine kopeks, a ridiculous commercial affectation in a country where nothing was ninety-nine, it was all either a sensible fraction, or the whole damn thing and nothing less.

"Prostitution," Arkadi commented, meaning the two young blondes.

"How can you tell?"

To me they looked no different than the last dozen sweet things on the street.

"For the sailors. But it's quiet yet, the season has not started."

"Look at that soup they're eating." A corner restaurant was filled with chomping people, served by a squadron of sweating young women with huge innocent eyes, dressed in eye-popping red sailor suits. Their customers had the happy frankness of gratified trenchermen. We sat down at a shiny maple table so wide my dining partner had to wave just to get my attention. The shaved-headed business-goon at the next table (to be distinguished from the street-hustling dandy-goons of Kiev, and the ubiquitous pocky-goons lurking on the roadways) was speaking on his cellphone, Insincere English:

"Sure, no problem. Delivery is September 15th, guaranteed. They quoted seventy-five, it's still a very good price . . . No, of course I am a broker, naturally . . . Could I just say this, just let me say . . ."

Whatever it was (an atomic sub for the Iraqis?), the Other Side wasn't happy, and his voice got softer and softer until it drained away like melted butter. Did the shaved head help or hinder his business dealings? When the women of Eastern Europe begin shaving their heads as well, then we'll know they are really in trouble.

A lavender-eyed sailor girl took our order and brought us cool *kvass* in brown ceramic mugs and heavy bread rolls sprinkled with salt, for starters. We had huge bowls of beet borscht, with heaps of dill and sour cream on top, followed by caviar blini, buckwheat pancakes, freshly pressed cherry juice, and sweet egg-bread with crushed garlic spooned over it. I didn't trust the food, not any of it by now, but I ate it anyway. It was delicious.

So far I have eaten seven or eight different types of bread in Ukraine, and I have barely scratched the surface. There are more than five hundred kinds.

The dark-brown rye, the soul of the country, is of course called ukrainski, the classic bread of novels and survival. Among the white breads, a nice poppy-seed eggbread with a slip of egg-white sheen painted on its crust is challah; to my mind it is chewy, a choice accompaniment to smoked ham with fruit preserve. Lavash is sold as "diet bread," meaning it is healthy, being a flat, yeastless elemental meal of wheat flour, water, salt, and baking soda. It is as ancient as India (from whence they say it originates) and it can be baked on the run. Probably the Scythians ate it too. Pumpushkeh, a glazed roll, is compact, dense, and perfect for soaking up a mince of pork fat and garlic, if you're so inclined. Finally we had the common roll, bolyshska, slightly sour and firm, something to munch on while you are perusing the poetic transliterations on the local menus, such as *ship's tongue* – or even more delightfully, *sheep's language.* In this respect the Ukrainian tongue is like Innuit and its famously multiple species of snow; except that, unlike the ice-hunters' speech, the language of these wheat farmers does contain a word for their supreme element in its natural, transubstantive essence: *chlib.*

Bread. In Soviet times this slogan was plastered everywhere, Arkadi recounted, on café walls and in railway stations alike: "*Chlib Stumo Holovah.*" Bread is Everything to the Head. Another common motto admonished "*Berjik Chlib,*" meaning "Take Care of the Bread," with its unspoken corollary, *and it will take care of you.* Bread was one of the chief reasons why the ancient Greek colonists came to this peninsula on the Black Sea in the first place, soon after 1000 B.C., to found a town they named Chersonessus, the "peninsula."

Bread, and wine.

Chapter 9

The Two-Centimetre Question

"And in our little museum, we have things we found here dating to 1399 A.D., when a huge conflagration destroyed all of Chersonessus."

Taissa Bushnell, the twenty-eight-year-old executive director of the Chersonessus Foundation, a project of the University of Texas, is cheerily guiding us through the ruins of the ancient, many-layered city. The lucky grad student is employed as a researcher with its Institute of Classical Studies, exploring the ancient port's remains on the coast of the Black Sea near the city of Sevastopol. A glorious June morning greets us from the knife-edge of the cobalt sea.

"We've had a lot of rain this year, so everything is really green."

The sea breeze carries her voice away through a mix of maritime and Asian wildflowers. Cyprus trees, red poppies, fragrant cedars, walnut and pistachio trees, rowdy splurges of tall blue and yellow phlox, even dusty pink hollyhocks, all provide a living chorus to the deserted foundations of marble and limestone. Suntanned workers, stripped to their waists and perched on scaffolds, are busy restoring the walls of the Byzantine city that stood here, successor to the classical Greek town, until it fell on that fateful day in 1399 to nomad invaders.

"You can see it happened quite quickly. Very hot, that fire," Taissa explains as we enter the tiny museum.

"The Tartars?" I ventured.

"Yes, an army under Khan Nogay. They attacked several times in the decades before, but this time they completely destroyed the city."

"Why?"

She was silent.

"These are the iron nails we found, all fused together."

"And this, is it glass? Also melted in the flames?" The pretty little heap set beside the lump of nails was a medley of blues and pinks and greens.

"Yes, burnt."

"And this black stuff here?"

"That's a piece of house timber, completely burned."

"And what about this black material?"

"Rope, burned black."

"This attack must have had an exact date and time. All these things are like a clock that stopped ticking. Living things."

"Yes," she agreed. "See this black lump here, at the top? That's a loaf of bread. It was all burned in the same fire."

The black loaf of bread was worth a photo, I decided. A memento mori to that exact minute, six hundred years ago, when the Tartars decided to torch a city that, as Professor Carter, the site's director and chief archaeologist, proudly told me earlier, had already survived "the Scythians, the Sarmatians, the Goths, and the Alans" through a heroic combination of statecraft and populist determination. Carter had been directing the dig here for ten years. Celebrated for his discovery of syphilis in an indigenous European population (pre-1492 Italy), he had arrived in Sevastopol in 1991, when it was still a closed city within a closed country, and he had worked hard with local archaeologists and the Ukrainian government to explore and preserve this national heritage site. The Ukrainian National Bank had decided to put the reconstructed marble archway dominating the ruins on their one-hyrvnia banknote. Accordingly, I took another photo of Taissa, holding the bill up in front of the monument, telling her she should have been engraved on it as well.

Carter himself was proud, and more than a little protective, of the buried city, as he welcomed us with a tour of his dacha headquarters. His team worked from a pre-Revolution wooden house with a terrific view of the port's harbour, and he told us the cottage had once been occupied by Konstantin Paustovsky, the Russian author of *My Life*, a groundbreaking recollection in the manner of Proust.

"Anna Akhmatova, the famous poet, lived on the other side," the director pointed east. "And Tolstoy came here to report on the Crimean War. This city is a battleground. It heroically resisted the Nazis for 240 days. As heroically as St. Petersburg, since they had no army, just citizens fighting from caves. And it always springs back, a beacon of civilization in the middle of tragedy. Now it's trying to spring back from a declining economy, and it's evident in the Tatars' return."

The Tatars were an ethnic group that had been deported by Stalin at the first opportunity at the war's start, the dictator claiming they were Nazi sympathizers. Muslims, an ethnically distinct Turkic people, endogamous, itinerant herders and petty farmers, they were suspect on every ground by the Bolsheviks – never mind their ancestral history as the implacable foe of the Russian people. Now they were coming back to the nearby town of Bakhchysaray in increasing numbers.

"I had the pleasure of dining with the Crimean Tatar leader, Mustapha Sulim, and a good friend of William Green Miller as well. He's the former U.S. ambassador." Carter led us into the tiny kitchen, where he poured us each a glass of mineral water. "Our local spring, it's very good."

I peeked into the next room. A narrow bed, some sparse wooden furniture, a few books. A monkish life this, summer after summer. I spotted a dog-eared paperback in the hall.

"You read Edith Wharton? She's one of my favourites." It seemed a good read for this dazzling semi-Mediterranean coast.

"Not mine," he hastened to correct me. "I only read detective novels and Russian literature, myself."

"Isn't that the same thing?" I opined cheekily.

"I'd like you to meet our assistants, Natasha and Andrei."

Natasha was exactly the CIA's dream of a Russian spy, tall, ash-blonde, thick lips. Pouty as Bardot. She was translating a chunk of dense text. Andrei had quick black eyes, a beet-pulp mouth, a relaxed and open manner. He said he was Romanian, and showed off his clay pots and amphora, all painstakingly pieced back together. Wine jars, I assumed.

"These contained resinated red wine?" I stroked the rough clay.

"I wish you could tell us," Andrei said, shaking his head. "We know that they were of local manufacture, from the Greeks' pottery works. We think they traded wine with the Scythians."

I could see immediately what the problem was. That heap of litter sat in the site office with a stunning view of the coiling sea. Had it been me trying to work here, me the product of a once-Presbyterian city that had produced precious little other than the principle of work for work's sake (a lakeside northern city that calls me, even now, even here, pulling me away from this indolent coast of drunken merchant ship captains, and merciless, well-oiled, and near-naked women, sunbathing mere yards away, displaying themselves like an array of greasy delicatessen meats on special), if it were me confronting these potsherds, I would spend precisely five minutes a day here on actual work (whatever that was) and the rest denying my past in idle contemplation of these moody, half-wild cypress groves and the curious ways the afternoon light slants over the crest of the sea.

So what hope would a cold-cocked Slavic fieldworker have, faced with such melting, indelicate mornings and incandescent afternoons? I shuddered to think of the evenings in Chersonessus, evenings with the moon cascading dreamy opalescence into every half-opened eye. What would I do with my evenings, if I worked here? Suffer the torments of eternal sweet damnation, that's what. Yearning, idle hungers, fitful cravings. Restlessly stalking the perfumed beach, a lonely satyr in love. Layers, that's what we had here. Layers of history, layers of light. Layers of meaning, of intrigue, layers of wild romance and wilder beauty.

Carter showed me a poem that ended his annual report of the dig's results. He said he loved Novy Sfect, the local champagne. Although it was only mid-June, he was brown as a hazelnut. He told us that he enjoyed the confidence and support of the Packard Foundation, that David Packard had even contributed his HP computers, and the project staff was now busy digitalizing the extensive database of old research papers, creating the digital infrastructure of Web sites, e-mail, and GIS, satellite imaging, the whole high-tech works. Government ministers Bohufski and Leonid Marchenko kept extending their original invitation and support, and former U.S. ambassador William Green Miller and his wife, Suzanne, provided their diplomatic currency and personal charm to the enterprise; it all made the director a happy man. Yes, it was coming together, ten years on this beachhead, like the Greeks at Troy – but with good meals and crickets singing through the open windows at night. I asked him about the Greeks, his Greeks. He looked out the cottage window to a sky as blue as chicory blooms lining the rickety fence.

"These Greek colonists, they had to face nature, war, using all their resources. They resisted oligarchy. They were democratic, I think. And although it went back and forth, from oligarchy to democracy, I think that democracy was the secret of their success. In Athens it was different, after the Macedonians."

"The Macedonians? You mean Philip, and Alexander?"

"Yes, of course. They spelled the end of Athenian democracy."

"You sound like a Jeffersonian."

"I am! Like in Virginia, in the U.S., the early Greek settlers here in Chersonessus had a free, egalitarian society. They had to collaborate, so as not to isolate themselves from the rest of the people. This city resisted the trend to oligarchy, it continued to have a democratic government long after Alexander the Great's conquests."

"But don't Alexander's conquests, like Genghis Khan's, show the work of individual will, of personal intent? I mean, look at Jefferson. The revisionists now talk about his slave mistress."

I meant Machiavellian motive as opposed to Jeffersonian egalitarianism, of course.

"Careful what you say," Carter happily warned me. "My family traces its ancestry to Jefferson's field commander."

"A Russian submariner told me last week that it was only Kennedy and Khrushchev who stopped the Third World War from happening in 1961. He was a captain on a nuclear sub off Cuba, waiting for the final order to fire."

"They had their fingers on the buttons," Carter grew testy. "They didn't *invent* the button."

"Okay."

"Writers of ancient history are always attracted to the leaders, but modern historians look to the underlying causes of the whole period. You should really have a look at Rostovtzeff's *Social and Economic History*. Five thousand pages, it's all there."

"But these Greeks at Chersonessus, they had a symbiotic relationship with the Scythians?"

"Yes, the Scythians could have wiped them out at any time, but they enjoyed their presence, I think. They had their own capital city, Neopolitis, not too far from here."

"It must have been odd: two radically different civilizations, holding court so close, and for hundreds of years?"

"I think they both gained immensely from it."

"Like you and this place?"

"I fell in love with this place on my first visit. Since I came here, the country has got a constitution, renounced nuclear weapons, struggled with the economy, and everybody works much harder now, because they are connected to the rest of the world, not isolated and cut off."

We were standing in the courtyard, between the ruins at the shoreline and the vine-clad research buildings. I took my leave of Carter, and Taissa led the way across the beach. Healthy Russian women in shoe-string thongs flip-flopped across thousand-year-old mosaics, young lovers curled up in the shade, indigo mud swallows chased each other relentlessly. It was a happy place once; it would be a happy place again. A few kilometres away, downtown, in the modern port of Sevastopol, the Party members' grim houses were being renovated by the newly rich. The cycle was on the upswing again. The only jarring note was this last blackened lump, found at the foot of a complete skeleton, set in a glass case by itself.

"What's this thing?" I asked Taissa, more out of automatic duty than any real interest at this point.

"That's the slave's leg shackle," she replied. "Iron."

I looked again. A heavy, custom-forged ankle-lock, it was intended to hobble its wearer permanently, and exhaustively. Now whose slave was he? The Tartars'? The Venetians'? The Byzantines'? The ancient Greeks'? Even Thomas Jefferson, above all Jefferson, had kept slaves. Who was he, in this glass case? The Unknown Slave? And what special human quality or feature did he possess, that permitted his subjugation, his living ruin at the service of one civilization or another?

And maybe the next civilization, after this one.

◈

Today Arkadi and I are driving out to Bakhchysaray, to see the modern Tatars. But first we must have breakfast in Sevastopol and study its women. One more time.

They are extraordinary, walking around nearly naked, right here on the busy streets of the hilly town. The first one goes by in a floral-print shift so sheer I can examine her white thong panties, like a lascivious Superman in his raging hormonal years. Now two gamines with freckles, real red hair, and microskirts saunter across our path, holding hands tightly.

"Twins," Arkadi comments, looking back with deep interest.

Two more dollies arrive on the scene, a blonde with a huge bosom threatening to pop and a brunette teetering on four-inch heels, all legs.

"*Not* twins," I pronounce sagely.

"Ah, there you are," Arkadi puts a forefinger up to the wind, a lecturer on technical social sciences holding forth. "Two kinds of women. Twins, and not twins!"

We get our good eyeful and hail a cab, both relaxed after a few days of easy sun and fresh sea air, and nothing to do but laze about and think of jolly things to say. But really, this fleshy opulence is astounding. No coyness, no flirtation. Here's what we got, boychuks, take it or leave it! Such generosity! Or maybe it's that the men here don't respond to such basic cues. Even Taissa Bushnell had commented to us yesterday at length about the lack of male magnetism in this country.

"The men are so out of it." She shook her head.

"It's a real sexual dimorphism," I tried to impress her with academic shop-talk. "Pixy princess on one hand and the dull goon or mamma's boy on the other."

"And it's like that through the whole country," she quickly agreed. "Even western Ukraine, where they're not so backward. I just bought an apartment there for myself, in Lviv. It's really quite extraordinary . . ."

Arkadi and I discussed this issue in the cab, as we exited Sevastopol through a series of confusing switchbacks and busy, police-guarded overpasses. The countryside was hilly, and everywhere large apple orchards following the easy curves of the somnolent earth. Who was going to harvest all that luscious fruit? The doctor was of the opinion that local women who studied hard and went past their thirtieth birthdays without marrying took extreme social risks, and knowingly. Most men married

in Ukraine at twenty-five, hence there was nobody left for all these educated singles.

"It's the same in my country," I said. "The braver men also come under
heavy fire, and few but the cowards survive the first onslaught."

We were looking down at an ancient limestone valley that had once been a
coral reef blockading an arm of the Devonian Sea in the Paleozoic era, and
was now a green upland thrusting five hundred metres above sea level.
Swallows darted out of the cubbyholes they had pecked in the volcanic tuff
over our heads. And far above them soared European kestrels, whose eye-
sight was so acute they could spot roving field mice from the pinnacle of
their updraughts, swirling pillars of warm air a mile high. And flying above
them, so far up as to be invisible, undoubtedly glided the great gryphon, the
eagle-winged leopard who had made the Crimea her lair since the Scythian
era, three thousand years ago. Then, the mythic creature had appeared on
gold bucklers, tearing horses apart; now the gryphon sells beer and soda
pop as a trademark of Crim Industries.

I am thinking about cold drinks because we have been hiking for over
an hour now, under the commanding peninsular sun, mounting ever higher
as we follow Savri, our seventeen-year-old Tatar guide, on his shortcut route
up to the tomb of the Tatar Princess. First we must pass through the
troglodytes' caves and a fortress. Far below us we can see the regular path on
the right, a paved trail that runs directly through the Uspensky Monastery,
built into the side of the cliffs like a gold-plated Orthodox version of Lhasa.
We are not on the regular path, we are on the far side of the ridge, following
a precarious goat-trail through blazing patches of lavender, butterwort, and
a sensual purple flower that hugs the ground in a triumphant amatory
embrace. Someone on the hills across the valley is playing a *sapilka*, a
wooden pan pipe. Birds trill in the forest glades hugging the cliff face; a fantastic battery of rough pistons turns out to be the local species of cicada,
crooning to his heart's desire in the dress-parade voice of a major-domo. A
strong musk smell of animal hits us in the face.

Around the next bend sits a series of goat-pens, and standing in the
stinky muck with his shirt off is a darkly handsome guy with a ponytail,

pitching grass to the goats. He says hello in Russian, and a hundred paces on, Savri points out the goat-herder's house, an immaculate whitewashed cube with a steel roof, set into the face of the living rock. A troglodyte with bourgeois leanings, it appears. What's he doing here in this remote valley, living in a cave-house? Earlier Arkadi had explained that the Crimea was full of Siberians, emigrants who took their quintuple remoteness pay and headed off to the soft South, easy landlady to a thousand dreamers. Goat-herding in the green Arcadian hills above Sevastopol was probably something this engineer had planned in his private moments, during long years of forty below.

We climbed, higher still. We could see other hills, other valleys. Now the location of the upcoming cave-city began to make sense. A single sentry posted here – on a clear day like today, with the wind scarcely moving, and the whole world stilled into timelessness by the ascent of the June sun – could have spotted a lizard scuttling, a twig breaking, a line of horseman approaching from a full season away. This wall of bare, placid rock, with ragged holes and caves cut into it, was known today as Chufut-Kale, the Jewish Fortress. A Jewish reclusive sect called the Karaites had fortified it and then left in the 1850s. Long before that, it had served as the final refuge for Tokhtamysh, a ruler of the Golden Horde Tartars, whom Tamerlane had smashed back in the 1390s. The Golden Horde Tartars were the most westerly branch of the Mongol dynasties that owed their origin to Genghis Khan's victories, and our guide Savri, the black-haired, brown-skinned teenager in an Adidas T-shirt, was a direct descendant of those armies. His ancestors had lived here until the 1950s, when Stalin deported them and brought in European settlers, Ukrainians, Russians, and even ethnic Germans, whom Boss Joe trusted more than these Asians. Long memory, or *realpolitik*? Hundreds of thousands of Tatars died in these forced evacuations; now they were drifting back from Uzbekistan and farther east.

I studied Savri, my first Tatar. His eyebrows grew together, as I had noticed in other Tatars we'd passed on the road. And he was bandy-legged, all right. But with his big eyes and aquiline nose he looked more like a Tajik, a hill-tribe Iranian, than an eastern Asiatic.

We came to the fortress gate and looked up. More steep elevation. Ahead lay a cobbled road with deep wagon ruts worn into it, from the long passage of centuries. Up we went, through Russian thistles, chokecherries, two or three types of white Queen Anne's lace, giant yellow hollyhocks leaning softly against the sunny sides of the crumbling stone walls. A wind came up, blowing steadily. We were crossing the cleft to the gusty side. A grassy meadow, a deep plunge beyond. The breeze was cool on our sweaty faces, and we stood facing it, transfixed by the rise and fall of the world to the north and east, the sudden lapses of the earth, and their patient recovery; and by the sudden discovery of our own insubstantiality, clinging like ants to this single volatile hill, one hill among hundreds stretching away, each grander than the last and profoundly indifferent.

The wind is strong, it feels like we are flying. I dare to peek over the edge of the chasm, and almost lose my cap as a volley of cold air rockets up the cliff face like an adult carnival ride. Two teenage girls in gauzy costumes are careening around the topmost meadow, and their red-and-blue veils fly across their faces and stick to them as their boyfriends shout instructions over the air torrent, holding out their clumsy Russian cameras, as if the gesture alone will still the bluster, and get the girls' poses ready. At the pinnacle, a riderless bay horse awaits the hire of a would-be Cossack chief; a new sabre is stuck blade-first into the turf. It's a photo-hire spot for tourists. But it's the girls who are playing dress-up today, and the boys' job is to assist in the production, to pay ten hryvnias for the costumes, and help them to choose an appropriate backdrop from the haughty peaks.

It's hopeless. The girls laugh too much as the veils flap in their faces. Beside them, ignored by the festive group, sits the stone tomb of Princess Dzhanike-Hanym, favourite daughter of Khan Tokhtamysh. I peek through the bars of the crypt. A marble sarcophagus sits alone in the dark recess, untouched since 1437. "She must have been virgin," is Arkadi's only comment.

Back in Bakhchysaray, the Tatar capital, where the Khan's restored palace was located, we sought a decent restaurant. Over bottles of cold Crimean ginger beer, I asked Arkadi to tell me the story again of Roxilana, the Ukrainian enchantress who had bewitched the Great Khan, Suleyman the Magnificent. Indeed, just across the street, and only a few doors from the Khan's Palace, was a restaurant called Roxilana. The sign showed a slyly smiling woman dressed in the same faux Oriental getup, red chiffon veils and so on, that the girls were fooling with on the mountaintop.

"It was like this," he began, eyeing the two sloe-eyed beauties who worked the little bar. "Tartar troops came to western Ukraine and captured women, including one very beautiful girl from the town of Rogatyn. And Suleyman, he bought her, as his slave. He loved her, and they had three sons, one of whom became Pasha. For thirty years after, Ukraine was never invaded by Tartars."

"That's it? The whole story?"

"I don't know if it's true or not. Maybe it's only a story."

"But, Arkadi, Lidia's version of this story – Lidia the publisher? What she told me and your wife at the Cossack Restaurant in Kiev was that Roxilana single-handedly brought down the house of Suleymen, that she was some kind of Ukrainian Joan of Arc."

"Maybe. I don't know."

He turned and ordered another ginger beer, and began talking to the two waitresses. Ulia was the porcelain doll with the white skin and flawless blue eyes, while the tangle-haired blonde who looked as if she enjoyed sleeping in late was Ludmilla. "So nice for the people," was how Arkadi flirtatiously translated Ludmilla's name, with a quick flick of his tongue to show his approval of her daylight charms. Then he began a serious conversation with them in Russian, to which they both attended just as seriously. I made out individual phrases: Chamu . . . Russki . . . Ukraine, Crimea, Lithuania?

"Why do Russians want to live in other people's countries? They have their own country," he asked them. "In twenty years, as the Tartars move back and have more children, then what?"

A large-shouldered and rough-faced blonde woman in a Puma track suit loped up the bar stairs and ordered a *kvass*, the cheap, old-fashioned bread drink, listened a bit, decided she didn't like what she was hearing, and actually knocked against my slouching torso in her eagerness to get in on the issue. Arkadi translated her staccato outburst:

"I would kill five people to save one Russian. I am patriotic, that's all!"

"Five people?" I asked aloud. "What five people? Tartars? Englishmen? Anyone?"

Arkadi ignored me, but Ludmilla twirled her finger in her ear as Puma Woman departed, making the age-old sign of the cuckoo clock for my benefit.

"What do these two think?" I wanted to know.

"This one," Arkadi pointed to the blue-eyed doll, "she is Russian, from Siberia. Her grandfather was *kulak*, rich farmer from near Moscow, so they were deported to Siberia, and now she comes here to work. The other one, she is half-Ukrainian, her mother, and half-Russian, her father, and she doesn't know who she is. Ulia, she says everyone should live together in peace. They are new generation, I think. They have open hearts."

"How was Siberia?" I ventured to ask Ulia.

"*Zemno!*" she laughed, then said in English, "Cool, very cool."

Arkadi studied them with renewed delight. Across the road in front of the Sultan's museum palace, the tourists had dwindled as the hot afternoon wore on, and now there were only a few customers for the thirty-odd European (Russian and Ukrainian) women selling homemade baklava and other Oriental sweets. I did not see a single Tatar woman among them, and wondered if these Slavs had an exclusive hold on the marketplace, or the Tatars a disinclination for trade. The matrons sprawled on their blankets, easy as lifeguards, with as few clothes on their large brown bodies as they could get away with, supremely comfortable in the flesh.

The inscription on the Iron Gate above their heads read:

> Erected by the tremendous Order of the Khan of the Two Oceans, Khan Mengliquilei.
> May God forgive him and his parents in both worlds.

The Khans had roamed the whole of Asia looking for female slaves. Now the women came here of their own accord, spitting black sunflower seeds into the dust and paying good money to dress the part of the All-Conquering Slave Girl.

Chapter 10

Spiritual Danger

Just as the Black Sea inveigles itself into the ribald, fun-loving southern coast, nibbling away at the old sod when he isn't looking, picking his pocket of loose change, piece by piece, boldly inserting its blue hands into every crevice and cavity (Professor Carter said that, due to local conditions, the waterline was actually growing higher here than in the Mediterranean, and that the Black Sea was unaccountably rising, not shrinking), so too the enormous reach of global modernity was eroding Slavic Civilization, blunting its finer edges, washing away its traditional perceptions and judgments, and leaving uneasy tumult and rank confusion in its wake.

Europe, with its funny little postage-stamp countries that could be crossed in an hour, perhaps while reading a business journal and eating a piece of *strudel mit schlag* heaped on top, was far too easy to resist. And China was simply *them*, indistinct faces across the freezing Amur River. Who cared about the Amur and its hordes of mosquitoes? But this plutonic realm that seethed below the surface of local life? This subterranean force that smelled bad blood and wouldn't let go? A shadowy continent lay here beneath the pretty appearances, a Presence, older than clocktime and mightier than any chronicler could encompass.

It had no name, no real character. The blue sheen on a fly. You merely sensed it, its tentacles grasping for purchase everywhere on this frontier with Asia, a kind of invisible spiritual parasite that had attached itself to the underbelly of this sunny land, a power that summoned the incubi out of their dens – and to what purpose? To do its bidding, to feast on the downcast people of the post-Soviet empire in their beds at night. The Fisher King? That's nothing.

Listen to these women, and welcome to an *empire* of fisher kings.

Words and phrases that I heard during the day always came buzzing back to pester me at night. *Tak dalushy*, and *slukai*, and *Ya presnaslo!* In the morning I would throw them back at Arkadi and wait for his reaction; it was my attempt to exorcise these great swarms of sticky Slavicisms that ended sitting deep in my chest like fine grit. "And so on" is how he translated *tak dalushy*, while the second was "listen!" and the third, "I bought it." It was obvious café drivel, not Pushkin. But the steady diet of cold boiled carp for breakfast, and tough lamb rinds for lunch, was toughening me up too. The pulmonary cough that plagued me in Kiev had almost gone here in Crimea, except for the odd, eye-bulging spasm that left me breathless in the middle of doing nothing.

I was losing weight as well. I might even lose more weight if I could manage to use the toilet one of these days, but my rectum turned up its nose (or whatever you might call it) at the condition of the Crim Hotel bathroom and refused to budge. Clamped shut. A rash on my thigh was responding to the steroid cream, but I must be judicious in any future applications. Horde my medical stash, keep the caps sealed on all my nostrums. I had eleven thousand kilometres to go, and pharmacies were already getting mighty thin on the ground.

"*Prosyvateh!*" I yell out to Arkadi, who lies half-dead with exhaustion after following my antics all day.

"Working," he says, with a deep sigh, not stirring an inch.

Okay, let's talk about the gods. The gods of the Slavs, or at least the gods of these vast Crimean steppe lands. Are they titanic like the spaces they inhabit? Or are they small like us, a people dwarfed by the sheer unforgiving magnitude of the world-continent, a limpid abstraction so real it defies comprehension? We're talking about scale here and, more than that, about the horizontal Abyss, the green Chasm, the blue Spectacle. It wounds one to look out for too long on this absolute Space called the Crimean horizon. Is it pretty, the countryside of the Tartars? It's an uneven sky, a tentative sky. Uneven and shocked by asymmetry. The steppe lands contain too many missing pieces to fit together nicely, one's eyes grow quickly weak with looking, and sting by noon. Mornings are hard, the afternoons, impossible. Is it better to go lock yourself up in a dim room somewhere and study? Read books and forget the view? Cross yourself in the dark and light a beeswax candle? Millions of Russians do. Do such things not from choice or pity, but because they are forced to; it's their only path out of the bright emptiness that surrounds them.

I can feel it, whispering at my elbow: Tartarus. The idea of hell came from somewhere, somewhere real. This steppe land was scenic as anything; sweetly pastoral, yes, on the surface, but shot through with a glittery, mocking darkness. What is it like for them, these people who have breathed it in, this intimate, ghastly apparition of history, flickering at the edge of their lives every hour since earliest childhood?

Below the Byzantine settlement at Chersonessus, Carter's team found the remains of a Jewish colony, two carved menorahs. And below that, the cryptic emblems of Isis and Serapis, Egypt's Moon-Goddess and the Bull-God. And below *that*, the Tauric Goddess whom the Greeks simply called the Maiden, Partheos. In Euripides' play *Iphigenia among the Taurians*, written in 414 B.C., the heroine princess declaims:

> "Would a Goddess desire such things? Would she take pleasure in sacrificial murder? I don't believe it. It is the men of this land who are bloodthirsty, and lay their guilt upon the Gods."

Only a third of the Chersonessus site has been excavated, a site that is a tiny enclave on a little spit of land, four hundred hectares, holding ten thousand people at its peak. The Greeks were not the only ones here; they were but a thin slice of farmer's cheese wedged in a fat Dagwood of cultures, and nobody knows anything about their mysterious predecessors, the enigmatic Taurians. Herodotus wrote of them:

> It is the custom of the Tauri to sacrifice to the maiden Goddess
> all shipwrecked sailors and such Greeks as they happen to capture
> upon their coasts; their method of sacrifice is, after the preliminary
> ceremonies, to hit the victim on the head with a club. Some say
> they push the victim's body over the edge of the cliff on which
> their temple stands, and fix the head on a stake; others, while
> agreeing about the head, say the body is not pushed over, but
> buried. The Tauri themselves claim that the goddess to whom
> these offerings are made is Agamemnon's daughter, Iphigenia.

The Chersonessus Museum displayed the carved stone head of a Tauric soldier, but his eyes are closed for eternity, so we cannot peer into his soul. In a nearby cabinet sits the grossly deformed skull of an adult male, who was kept alive by the Greeks for years, despite his bizarre medical affliction. A whole burial plot, filled with such poor freakish creatures, twisted limbs and grotesque heads, was also found nearby. A hospice?

Or the human horror collection of a sadistic slaveholder?

Nietzsche says in *The Birth of Tragedy* that the Homerian epic was the Greek's "victory-song over the terrors of the battle with the Titans." This, of course, was the peninsular, dynasty-founding victory that Zeus owed in part to his allies the Centaurs, as Robert Graves reminds us in *The White Goddess*. Victory-songs, yes. But over what? The Titans? Who were the Titans? The gods of monstrously earth-rooted aborigines, like Atlas? Or stoutly resisting tribal warriors like the Taurians? The learning curve accelerates past the unknowable and straight into the insane, and before you can avert your eyes, the mystery doctrine of Tragedy discovers and proclaims that "individuation is the root of all evil." Monsters are always unique.

So watch out, comrades, and fear what Ukrainians call *drabyt* – the fractioning off, the bitter loss to the Void – of your soul.

Example of something, I am not sure what: On the way back to town from our daily excursion from Sevastopol into the Crimean countryside, Vladimir the taxi driver cocks his head at the motor. There is a harsh scraping sound, like seagulls fighting over fish heads, coming from within. Then the engine dies like a dog. Then silence: all the motor-animals have expired with it. Panic. We're poised at the top of a steep hill. Busy traffic, narrow lanes, no place to turn.

Vlad goes for it.

We coast down the hill, accelerating faster and faster. Now we are rounding the curve, he spots a gas station coming up on the left, and, without further ado, he pulls the Lada across two lanes of oncoming traffic, led by the stalwart Angel of Death herself, dressed as a sixteen-wheeled green army truck loaded with munitions or kerosene coming straight at us. He just squeezes into the asphalt lot ahead with the last puff of our momentum. Vlad hops out and pushes the car over to the pumps, smiling with relief.

I understand now. He was simply out of gas, and he's made it to the pumps with a few manfully sweaty pushes. *Bey problemo.* He gets four dollars' worth of the very cheapest benzene, number 76. Almost pure water. The car wheezes to life again, and we're off.

This time for good.

It's already hot at 9:00 a.m., and I'm glad I brought hiking shorts and sports sandals after all, so I decide to wear my socks too, *à la Russe*, braving the sartorial danger this outfit poses to my keen fashion-soul. Vladimir is taking us out to a good swimming spot on the coast, but the only name he is able to give the area for my notes is Dacha District No. 9. Soon enough we are breezing over a coast road dancing with architectural mirages, unfinished Norman castles, French châteaus, and Victorian manor houses, all blindly staring out at the world, windowless as doomed souls, as we sail by in a cloud of yellow coastal cake-dust.

"They are unfinished because owners are dead or in jail," Arkadi explains. "This whole catastrophe is Second Chernobyl."

"*Da, da,*" Vladimir nods, slumped over the wheel like a Texas cowboy, all skinny brown arms, wraparound shades, and lazy eyes looking at nothing (least of all the road).

"Yes?" I am in the back seat, getting used to the smell of good old-fashioned male sweat first thing in the morning, realizing it's not going to kill me. "Second Chernobyl?"

"*First* Chernobyl, some die, some get sick, but live. Second Chernobyl, Soviet collapsation. Some get rich, others get poor."

Collapsation, I liked it. He repeated his idea a few minutes later, but this time I heard Soviet *corruption*. Arkadi was working on mapping out the big picture for himself.

We stopped at the peak of a grassy cliff. Vladimir kept edging the Lada closer and closer to the jagged brink, until Arkadi told him enough and opened the door to bail. A panorama from Mars greeted us: red and orange buttresses soared over an ink-dark sea to our right, an enormous green mound surged straight out of the water on our left like some aqueous deity, and over the cliff edge below, a tiny grey pebble-beach beckoned. A few snorklers paddled around the white plinths that had toppled over in the great battle between the land and sea. We took our time negotiating the goat-path down to the sea edge; it was steep and illogical, but there was no other way. I marvelled how the young children and the women in cheap, high-heeled plastic sandals made it down without breaking an ankle or two. Relaxing was always such hard work in this country, and they were clearly used to it.

The plunge was cold and refreshing after our sticky, scratchy descent. I sat in a salt-tingly stupor, drying out on a smooth boulder, watching the young couples (the steep path prevented the ubiquitous babas from attending, which may well have been the whole point of the beach) enjoy their summer vacations. Already well cooked, they deliberately burned themselves further. The women applied their sun creams only after they got beet red. I observed they all had Caesarean scars, and some before their early thirties too. Also good gold jewellery, and attentive, executive husbands. It made me think this medical procedure was more a current fashion statement than a medical necessity. Out beyond the last swimmer, a single black cormorant searched the flat ink for a fish, and on the horizon a fishing trawler did the same. Doubtless there was a fish out there, somewhere, that one of them might scoop up if it was quick about it. Carter had agreed that the Tauric goddess was hostile to shipwrecked sailors and demanded their sacrifice. He didn't say why, but I could believe it now, looking up at these scalding red cliffs that stretched away to the west, impassive as the idols of Easter Island. Hundreds of feet high, they reigned supreme. The lordly and bloody gods of summer.

The Greeks who had come to these shores had accomplished something rather extraordinary. They had avoided the usual fate of other invaders, reaching an accord with the Tauric natives and, later, solid treaties with the Scythians and the Sarmatians. It was only in its incarnation as a Greek Byzantine city that Chersonessus finally fell to the Tartars in 1399. Otherwise it enjoyed an incredible civic run of almost 2,500 years and, despite its many permutations, remained an essentially "Greek" city throughout that entire time span. What was this concept of theirs that had worked so well for them?

Trade. And what was this trade but a profound and institutionalized policy of self-deficiency, creating a necessity for the other to come and complete the whole? I could see it in their demi-gods and monsters, the Greek prodigies, always half human, half something else: gods, animals, even trees and landforms were unfinished until joined to humans. The essentially incomplete drama of the giddy Centaur, the artful effigies of a synthetic Gryphon. These puzzles pointed to an order always in the making, a provisional and capricious connection. The Greeks of Chersonessus produced red wine in great quantities, using slave labour, but not "fine" wine, and no olives; and as every Greek must have his oil, there was always good reason to trade with distant Galateria on the Black Sea's distant south coast.

And because wine-growing is labour-intensive, the Greeks of Chersonessus must continually trade for slaves from the Scythians of nearby Neapolis. The nomadic Scythians admire the Greek artisans' goldwork, so they are persuaded to bring in grain and hides for exchange as well. And is not the exchange of jewellery the sure sign of a lasting bond? Neither "side" attempts to capture the secrets of the other. No, instead they concentrate on exploiting their differences and even emphasizing them, a development you can still see throughout the Mediterranean today. A coastal rather than a continental strategy.

With the Tartars, everything changes, not just here but across the known world. Genghis's hordes want control of everything, they will burn the bread loaves if they want. What they cannot control they will inciner- ate, leaving only ashes behind, to fall like snow on the ground. The Tartars, "the men from hell," or *Tartarus* (as distinguished from ethnic Tatars), take Crimea, and Baghdad, and the towns of Rus, and Herat, and all the trade centres of west Asia too. They never attack Constantinople, the Queen of Asia Minor. Why not? Of course they make the necessary military calcula- tion, but perhaps it is too alien for them? It's the heart of a vast trading empire, and too spiritually dangerous for their narrow souls. Their succes- sors the Ottoman Turks simply camp on the nearby plains for generations, waiting patiently for Byzantium's inevitable fall, until 1453 when the depopulated city gives up its ghost.

It is clear that the strategy of Russia, ever since Peter the Great (b. 1696), had aimed for this same continental self-completion. Everything of Russian life, from its long tradition of monumental war architecture to the shame-based farces of daily experience, speaks of this inner yearning for total absorption, for total possession. Possession, and absorption. Even the standardized mosaics decorating the Russian bus shelters create a burlesque fantasy of all-absolving modernity. We may be forced to wait for a diesel-leaking hulk for two hours in our cardboard shoes, but look at *how* we're waiting, so with the times! The facade of one Sevastopol apartment building we pass every day features a four-storey-high mosaic of a 1960s cosmonaut, done in hot-orange-and-green tiles. The work is already tartly nostalgic and priceless, beyond even abstraction in its fading and unsalvage- able mediocrity. The Russian sentimental attachment to childhood too, as the purest expression of the Future made manifest, offers a transparency and transcendence denied the masses in their other spheres of life. Even here in Sevastopol, in this former Party-and-Military small town, there is a large department store devoted exclusively to neon-orange-and-blue children's toys. Yet so few kids about. It's about the *idea* of childhood, who cares about the *children*? Whatever was once unique to this coast has been reduced to cheap sugary wine, bad sunburns, and godless steel monuments to fallen Soviet defenders – made to salute the idea of the Idea, with their stubby machine guns raised skyward in their death throes.

I am the only foreigner to be seen anywhere. (And why don't I ever get this fact from the peripatetic journalists of the *Globe and Mail*? Why is everything, from the moment I stepped off the plane, such a big surprise? Is anybody else awake from Our Side?) Yet these Russian girls of Crimea, unlike the Ukrainian women in Kiev, scarcely glance in my direction, while to the local men I remain wholly invisible. These are a people who have been taught to see only themselves; and I wondered how far it went, this solipsistic self-regard. During my trek past the Uspensky Monastery, an Orthodox cliff-retreat built into the limestone pillow-mountain, I had noticed half a dozen monks lounging on the steps of the refectory, knobby knees crossed, taking the air. They sported theatrically long beards and carefully washed ponytails, scrubbed faces, and they poised insouciantly on the steps, staring back at the tourists like haughty young cavalry officers just arrived at a gallop from the last century. The good century, when you could cut down pleading miscreants at will with your sabre. They were too good-looking, overly dramatic. I actually wondered, Were they real monks? Or were they some kind of professional troupe, actors hired in Moscow to play the role on behalf of a new government that was going to reinvent Russia on the foundation of yet another final Orthodoxy?

In the drooping heat of the evening we went out, Arkadi and I, searching for a new restaurant, walking for miles under the white-limed lindens. Nothing. No restaurants. Only the two cafés we had already tried, not counting the McDonald's, beloved playground of the spendthrift working girls. Kiwi Slurpees! Fifty kopecks! Arkadi refused to go inside, not even for a mere snack to fortify us on our nocturnal sortie.

"I know these people. They have their own cows, their own farms. They want everyone to eat the same food in the whole world."

He was not about to trade one world system for another. We kept walking. I didn't care any more. We passed a woman bleeding badly from a terrific wound to the right side of her face. She had either suffered a road accident or lost a terrific brawl, and while her shoes showed her to be solidly middle class (how categorical we are in our judgments), everyone else on the street averted their eyes. She stopped to ask directions of an old woman, the trusty bedrock of this civilization, and ignored us, two men in good shoes standing a few paces away.

Who is she, and what happened?

Arkadi is my Virgil, my resolute guide through this realm of terror and gloom, and like the great poet of classical antiquity, he admits to imperfect knowledge of the spectral visions we behold at every turn. He doesn't know.

A few minutes later we pass a calmly resolute baba leading a shrivelled teenaged boy through the main street, holding up a rough sign with her free hand. "Cerebral palsy," Arkadi translates quickly, as if to make up for his failure to diagnose the bleeding woman's state. Across the street, a young hoodlum with a mohawk out of *Taxi Driver* is sitting in a maroon Toyota Land Cruiser. Looking at us. No. Not looking at us. It's his twenty-year-old girlfriend, she is standing beside us, waiting for the light to change, and if her miniskirt were any shorter it would be a headband. The cheeks of her rump are perfectly exposed, two white melons divided by a built-in black thong, and it strikes me with gloomy precision that the Russians are waging the total war on this sexio-consumerist Front as aggressively as they once did in the age of ICBM march-pasts and bogus production statistics.

Chapter 11

The Styx Is a River That Runs from the Heart

It's evening, and the summer sun is setting over murky Sevastopol. I go outside to cool off on the crumbling concrete balcony of the Hotel Crim, treading lightly lest I disturb the delicacy of its original 1958 infrastructure. My wife would never forgive me if I came to sudden grief because the plate broke off and left me standing here on nothing, eight storeys up. I am thinking about Russia, this weird doppelganger of continental America, this half-sister of no mercy. She of the droopy eye and steely smile. Where is truth and freedom to be found in this unholy, and still smouldering, glowering wood?

From my existential vantage point I can see a black dog below, tied to a short rope in an ordinary junky warehouse across the street. And Blackie can see me. He gives off a bark as soon as I appear, as if I'm Mussolini taking his daily salute, and then he goes for a quick, excited circle around his wooden peg, only to return and wait wagging for my next move. If I do nothing and freeze, he will desist; but if I move across the eight-foot decaying floor to check my drying underwear, he will bark joyfully at each step.

Two steps, two barks. See?

We have a relationship, Blackie and I. There can't be too many other guests on this side of the building. The hotel has three hundred rooms, but most mornings fewer than a score show up for the included breakfast of cold boiled fish and rigid bread rolls. So I am Blackie's only solace, of necessity friend and enemy both. Is he a Russian dog, somehow different in temperament and training from his Western cousins? Or is he just a dog? Earlier today I had stepped over a bustling line of ants and I realized with a start that they were oblivious to human history, except for the crumbs they toiled over. The swallows too are free of conception. But not the trees. The poplars and birches have cryptic messages gouged deep within their living bark. That's how far I've gone already.

Envious of ants, and suspicious of trees.

Balaclava, scene of the great battle of the Crimean War between Russia and Britain, is not to be found in the guidebook, and it takes me a great effort to wheedle out the name of this seaside town from Vladimir, our louche cab driver, apparently because it's so self-evidently Balaclava that he can't comprehend my ignorance.

"Balaclava, *da*?" I repeat, pointing to the decent little harbour of private boats and ferries.

Vladimir shrugs; it's infuriating. Maybe the Soviets changed its name to Diesel Station 129, what do I know? It does not help when I try to explain, through Arkadi, that in my country a balaclava is "a kind of woollen sock one wears on the head, with holes cut out for the eyes, to rob banks." They look at me as if I'm deranged. It's reaching thirty degrees Celsius already, and the aromatic sweat is dripping down Vlad's armpits in a bejewelled festoonery of masculine glory.

"What did he say, he wants to put woollen socks on his head?"

I understand what they are saying, sharp splinters of light cracking through the great silvered mirror of culture between us. I try again, reaching for the handle that opens the door, the Ridiculous:

"Do they make baklava here? I have a real craving for it suddenly."

"What did he say?"

"No baklava, *Balaclava*!"

"I am getting a real backache-ola from this cab," I blithely continue, rubbing my neck and grimacing. "Say, what's that up there?"

I point to a yellow rim of dressed stones on a bare hill above the town, whatever it's name. (Later Arkadi will allow, "Of course it was Balaclava, everyone knows that, it's famous!" Arkadi and Vladimir bend heads, confer, pooling their meagre informational resources. Their palaver ends.

"A fort." Arkadi stoutly declares.

"A fort? Tartar fort, Genovese fort? What *kind* of fort?"

They ignore me, so I walk to the edge of the cruddy, salt-encrusted pier to admire the pretty little town, its colourful and pastel quayside – charming, except for that black submarine hanging its head shamefully in drydock, creaking in the breeze . . . Is there one glorious view here without its sulphur-belching smokestack? One afternoon of peace without the cockroach of death rustling in the wings?

"Ready for a boat ride?" Arkadi calls out, triumphant from his negotiations. "The ferry goes to nice beach on seaside." The venomous, sly water laps at the pier. A burnt boatman sits at the motor, ready to ferry us across to the other side.

Vital Zubar, the archaeologist in Kiev, concluded that the nomadic lifestyle was a dead end because it "didn't go anywhere," demonstrating its inescapable ecological cycles with a twirling finger that in the end described the hard fact of zero. Fine, but where exactly are *we* going? Can we pretend to rule the autonomous forces rustling the curtains of our late industrial culture? Do we even need our physical bodies any more? Or is the silent scream of the protesting mind the best we can offer? ("The isolation of atomized individuals is the basis of totalitarian rule," according to Hannah Arendt in *The Origins of Totalitarianism*.) I get in the boat, the boatman pulls at the motor, it sputters out its bit of noxious fumes, adding to the billions of cubic somethings out there, and we were off, heading across a sea that has condemned to oblivion every civilization before this one.

Last night, June 21, was Graduation Night for the nation's high schools. I didn't sleep a wink until dawn. The kids finally dispersed as the sun came up, after a long and screechy all-nighter, complete with hazardous fireworks and smashed beer bottles down in the parking lot. Poor Blackie! He was hoarse from barking by dawn. The last time I went out on the balcony to see if they had set the hotel on fire (the acrid smoke in our room turned out to from a brush fire, set in a park by another jubilant party), the moon was a brown bottle cap, sinking low into the western seacoast. Its stained shade showed exactly how much dust sat in the air, unmoving, despite the stiff ocean breeze.

I was thinking all night about the Centaur. Was he a horse who dreamed of being human, or a human dreaming of life as a horse? The correct answer, of course, in the cool grey logic at 4 a.m. was not either, nor both, nor neither.

Neeither! Neeeeeither!

Chapter 12

Flatheads at Twelve O'Clock High

The writer D.H. Lawrence didn't like Russians. Or, at least, the Russians portrayed in their dense literature. Too creepy-crawly, skinless, gloomy-paradoxical, and insincere in their easy hysteria.

Or, as he wrote in his deadpan Roundhead English,

"They bore me, these squirming sorts of people: they teem like insects."

What he said of Dostoevsky's characters might also be said of Russian TV, a mendacious medium that I have been forced to watch for hours on end, owing to an intractable sore throat caused by my aversion to the cadaverium and sleezium enveloping the port city of Sevastopol. On Channel 3, the black-and-white documentary rerun of the Second World War enters its fifty-seventh glorious year, with blond, eternally young Nazis chewing their pork-fat sandwiches, *ja-ja*, *ha-ha*, as starving, unshaven partisans skulk in the shadows of bombed-out factories, waiting to exact revenge for the stolen sausages. The comedy channel features robotic domestic pratfalls that make *The Osbournes* look like the pinnacle of Aristophanes' art. The news channel brings us another reburial with full military honours, thirty shiny new coffins for the mummified soldiers found in an unmarked mass grave in Stalingrad. Glum-faced plant managers do solo interviews for the business channel, their faces a bit shaky and greenish, as if the cameramen had downed a hearty liquid breakfast with them before the taping. Farmers give their views on the pollution problem of Donesk, with a cutaway to the sulphur-spewing water well sitting in the middle of an oat field, unable to explain how they got their lines crossed with a chemical plant miles way. And then there is the kick-boxing.

It's Mafiosi Theatre, short, brutal, and to the point. Big Destroys Small, that's all you need to know in this life (and possibly the next). The match-maker in our jurisdiction would be charged with criminal manslaughter for arranging such a no-contest, pitting this trembling little ducky against the iron-jawed stone-killer from Sverdosk. The sharkbait backs himself into a corner at the beginning of the second round, and very intelligently stays there, desperately flailing off what will be serious brain injury as soon as the referee permits it; which is just about now, because the ref is turning around to take a good look at the pouty card-girls, and actually turns his back on the mayhem, to converse at length with a big bald guy in the audience.

Hamburger Helper makes it to the bell, but he's so out of it he goes to the wrong corner; the fight continues after a wide shot of the grim audi-ence, a score of flathead diehards and their gum-chewing doxies. We cut to a close-up of the sponsor's logos, Casino Royale and Casino Atlantis. Wonder who owns them, huh? And now it's back to Round 3, and our brave little dogmeat gets it in the solar plexus in a quick jab from Lockjaw's tita-nium knee, and oh!

He's *down*! Down at last, slipping downstream along the pituitary artery, to dream of his childhood home in Pskov, now he's running to show his mamma the slippery tadpole he just caught in the river . . . Who says Russians aren't merciful?

Like it or not, that's where I am going. Straight north, into the heart of Mother Russia. Yes, I am leaving the Crimean's swelling summer haze for cooler climes, with my fingers crossed, hoping for cleaner air. It's looking good: Arkadi insisted I fly to Moscow, and the view below is so far encouraging.

Moscow, on our Aeroflot jet's approach from the south, is astonish-ingly green and boreal. The telltale brown pike streams meander through algae-bright swamps, then wander off again, only to turn around and lose themselves in another iridescent duckpond that flashes in shock at our brave passage in the tawny miasma above. Two residential orders of magnitude compete for our attention down there. First come the local villages, camouflaged in the wild thickets, hundreds of lowly wood dwellings scattered through endless fir trees, all following the cold logic of father winter and his prevailing sons of winds. Remnants of old Russia, one supposes. Fast on their heels come the huge apartment blocks, stacked in rigid rows like chewed-up dominoes. Two orders of life, two stances, the insouciant and the impositional. I have already met the watery man of rural yore, in the musky person of Vladimir the Crimean taxi driver, who moved from sunny patch to sunny patch with all the instinct of a comfort-loving creature, perhaps the common ancestor of man and tabby cats. Vlad was profoundly indifferent to the presence of Large Hard Objects, like these scabby apartment blocks and the need to make money. I recalled now what he said:

"I pay 150 hyrvnias for the car rental, one month. Plus gas and all repairs."

Thirty dollars, a month's wages for a worker. This did not include his own efforts to keep the cab together, wiring up its doors, hood, and trunk with telephone cables and the odd scrounged bits. The whole contraption looked like a Calder mobile; even the taxi sign on his roof slid around uncontrollably, ready to sail off on a whim. At one point we were driving on the highway and the passenger door unaccountably flew open. The blurry outside world suddenly gaped in alarm at our happily dozing Arkadi. Much awake now, Arkadi slammed it shut again in a fury, but I could see our unperturbed driver eyeing the problem speculatively, as if it were merely a prompt for designing yet another contraption to prevent loss of future clients.

Still, he had to pay a certain percentage of his fares to the owner, *da*?

"*Da, da.*" Vladimir nodded absently, a hopeless heap of receipts on his dashboard, all doodled over with meaningless numbers, a testament to his slouchy defence against the taxman's depredations; the tax collector in this case being the small-time entrepreneur-owner with three or four rusting Ladas under his belt and a barter-deal going with a local garage, such a man as the foreign-owned business journals might describe as "one of Russia's emerging middle class." But the fleet owner was also what Vlad and his beleaguered countrymen generally considered a cold stone with feet, that strangely incomplete creature of modern times, the *bizinessman*, someone to be avoided, outducked, outrun, and secretly condemned – but never, ever, to be taken seriously. Nor accepted as fully human. Perhaps we might think of summer-stock actors in the same way, should we ever meet one socially. Slick with their self-adoring immateriality, and never enough of that grounded balkiness we consider a sign of true character. So how much does Vlad pay his car-lord out of his receipts?

Tak dalyshy – whatever it takes. This is Vlad's fief, his sagging empire: a car held together with coat hangers, a bad road ruptured with potholes big as bomb craters (or maybe they are just that, fifty-seven years since the war and still counting), slimy chemical spills and a half-dozen palms-out police checkpoints to get through every hour, despite Sevastopol being an "open" city these days. And still we had made it to the airport within a minute of his original estimate.

Thanks, Vladimir. Here's to you, and old Russia. *Tak dalyshy!*

Now, as for modern Russia, here we are, streaking in like wounded banshees on the commencement of what they call a military landing (sharp bank, steep descent, slammed brakes, no chance for an enemy's hand-held rockets to engage), and on time. It's not all hopeless, for here I am flying down over the great city. The food on the airplane has already made me absurdly happy: a beet salad, a plain piece of cold chicken breast, a roll with soft butter. The simplicity of the unadorned internationalist cuisine feels like a solemn religious rite after the creamed mystery-dishes of Crimea. (Except for the bread, the food there tasted like the place sounded.) I eat the bread roll slowly, enjoying the contradictions of its textured fibre against the slippery, angelic butter, as the engine's choruses reach their crescendo and the Tupolev dips and banks and the schoolchildren onboard go *ahhhh* in unison, little cats awakened from their afternoon naps. Through the port window I see another jet streaking ahead of us, leading the way down through the strange metallic clouds of northern Russia, tarnished family silver rattled by the swiftness of our passage.

Rather close, that other jet ahead. Did the controllers show for work today?

On the ground, the impression of a boggy, coniferous dominion continues. Late June, and fat raindrops splatter the wide roadway, striking

cold and mineral. The landscape is like Temagami or maybe Moosonee.
Why Moscow? Why here? My taxi driver is eager to show me something. He
abruptly pulls the Mercedes off into a muddy lane running through a
primitive park and barks at me, "Port, port!" An antique wooden building
with a wide veranda appears through the hemlocks, great panels of cracked
green stucco on its sides, as if the architect couldn't make up his mind.
They're blank too – lost murals. We stop. No signs, no further explanation.
People stand silently on the dripping veranda and scan the dishing torrents
without hope. I conclude it must be our hotel until the driver backs up and
suddenly we're off again, out into the heavy traffic of Leningradsky, the
major thoroughfare, running hard and fast. Compared to Kiev, it's orderly
too. A local motor-system is at work here, you can feel it; the intimation of
a power grid to which these motorists, and their prey, these loping, rain-
soaked pedestrians, warily attach themselves. Willingly or not.

The next morning, my twenty-four-year-old student guide, Anya, escorts me
the fifty long blocks from my commercial hotel to my family guest apartment, where I am to lodge for the coming week. This apartment is the private
dwelling of a medical doctor, located on the eleventh floor of a concrete
tower from which I can see them both, the two Moscows. The bright, flag-
draped cranes of the brave new city and the rotting squat towers of the old
Soviet capital that saw better times with Brezhnev. This wide view, loaded
with historical irony, is undoubtedly shared by thousands of immediate
neighbours. My unit is laid out exactly like the physicist's apartment in Kiev,
plumbing fixtures, light switches, and everything, only it's bigger. The doctor,
a regal woman in her late sixties, escorts me into the dark and fussily decorated living room. My quarters, for fifty dollars a night. Crystal candy dishes,
two brown-brocade sofas, and 1930s-style family photos, set like mini-altars
along the laminated cabinets, the rotund faces carefully retouched with
heavenly pink pastels. Unaccountably the photographers leave the warty
birthmarks alone, perhaps they illustrate important genetic information.
The larger couch is already made up into a bed. Victorian-sibilant voices
drone from the other rooms. The doctor herself is a magnificent lady, a
silver-haired aristocrat. How did she survive the Purges? The living are all

guilty – of some sin, something terrible, that's the horror of old Europe. She brings me a mid-morning snack, black tea and bread with homemade raspberry jam, and ice-cold mineral water. I eat. Everything tastes Russian.

Olga is seventy-two years old, a pediatrician. She proudly shows me the seven red roses the schoolchildren gave her this week, at year's end. She is still working full-time. She ignores the sudden clamour from the other rooms. I suspect she doesn't trust the others in her domain.

I fight the urge to take photos of her narrow bright kitchen and its odd condiments, the Uzbek tea and the black Crimean flower-honey, afraid I will offend her. She is affable, patrician, nothing at all like the lunatics on the streets outside. (We'll get to them soon enough.) How does she live? By using her wits, every bit of intelligence. You can see the clever sapphire in her eyes. She introduces me to her white Burmese cat, Sumi, "the most beautiful cat in Moscow." Adjacent to the apartment building is a grubby park that has been taken over by allotment gardeners, and the children who play on its rusty slides and broken swings must be careful not to trample the precious dill, tomatoes, and green onions growing in neat rows around them. Life at the edge, Moscow-style. Standing on the decaying balcony, I begin to cough, hoping it's just the cat.

Back at the hotel yesterday, my first evening in Moscow, I had met Sarah, an American returning to the city with her teenaged daughter for a short visit. Sarah said she had been "posted" to Sofia, Bulgaria, and from the way she led her daughter in a drawling prayer over the cold buffet of fish eggs and peach yogurt, I had decided she was an emissary of a Southern evangelical group. Surprised to hear her speaking good Russian to the waiter, I ventured a bold opening.

"So how do you like Moscow?"

"I love it here, but three years is enough. The city was getting to me, the bad air gives me asthma, right? I had to be hospitalized. If I stay here, I'll die."

"Asthma?" I told her about my persistent cough, sore throat.

"That's how it begins," she nodded knowingly. "Then it goes into not being able to breathe. At home in North Carolina, I had your typical allergies, dog hair, mould. But nothing like this. It's *real* bad here."

She recommended a few over-the-counter medications, and I dutifully wrote them down.

Now, here at the apartment, I soon met one of the background voices –
Alexander, my landlady's middle-aged son, a morose, out-of-work nuclear
physicist. He nodded silently at my request for the nearest location of a
good pharmacy and disappeared without a word. Funny people, I said to
myself. I contented myself by playing with Sumi, wondering how Russians
got pets like a Burmese cat. Fifteen minutes later Alexander reappeared and
mutely handed me a plastic bag. Inside was a brand-new inhalator and two
kinds of foil-wrapped pills.

"German," he said, pointing to the manufacturer's name under the
Cyrillic instructions.

"How much?" I said, reaching for my wallet.

"For you, no charge. Is okay."

I looked up; he was staring at me with the bleary drifting eyes of the
ecologically betrayed. "You too?" I asked, and he nodded unhappily, "*Da,
da*. Asthma."

My heart sank; the American woman was right. Moscow was an
omen.

Shall this be a guidebook to hell, then? Directions to the labyrinth, a
catalogue of the ways the human race comes to bitter grief with itself? An
investigation of the final florescence of meaning that attends global
destruction, an exacting inquiry in all its excruciating particulars? The
white Burmese seems to like me, her eyes glow, but I am still glad I am
bigger than her.

Anya, the student tour guide, returned to the apartment at noon. Over
more cups of black tea, I tentatively decided on a half-day walking trip
around the central downtown core – tomorrow. "And nothing too strenu-
ous, please."

She nodded. I asked her about life in Moscow, during the recent political changes.

"Pavlov said, 'A frog should not be made to suffer the experiments,' the
way that our people did." My apprentice guide began expounding a social
history, without prompting. "When collectivization came in the 1930s, to
Moscow, it was social collectivization. My family had a six-bedroom

apartment. So, six families must move in, although only one bathroom. And *nobody* can wash."

"So, experiment after experiment. And now?"

"Now I go to tourist studies, in university. This is my practice."

Anya then looked at me with direct, abiding interest, displaying the intelligent curiosity of the local tree-crows dangling off the garbage bins outside. First one feral green eye, then the other. Trying to get it right, her fix on me. Tourist studies? I kept moving, the lone hunter in the wild wood, using every bit of ground cover as backdrop, breaking my outline.

"So, Anya. I am your practice?"

I began rummaging hurriedly in my bags for the camera.

"*Da, da*," she laughs, easily pleased. The practice speaks. The practice makes jokes!

"Ah-hah! What's this?" I show her the label of the blue Crimean mineral water bottle, packaging I have saved for its curious semiotics. It shows a brave young couple at the wheel of a tipsy white sailboat. Anya studies it carefully, and sighs audibly.

"The woman, she is Russian."

"Why Russian?"

"Because she is beautiful." Emphatically now.

"I see. And the man? He is *not* Russian?"

"He is good-looking. So I think, not."

"What is he then?"

The green flecks in Anya's eyes dance, playing over the icy distances of the image.

"Something far away. Far away and romantic."

You see? I am in Hell, all right. Deep inside an endless corridor where the same door keeps opening, and the same person comes out and says, "There's no one here." And you turn to ask a question, the real question, but she's already gone, and you can't even remember who she was, or what the question was in the first place. Just as Anya is about to leave, her tour-agency supervisor telephones, but only to warn me not to give money to policemen, even if they demand it during our little street tour tomorrow.

"Just refuse."

Okay, just refuse. Twelve hours in Russia, and already I am a refusenik. The entrance to the doctor's apartment consists of two doors, the outside of such hard tensile steel it would suffice for a jewellery shop in the Bronx, and the inside door a fat vinyl-wrapped behemoth that opens only to three or four complex keys applied in exact order. All this for the security of their ersatz crystal, and a small colour TV. Or maybe not. Maybe "they" come in the night, and *do* things to you. For their amusement.

I venture outside. By myself. The apartment keys jangle like knives in my pocket. I make it to the subway entrance, two blocks away. Walking slowly, blinking at the brutal traffic. Down we go, into Aeroport Station.

I soon discover that Hell's northern precincts are populated by *rusnalki*, forest darklings, the bright-eyed foundlings of Time's subterranean minions. It's a dark carnival down into the murky depths of the Moscow subway system, a crashing midway where they march freely, these many leggy legions of Russian women, all profoundly and wildly beautiful, burning like torches with a raw, urban incandescence. It's almost fun, despite the din, a ghost house filled with babes. The ratchety escalators raise them up out of the gloomy depths, and then plunge them back down again, rickety cataracts hundreds of feet deep, a living movie rolling along at five astounding faces per second, and presenting each woman to her illuminated fate, which they confront with the equanimity of angels. I find my own precarious place in this wobbly, fun-park dimension, and hang on for the ride – a mostly emotional one, it turns out, for I endure an inconsolable sense of loss, whether I am rising or falling with them. The subway's addictive; and I'll never seen any one of them again.

Speaking of light, darkness, and film stock, Arkadi had mentioned to me something I originally dismissed as another one of his pet personal phobias: the twenty-fifth frame. I was wrong. The twenty-fifth frame is big news here, and it refers to subliminal coding, a ruse supposedly used by Russian TV producers who secretly insert an extra twenty-fifth frame within the usual twenty-four frames of film, which bit contains a fleeting slogan such as, "Sit and watch only ATN-TV," and "images of children . . . in banking and real-estate services," or children "showing disrespect to parents" (Lays). This is all according to the June 26 issue of the *Moscow Times*, in an article entitled, "State Has Its Eye on Subliminal TV Ads."

There is little proof cited in the magazine article about this famously arcane practice; instead the Russian reporter quickly reverts to a traditional consumerist attack on misleading ads and product misrepresentation such as "bad liquids" being sold as "juice." The interesting thing is how this phenomenon exactly mirrors our own recent cultural history. Canadian professor Dr. Wilson Key published his book *Subliminal Seduction* in 1967, whereupon he was nearly ejected from his office by some members of a hostile university board. In his work Key had attacked the use of "embedded subliminals" in TV and print ads, such as sex-and-death symbols hidden in liquor and cigarette ads. His oddest find, a full-scale naked orgy in a photo the Howard Johnson's chain used for its clambake lunch special, became the centrepiece of a sequel book. The attendant public paranoia, anxiety, horror, suggestibility, or whatever was obviously real enough in North America (Key's books were best-sellers and counterculture staples), and it suggests that Russians (or Muscovites) are going through the same crises of psychological disintegration we experienced in the decade following the introduction of colour TV and mass advertising. But enough theorizing. I should really go out and face the police, the keepers of these fifty-calibre bullet lanes, as manfully as I can. Another reconnoitre, no? Shut the tube off.

Ignoring the back streets, I take an afternoon stroll down sunny Leningradskiy Prospekt, a fourteen-lane artery with two additional lanes of light rail running down its middle. The road ends in St. Petersburg, four hundred kilometres to the northwest. Thousands of small sellers take advantage of the summer day, offering flowers, cigarettes, second-hand books, wrinkled sausages from meat wagons. Village women squat for hours beside dishes of homemade pickles and little pyramids of tomatoes. I decide to head north for the Moscow Bank Building, an architectural mirage that gets no closer after ten long blocks of hard walking. The city's scale is set to motorized, not pedestrian, traffic. I must sit down.

A small pizza, a Coke, and a coffee costs me thirty dollars at an ordinary sidewalk café. The fact that I can't understand the bill troubles me more. Three young businessman at the next table explain that each topping added three dollars to the toll, starting with cheese. They are in their early

thirties, drinking Heineken. Pyotr tells me in good English they all got their MBAs in Akron, Ohio.

"You've heard of it?" he asks hopefully. He is good-looking, ash-blond, in that young Soviet soldier, about-to-be-machine-gunned, sacrificial, war-poster kind of way. More Aryan than the true Aryans.

"Sure," I say. "It's not Princeton or Yale, but it's pretty good."

They laugh at this. Pyotr tells me they are in business. What kind of business?

"Liquor business." His eyes shift; he's no longer looking at me. "Sleazy business."

"Most sleazy business," the dark one in the corner adds.

"The companies buy each other. Heineken bought this one," Nikolai smiles, showing me the brown bottle of an unfamiliar beer, and sighs meaningfully.

"Big fish eat the little ones." I make the gesture with my hand. "Soon only big fish."

"No, no," they protest. "Lots of fish here. Lots of business."

They sound more hopeful than convinced.

I ask if there is anything beyond the Moscow Bank.

"Only thing is St. Petersburg." They laugh.

"Everybody shoves here, in a hurry. Can't sit and enjoy life," they complain in a happy chorus. "St. Petersburg is the best place in the world."

It's decided: I turn my back on the shimmering money-mirage and take my life in my hands as I cross the Prospekt at full tilt. Cars whine past me, one hurtling Mercedes is already honking at a distant woman struggling to cross over with her bags, three or four hundred metres farther down the road. Two leather-jacketed bikers, black-faced with road grit, come out of a liquor kiosk. They good-naturedly tell me to screw off when I ask to take their picture. I am suddenly happy again, ready to see more of this curiously imperial capital. What do I mean by imperial?

The free weekly glossy, *Where?* magazine, says it all:

> Ivlev, the chef here at the Boulevard, is an innovator, a devotee of "extreme" cuisine, full of innovative flavours. . . . "I use the most exotic ingredients," says chef Ivlev. "I like to translate them into what Russians love."

And what do Russians love?

> Is there any other Moscow cook who could offer you a soup of frogs with green-tea noodles, shallots, ginger, garlic, and oyster sauce?

No, I don't think so. And at prices starting at U.S.\$150 per entree, I don't think I'll be dining on rare amphibians at the Boulevard any time soon. Nor will I be going to see James Brown at U.S.\$300 for a decent seat, much as I am a fan of the Godfather of Soul. I wonder, What does the aging patriotic hipster make of his renewed celebrity in this part of the world? Moscow is a strange city, a mandated empire-city, not an organic entity arising from its nexus to this or that wellspring of life. Imperial is as imperial does.

The city has been burnt to the ground at least four times. In 1239, Mongol raiders under Batu, Genghis Khan's grandson, torched medieval Moscow's wooden palisades. Then the Golden Horde of the Crimean Tartars fired it twice: once in 1382, in retaliation for their first-ever defeat by a Russian army, this led by Prince Dmitri; and again in 1571, when the Crimeans retaliated for Ivan the Terrible's conquest of their Kazan Khanate a few years earlier. Then at the Battle of Borodino, with Napoleon newly installed in the Kremlin, a terrific fire broke out in the stables and engulfed the entire city. There is some question as to who started it. The scorched-earth policy had already been used earlier against the invading Swedes of Charles Gustav and would prove useful against the Nazis in the future.

So where is the city? What is "Moscow?"

There is no city but an imaginary one. Moscow is a re-creation, a pastiche done up from the plans and memories of its former builders, erected against nature and the long odds of history. A current show at the Kolomenskoye Museum celebrates the architectural work of Pyotr Baranovsky (1899–1984). Like his counterparts in Kiev, the curator Baranovsky took precise measurements of the doomed Kazan cathedral in Red Square, erected in 1642, just before Stalin had it razed in 1936 to make a marching plaza. Similarly, the jewel-like Church of St. Nicholas in Tolmachi, dating to 1625, was closed and destroyed by the Bolsheviks in 1927; both churches have now been reproduced under an impulse the official exhibition calls "creative memory." These churches, and the icons that fill them to the rafters, are the gilded victors of invisible psychic wars in the folk memory of popular legend. I read with more than casual interest that St. Nicholas, the fourth-century A.D. sage, is the Russian patron saint of travellers and orphans, and the ailing. In other words, me.

The "Virgin of Vladimir," an icon brought from Constantinople to Kiev about A.D. 1150, is credited with warning off rape-mad Tamerlane and his hordes in the fourteenth century; while the Don Monastery, built in 1684 by Peter the Great, once housed the thirteenth-century "Virgin of the Don," a relic honoured with repelling an attack by the Tartar Khan Giri, who retreated from battle after the icon showered him with fiery arrows in a dream. Both supernaturally powerful icons are today housed in the great collection of the Tretyakov Gallery in Moscow's centre. The "Virgin of Vladimir" herself now sits behind bulletproof glass. The early cities of the Rus people were whole city-states, independent and proud – Kiev, Pskov, Tvir, and Novgorod. But Moscow learned a lesson in statecraft from the marauding nomads. Early in the rise of the Golden Horde after 1300, Moscow saw its political possibilities: it soon brokered its position as chief tax-collector for the Tartars into a suzerainty it maintained with a ferocity that would spare no one, least of all itself, whenever it fell to the enemy. Did the Tartars ever actually burn this city? I wonder.

This week in Moscow a gang of robbers took a 7.5-kilogram emerald from the safe of the Diotimo Gem Company, and, still hungry for loot, lifted a 2-kilogram topaz as well. Overkill! Over-the-top madness! Where are they going to fence such million-carat behemoths? You can be sure that, when they do, they will be celebrating their coup with an extreme dinner of frog legs in green oyster sauce (Green? How green? – Fifteen pounds of pure green!) All the loot squeezed from ten thousand miles around Moscow ends here: Byzantine icons, chrome-plated Mercedes SUVs, hot U.S. banknotes in the billions, all of it, a great hungry funnel of plunder. So the colossal gems cannot have strayed far. Perhaps they're already lodged in the private hoard of a new Pan Tretyakov, who now sits gloating behind his bronzed doors and surveillance cameras, in his International Trading Company, with its own badly designed green-and-purple banner.

I could probably meet him, Mr. Big, because, for all its self-important pomp, his corporate compound will always have its public restaurant, built like an afterthought into the side corner, as if the boss could not resist his deep-seated urge to haul in a piece of that pocket cash going past on the busy streets outside. And he will always leave the heist to put in an appearance, and check the till. Believe me, the Emerald Grand Restaurant will stay open, even if he gets away with it.

Chapter 13

Crocodile Shaslyk, *Anyone?*

In answer to your questions, yes, I would like to visit these over-the-top Moscow restaurants with their instant gratifications, anything the newly rich desires, and cheerfully pay their five-hundred-dollar champagne cocktail bills. Yes, I would peruse their fat menus designed around twelve *real* cognacs, then later enjoy the rollicking group sex offered by the Night Flight Club, with their gorgeous model-prostitutes, perhaps to breakfast at dawn in the Limpopo's VIP room:

> Two rooms stylized into huts of an African village with stuffed animals. Specialities: Grilled crocodile and crocodile *shashlyk*, kangaroo, and delicious tortoise from the Cape of Good Hope.

Then, too, I would certainly enjoy a lunchtime visit to La Veranda, with its menu that "combines the Mediterranean trend with a French accent and the Bavarian beer-cuisine."

But sadly, I will miss its offerings of the pop theme from *Titanic*, performed by a duet of traditional accordions. I can resist the lure of the extreme, the exotic, the experimental, all this explicitness the ex-Soviet society needs to experience. Of course, I do feel some inner need for these and other human delights, and sense within myself an appetite for endless novelty too, for total power is a trip like no other. Muscovites take things to their logical conclusion, a metaphysic that continues to lead them, unshakably and even cinematically, into living in freefall like Eisenstein's bouncing baby carriage. What is this metaphysic? Gambling, sex, and drugs are its holy trinity, its supporting actors, but its leads are Force and Strangeness – the one grimacing, bleak as the groundless centre it must occupy, and the other, offering up a thousand different smiles, each more devastatingly funny, sad, or enigmatically endearing than the last.

It's Scheherazade, of course, the exotic compelled into uneasy life by the violent vortex at the epicentre of the Russian spectacle – the man counting his loot, and the woman adorned with it. But the robustness of this system is its own weakness. Its main authors were Prince Donil Donatsky, Ivan the Terrible, Peter the Great, and Lenin. The dynamic they edged into being is inherently unstable. Authority comes from a position staked at dead centre, and the centre keeps shifting, based as it is on the perceptions of a numinous reality – all the input, all the time. It's relentless, this vigilance, for nothing is irrelevant to its concerns. It's nomadism, the raiding party institutionalized. All roads will be lead here, like ancient Rome's, but celebrating a paranoid's marriage of plunder and display. In bygone days the names of this groom and his fabulous bride were the Czar and the Russian Orthodox Church; they swerved left into the Leader and the Party, symbolized by the lonely Star shining ever so brightly above Red Square, and the serviceable Hammer and Sickle below. What shall they be called now?

"Stalin envisioned the Metro as his subterranean Socialist paradise," my city guide, Lena, advised me as we descended the vast flight of stairs at Aeroport Station on the Green Line and headed downtown for a brief tour of the Kremlin. "This was Nikita Khrushchev's first big construction assignment, and their idea was to create an alternate world down here. Perfectly organized, efficient, with inspiring art. The essence of modern life."

I can barely hear her commentary in the dull roar of surging trains.

"But it's so dark," I ventured to say, trying to follow the nuances of her little pep talk. My own feet disappeared quickly in the basement gloom.

"You get used to it." She watched gamely as our bleak train approached. It was battered and senile, but the faces of the passengers in the windows were lemony with faint hope, beeswax candles that needed only a single fresh match to bring them to light. A middle-aged woman in a torn coat harangued the others inside the car. They looked only slightly better off. I asked Lena if they had a lot of suicides, people jumping, that sort of thing. She glanced at me as if I were insane. We arrived at Red Square, and she insisted I join the short queue of fifty souls waiting to see Lenin in his red-and-black granite tomb, and I obliged her, although I was already sick of these bloodthirsty Commies and their all-too-tractable victims. In our twenty-minute trip she had already told me too many stories: this newly discovered mass grave, found and reburied, something about fired generals pulled screaming from a nearby cattle barn, dangling on meat-hooks thrust through their necks, and a pale green building where the former top dogs themselves admitted they were all spies and saboteurs too, crying for mercy at their 1930s show-trials.

"What do you think of your karma?" I blurted.

I stepped behind a clutch of North Koreans in bad blue suits. They were being abused by a mustachioed souvenir-hawker dressed in a bright-green ensemble, trying to sell them programs. His outfit was even more absurd than theirs. The hawker was either speaking clumsy Korean or some kind of madeup, racist nonsense. I voted for the latter, after hearing "Hyundai" and "Seoul" peppering his aggressive diatribe too many times. I don't know, what about this gawky street-pidgin? Mass tourism studies is a borderline discipline, along with subliminal advertising and mortuary art, maybe it doesn't quite get the study it deserves . . .

"Whose karma?" Lena blinked rapidly.

My guide was in her thirties, short, intense, in stout physical shape from walking the streets in her counterfeit Nike sports-sandals. She said her family had moved to Moscow in 1928 from Byelorussia, the saddest land of all in a cheerless nation, in the northwest. Now called Belarus, it was even sadder with most of Chernobyl's wastes drifting into it.

"Yours, Lena. Your family's. The country's."

The line to the tomb was getting shorter.

The guards were checking everyone with metal detectors.

"I don't know." More blinks. "I never thought of it before."

"But you've obviously thought a great deal about politics, history. What did all this mean?" I was getting furious, but trying not to show it.

"I'll wait for you at the exit," she said, taking my camera as a security precaution. "Just follow the line, that brunette woman there."

I found myself descending into an unbelievably dark crypt, and given that most of its visitors were middle-aged and older, I guessed that an actuarially fixed percentage would inevitably come to sudden grief while plunging down the grey stone steps. But who were they going to sue? That pale slug in the clear box? Lenin lay flat in his glass aquarium like a Disney pirate hologram, the halogen lights plying his image so hard that, for a brief pulse of time, you had the illusion there were three Lenins in there, radiant triplets in identical black wool suits. I checked to see if his nails had grown in the past eighty years. They were carefully clipped. The attractive brunette woman ahead of me now dropped behind, exciting the armed guards' keen interest. They all leaned forward as she mumbled a few words over the prone figure. Then she waited for a reply. Apparently she had personal business with the Bad Elf of the twentieth century, the only man Hitler ever respected. (And vice versa, according to Hannah Arendt.)

Back upstairs in the late-morning sun, I was eager to face the fair breezes blowing off the Moscow River. A crow changed its course overhead, deflected by some unseen thing high above the city; it landed and began chanting a peculiarly raspy dirge from the red-ochre walls of the Kremlin. Here I was, exiting Red Square, happily walking past the graves of the century's greatest murderers, and instead of the icy frisson I was expecting all along, all I got was the simple satisfaction of the inevitable bird shit, coupled to a mild curiosity that Stalin's otherwise undistinguished plot received three times as many red carnations as anybody else's did in the long row of dead Bolsheviks. At least on this sky-blue day.

We walked for miles at a good clip through the city, Lena and I. She said she loved walking, loved looking at the new neighbourhoods going up, but was horrified at the constant change that kept obliterating her memories, one by one. And that she was forty-six, not thirty-five as I had presumed.

"There was this building constructed near my parents' apartment, it started in 1928. I grew up knowing it as a work site, year after year. It was finally completed in 1984. A theatre! We had no idea! But that was how fast things changed, back then. Fifty-six years to put up a single building. Now they do it in four months!"

She was shocked at this unexpected dimension revealed in her country-men. They had a secret capacity all along for overnight transformation, an unhinged febrility.

"You know, not everything is great any more. Before, we could travel, see the whole country, for cheap. And parents had special care for their children. Now everything is ruinously expensive, and our country always thinks it must destroy everything it has, and start from new. But there were good things, worth saving."

"Like what?" I asked.

"Well, you know, without its strong banks, a river is just a puddle. Now we have so-called democracy. But it means the extreme right wing, now they take the schoolchildren in, after class, and feed them, but they also feed them propaganda too."

"Ultra-nationalism? Anti-Semitism?"

"Yes, and even these countries, the Ukraine, Belarus, in such a hurry to be independent! For what? Now they are suffering too!"

We had reached the bridge over the Moscow River, and we could see the new gigantic statue of Peter the Great. The current story was that it was originally Columbus, which the sculptor had done for America's five-hundred-year celebration in 1992 of the discovery of the New World. After the Yanks had roundly rejected it, he simply added a two-headed eagle to the prow of the *Santa Maria*, a few Slavic cosmetic details to that pudgy Mediterranean face – and *voilà*, the iron-willed Czar Peter rises anew from an incomprehensible hodgepodge of brass and steel, to stare proudly over the duckweed collecting in dark pools along the river's backwater.

We came to the Park Skulptur, a garden to which the statues of KGB founder Felix Dzherzhinsky and his boss, Stalin, had been consigned. Joe's nose had been smashed off, in plain sight of a row of alternative granite Brezhnevs, which provided an object lesson in State Revisionism. Each rendition tried out a different smile; none were convincing. A young mother watched her toddler take her first perfect little steps under Felix's simpleminded gaze. This was all just statuary now, I told myself, without believing it. I said a short goodbye to Lena (Had she been named after Lenin?) and went on alone the few hundred metres farther to the Tretyakov Picture Gallery. There I took in as many rooms as I could, aware that the banks of my mental river were flabby and dull, unable to contain much more data at this point. Indeed the priceless gilded icons and operatic nineteenth-century Realist works were already slipping away downstream, even as I stood before them and watched them go.

To reward myself for the sheer effort, I paid a visit to the McDonald's across the street. Oh heaven. Oh sweet taste of cardboard nothing. Is it food we want from fast-food joints, or absolution? No history, no nothing. Every bite of oversalted french fries persuaded me I was getting closer to the elusive spirit of Modernism, convincing me it doesn't have to make sense. It never made sense and it never will. Forget the past; forget the dead. Eat your Happy Meal and shut up. Better yet, talk to that nice blue-eyed girl at the next table instead. Tell her she has the same Siamese cat-eyes as her pet in the plastic carrying box, eating bits of choice South American hamburger under the table. Tell her you wish you were her cat.

My landlady's son in Moscow, like my Ukrainian landlord back in Kiev, is a theoretical physicist. The Russian specializes in electromagnetic fields, and of course it was always the cream of Soviet science who got these large apartments – units that now qualify as tourist lodgings – in the first place. My sense of their material circumstances is that such physicists lived roughly at the level of our high-school teachers, but without the yoke of a house mortgage. Alex speaks English, passably well enough to tell me that he works "very hard with his head," and therefore he has ignored his body, which now protests his indifference to it by refusing to function without copious medications. Asthma, migraines, bowel problems. The whole chronic sideshow. Vowing silently not to do the same, I ask Alex if the pills he's given me remove any vitamins or other important nutrients from the system, and he regards me as if I have just asked him an interesting theoretical question. He goes straight to a heavy textbook.

"Ah-hah! See? It's cortisone – a steroid, the main ingredient!"

"Nothing about a loss of vitamin C?"

"No." He points to an exercise machine, gathering dust out in the hallway, a piece of equipment I thought belonged to his hulking son, Vlad.

"I got this machine to increase my lung power. If you like, I will clean it up and you can use it." He started wiping it off with a rag as he spoke, clearly

happy with the idea that I, at least, would get some use out of his neglected
investment in his own health regime.

"Did you notice the armless Virgin in that church?" Lena had asked me as
we exited Red Square. My guide was delighted with my squinting.

"Mmm." I nodded equivocally. I had noticed a lot of virgins. The
Orthodox idea was that you piled them up on the walls to the rafters, with
as little space between them as possible, so armlessness was a hard feature
to distinguish in this heavenly mob.

"The story goes," she continued, "that a village girl outside Moscow was
born without arms, and her mother looked after her as best she could, until
the mother died. The father remarried, and the stepmother did not want to
have this 'useless creature' in her household, so she persuaded him to take
her into the forest, and leave her for the wild beasts to devour."

"When a young prince came —"

"*Wait.* So the boy comes, and he saves her, takes her home. Says he loves
her, and will marry her. She protests, and prays very hard. The boy says, she
must marry, the date is set, and the night before the wedding she prays to
this icon, the Virgin Mary. And in the morning she wakes and finds she has
arms! And the Virgin in the icon has none!"

"Beautiful story . . . ," I begin.

"Wait! The story is not over. In 1941, the Germans were advancing on
Moscow. Stalin, it is said – this is a word-of-mouth story – Stalin ordered a
plane to take the Armless Virgin up in a wide circle around the Germans,
and this is what stopped them at Kilometre 41. The power of the Icon."

"Kilometre 41," I nodded, impressed, although I didn't get the point of
the story. Did the girl marry the boy or not? Was she made whole for love
or for God? Now that I had seen a couple of thousand pictures at the
Tretyakov, in as many seconds, I was obliged to think about these vast State
hoards, about their deployment, their function as a magnifying lens for the
collective will. It was not about this picture or that one, clearly; it was an
unrelenting sensory attack on individual assertion. Even Lena had let slip
the word *gallery* when she meant *church*.

"But of course in Stalin's time these churches were galleries," she said apologetically. "They were desecrated, then reconsecrated. The church that houses the Armless Virgin is, of course, recreated too."

It went without saying that the hundreds of icons in any given Church of the Annunciation were also brand new, commissioned from a catalogue of prototypes and aged to look a thousand years old with all the chemical tricks of the cunning antiques trade. Perhaps they used the same Egyptian death-alchemy that made Lenin look as if he'd died last Monday. My point is that the secular art gallery itself grew from the icon-stacked Byzantine Church and that this great gilded crowd, whether of ethereal saints or wanton *houris*, is, evidently, intended to defy rational organization; it is intended to produce a numb noggin in an hour or so of strolling around. Art en masse wants to overload the circuits, and leave us breathless and indecisive at Kilometre 41.

Ritual space, loads of ritual space. The images in the church and gallery both create a perfect vacuum around them, a shield or wall, the *iconostasis*, meaning literally, "where the icons stand or stay put." I am not talking about individual pictures, individual pictures are fine, and God bless Picasso. I am talking about the political uses to which the State puts artworks in the aggregate, about how this lesson was first learned from the Eastern Orthodox Church, and then aggressively deployed by all modern States, including our own.

So these are the familiar old tricks of settled states: walls of brick, or of the images of same; appropriation, eating the wild crocodile as it were, and rendering its evident dangers harmless; disputation, the logical ends of all argument tied neatly together. ("What would happen if Russia pulled out of Chechnya?" I asked Lena. "Oh, they wouldn't survive!" she said quite passionately.) And finally pasteurization, killing off the bacillus of the independent element with the calculated application of boiling heat and bright lights with mass transit and colour TV.

Walking the city was teaching me something too. Each block of the new Moscow stretched longer than the last. It was clear the First City of the Revolution was designed exclusively for motorized traffic. The subways, the underpasses, the apartment complexes belonged to an order of scale that far surpassed the limits of human frailty. The Russian pedestrian is made to feel his utter dependence on the System from the moment he steps out his door. Moscow is a program, all the more powerful for appearing to be just another European city, and staying neatly invisible behind its array of calculated effects.

Chapter 14

The Square Is the Icon of Our Age

At four o'clock in the morning, the vile hordes lurking within the city's corrupted atmosphere made their final death-attack. I fought back with everything I had, desperately rummaging through my drug kit. A shot of Ventolin, two shots, the Suprastine tablet, another one, then Aspirin and water. Still I was choking. I reached for the red foil package my host had given me earlier, accompanied with a stern warning.

"Very strong. Break in half, and half again."

Now I tried to break the pill; my hands were shaking. What had the American woman said? She loved the place, but it almost killed her? And Alex, my host, when he introduced me to his friend Valentin? He told me they both had migraines and high blood pressure, on top of the asthma. A congress of invalids hunched there in the computer room, a real zombie prom, restlessly pacing about the flat every night. I had sent out my e-mails, short ones, as breathless as I felt, to everyone I could think of: *I'm here in Moscow thinking of you.* A hollow communication, a one-way radio transmission into the void of space, a message in a leaky bottle.

Now the crisis came. I popped the whole red pill, some sort of Russian hormone, into my mouth, swallowed it, and waited on high alert, as if the black miasma hovering outside the balcony was a sentient thing, one that would quickly counterattack.

And come it did, another wave of spasms and breathless interference. All the micro-toxic junk of Moscow's hyper workweek, settling itself down in my guts on a warm Friday night. I slipped into a weary crouch. Sleep of a sort came, followed by my late father, mysteriously alive again but ailing, as he always is, in dreams of late. Dead but not-dead, chastising me for another hopeless career move.

"I left you a perfectly good law office, and look where you are now!" He shook his head, glaring at me with the supreme foreknowledge of the Undead. "You won't be able to do this book – now you're really finished!"

It was true. How could I go on with this stupid enterprise? It was hopeless. I would have to go on the next flight out, figure some way of repaying the publisher's advance. The money was already gone, on last-minute dental work and prepaid travel expenses. It would never be recouped. And worse, the shame! I could hide out in my house for a few weeks at least, before casually reappearing in public one day and telling my friends I was still working on it. Maintain the fiction for a few months, until they forgot about it.

Now the Big Red Pill seemed to be doing something. Now Metallica's drummer had set up shop in the hollow of my chest, and began to pound out the theme song to *Titanic* in triple time. I pulled on my earphones and played my Yes CD. *Hold on*, the lead singer entreated. I'm trying, really. Maybe another Aspirin to thin the blood away from the incipient heart attack? Each lyric of the Yes song became a way station on the approach to Central Headquarters, but whether it would be open for business or not when I got there, I could not say. I tried to take my refuge in the Buddha, counting my breaths, *one, two*. In and out. *Three, four*. Slowly I descended into a neutral space created by the medication, and slowly slid into a space that began filling with real air, as the quiet morning fluttered over the grey city and I awoke to find myself okay, at last.

What had happened? The city was quiet. A Saturday morning.

The weekend had arrived, millions of Muscovites had left for their dachas, and the air had grown relatively clean in their absence.

I went out for a walk. It was true. The cars on Leningradsky had all but disappeared. I was alone with the shuttered cigarette kiosks, free to ramble down great swatches of open sidewalk.

The city was actually pretty, what a relief! All pastels, pink and yellow. And interesting little garden nooks appeared. Open squares that had remained invisible behind the long week's endless streams of black Mercedeses. I took the Metro to the New Tretyakov, where they kept the Malevichs and the Tatlins. The subway car was almost empty. No missionaries or hustlers.

Now I got my Moscow frisson, my steely, high-wire thrill, now that I found myself alone on a wide deserted industrial block that stretched off for a clear kilometre. De Chirico-like, deserted perspectives. New buildings everywhere, in soft creams and cocoas. This was the sumptuous product for which all these lives had been spent, bloody decades bent on constructing a fantasy. A dreamy pastel cake factory, pink fairy castles and mammary onions in gold, and milky cloud vistas framed and tickled with intricate, agitated spires. The city was empty, deserted at the height of a glorious summer season, a fancy garden fête prepared by a band of light-shunning pixies, who had gone on to take their frenzied quarrels somewhere else. Deep into the magic forest.

The oil painter Kazimir Malevich's prophetic *Black Square* sits behind a Plexiglas shield on the third floor of the New Tretyakov Gallery, beside other seminal works of the twentieth-century avant-garde. Tatlin and Popov. The mine canaries of Modernism.

It is a simple work, two feet high, a foot or so wide. A poster-sized rectangle. The white border, three or four inches in width, is a kind of greyish, domestic white, the sort of white you get after washing your dishes in soapy water. Not the pure white of science or technology.

The black, on the other hand, is pure. A flat black, nearly dead. It neither emits nor reflects anything. But of course, in the embrace of the white it comes alive, it actually stirs. This is the sly trick that Malevich lays on us, this thing that rises from the dead of night. Was his work about the Father and the Mother? The unknowable, tantalizing Absolute, and its consort

Intercessory? Or was this the White North that had captured the Black South, the sterile union of Russia and Malevich's native Ukraine, an embrace that had failed to produce its own Red Child?

Either way, one could see that the black square was literally now falling apart, disintegrating into oblique crusts and spidery stipples. The picture itself was dying. An ecological Rosetta Stone now showed itself in the black square, brighter than its white border on account of the light reflecting off its intricate cicatrices. The strange hieroglyphs of decay and dissolution, the natural world's emblem of choice, had chosen this work to announce their eventual and triumphant return. Had the artist intended this effect from the beginning? It was Malevich, after all, who said that the square is the icon of our age.

Now the square was in rapture, leaving us to our fate.

On my way out, I came across a curious large-scale work, *The End*, painted in 1948, showing Adolf Hitler in his Berlin bunker, getting ready to take his cyanide pill. Who cares to imagine what Hitler's last moments looked like, from inside the bunker? Yes, this is gangster art, all right: social-ist realism, *ha ha* we won and look at you worms squirming now, the hated enemy's purple head torn off and impaled on the stake, but what an obses-sive compulsion *to see*! To imagine what we must see, to see what we've damned to hell. A thousand more pictures like this one too, hanging in pride of place throughout the gallery. Graphic as cartoons, and horrible, as if Disney had married a Dr. Frankenstein and began the opus with Snow Ice and the Seven Zombies. Here's a vast painting of a dead Siberian settler stretched out in the middle of the country roadside, his bereft wife and child horror-struck with sudden shock, and no one around for crow-screeching miles except the artist himself, ravenously seizing on every pathetic detail. This is hyper-pathos, an excess of nostalgia that leaves nothing to the corruptible individual imagination, because (I think) Russian art, too, is a symptom of the square, a sign of its power, the obedi-ent servant to its final urge to utter completion and self-abnegation.

Enough of the square. Slip into something comfortable and listen to the sound of nightingales in the strange night breezes.

My last evening in Moscow, time for a homage to the Russian pickle. It's the beginning of July, summer holidays, the city is liquid with limetree light. I am sitting in a hidden corner of a great park, perched alone on the foundation stones of Peter the Great's Moscow palace, examining my picnic loot. Spread out on the grass at my feet is a northern smorgasbord, items chosen at random from a smart little delicatessen around the corner. Plump, floppy little mushrooms, swimming in a green onion vinaigrette. A musky, peppery sausage, chewy and lean. Ice-cold Russian beer, a couple of cabbage rolls in a sweet tomato sauce.

But it's the lone dill pickle that surprises me, a spunky extravagance that bears no resemblance to the water-logged lumps we get back at home. No, this is an *ogurtsy*, alive, fizzy with effervescence; and each bite resonates, revealing a new dimension of culinary spelunkery. My tongue delights in probing the mysterious interior, the smoked salmon and brie lie forgotten. I do not even care to examine the dog-walkers and their charges; I just sit back and dream.

I am one of those distant figures fading off into the golden afternoon too, turning into soft light at will, as I bite my way through the green fruit of a tart paradise.

PART TWO

Black

Beyond the Urals

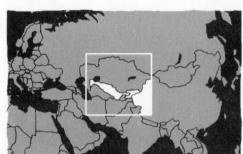

ASIA

UZBEKISTAN & KYRGYZSTAN

Russia

Kazakhstan

Caspian
Sea

Aral
Sea

L. Balkhash

Almaty

BISKEK

UZBEKISTAN

L. Son-Kul

L. Issy-Kul

Khiva

Narin

TASHKENT

KYRGYZSTAN

Turkmenistan

Samarkand

Bukhara

Tajikistan

Kashgar

Dushanbe

CHINA

Ashgabat

Iran

Afghanistan

Pakistan

Kabul

Islamabad

India

Chapter 15

The Choice Between Italian Shoes
and the Exotic

Dawn, the colour of old honey. The birds began their multiple choruses to the soft jazz-rhythm of gum leaves brushing against the window. From my bed I can detect eight early performers, at least. The martial roosters lead off. The cockbirds begin stridently enough, and quickly fall into the plaintive wails of overtired muezzins. A bubbly avian oboe with only two notes, high above the others, plays from the crown of a linden tree; a flustery, quarrelsome finch seems to throw its arguments back at itself; a chirpy fury from the hedge spits out its hot verbal pepper; while the rough insinuation without melody or pitch can only belong to that gang of streetwise crows on the next rooftop, they're not quite awake yet. A keening whistle that ends in a two-part drone tells me I am deep within a foreign land, and a high-register *wallop* that explodes in a vocal rainbow of chortles announces the morning sun has finally burst over Asia.

I am lodged on the second floor of a small hotel in Tashkent, which city from my window is a flat green city of plane trees, chestnuts, and walnuts, with pleasant one-storey houses set back on open courtyards and lanes filled with rose bowers and grape trellises. Imagine Tashkent, imagine Uzbekistan. Nothing comes, of course. It helps to put the words *Soviet* and *Mexico* together. Get the scissors and glue and try some mental collage or idle Sunday-afternoon découpage. Take away the baroque Catholic churches on the Aztec city squares and replace them with giant monuments to the eternally steed-mounted Tamerlane. Make sure his horse's teeth are of steel. Delete the saturated murals of Diego de Riviera and put up something more folk-abstract, cooler blues and acid yellows, and scatter them across apartment buildings that no one wants, judging from the current asking price of U.S.$1,000 for a one-bedroom flat. Put little dinky cars everywhere; the cheapest new auto is the product of a joint venture with Daewoo, the microid Tiko or Rabbit, and it costs U.S.$5,000 They must have multiple owners, judging from the people jammed in their front seats.

Most of all, it is the bleached light of the plazas, the wide, commemorative boulevards drained of all history except this season's, the packed, Ukrainian-made buses, and the expansive parks with their dedicatory fountains and acres of tea roses in bloom that says we're south of the border. The short, cheerful women in their bright florid dresses would pass unnoticed as local *mezitzos* anywhere in the New World. The brown, cheerful parts, that is.

Uzbekistan is the first of the three ex-Soviet Central Asian republics I will visit, along with Kyrgyzstan and Mongolia, each claiming a special place in the history of the ancient war between the settled and nomadic peoples. This country is the original homeland of Tamerlane, the horse-conqueror who claimed kinship with Genghis Khan, yet wrecked his ancestor's legacy by crushing the surviving Mongol Khanates in the 1390s, and ultimately leaving a power vacuum the Russians were eager to fill, beginning in the 1550s with Ivan the Terrible's Cossacks' inexorable advance eastwards. The Russians took this region in a series of sustained military campaigns that ended in the 1880s, and left behind them another power vacuum in 1991. While the Slavs and German settlers who arrived with these troops have now been emigrating out of Uzbekistan, its capital, Tashkent, is still loaded with historical oddities and the atonal music of clashing cultures.

We had been driving around the city less than an hour yesterday when the first policeman waved us over with his red-tipped baton, to tell us where to stop for his summary inspection. This despite the fact that our driver has a brand-new vehicle, a sparkling Toyota festooned with licences and permit stickers, and that his passenger is clearly a tourist with a battery of cameras and a baseball cap. Or maybe he saw I was a tourist, one of the few to enter the country these days (the airport had scarcely any) apart from the Russian *bizinessmen* and their spoiled, pouty wives, drinking themselves sodden on the plane. Despite the smooth Italian clothes, the Russians passed the wine bottle around like the Sunday-morning boys in the park. No, this is not the place for the casual Westerner.

While the driver does what he has to with the policemen, Zehar, my guide (a ringer for Anthony Quinn, hairbrush moustache, squashed boxer's nose, and all), leads me to the Tashkent Earthquake Memorial. Yes, this is exactly what I came to see, a cracked marble plinth on the baked ground, standing in the middle of nowhere, with itchy weeds growing around it. The rusty plaque said the 1986 tremor was 6.5 on the Richter scale, but 8.2 on the local scale.

"What is this local scale?"

I could be seven feet tall on my own scale; I could be *anything* on my local scale.

"This is our own scale," Zehar said proudly. "The Richter scale is, of course, good too."

"So if it reaches nine, on your scale, what does that mean exactly?" I watched some brown boys plunge into an artificial cataract under the next grand monument, a hundred yards down the road. What was it commemorating? The flood of 1987? The drought of 1989?

"Nine means more than 8.2 on the Richter, which is a vertical tremor. Nine means a massive wave, rolling along like the ocean. Like a tidal wave of earth. The next thing to collapse will be the subway."

"And ten?"

"Ten? Ten means God is finished with us."

Zehar took pains to point out the rottenness of the apartment buildings the foreign Russians put up after the earthquake. The literalness of the monument itself was more oppressive. A granite clock showed the exact time the earthquake went online, and the earthquake itself was denominated in black granite, while the red granite, represented "human hope and the power to overcome nature." I studied Zehar when he recited this last, because I did not believe an Uzbek would believe for a minute that man can overcome nature, and I decided he was merely explaining the stonework, not expounding his own view.

"Ten kinds of peaches," he suddenly cried out as we passed a fruit grove, embracing the lush view with his stocky arm. "Two hundred varieties of roses, and a hundred of cherries. We have the sweetest fruit in the world! Come, let me show you!"

It was true. The Eski-Jarah, the Old Market, indeed displayed two hundred varieties of grapes, and more fruit than one could sample in a lifetime. Watermelons, seven or eight types, a dozen unknown kinds of berries, heaped in tin buckets. The Koreans – the descendants of war prisoners exiled here by Stalin – were selling *chimchi*, noodles, and other chopped vinegar salads; a thousand people stood in stalls clustered around the huge domed market building of steel and coloured glass, while inside the enormous, gloomy cavern, the unceasing din forced everyone to bend, head to head, using hand gestures to negotiate their deals. The dresses of the market women were dazzling, shot through with gold and elliptical slithers of running silver. Everyone present radiated the sunny rustic glow of the open countryside, and directed expressions of easy interest towards our slow passage through their tightly packed stalls. It was staggeringly rich, loud with echoes and tinny music, effervescent.

"Try this. Of course, it is not yet the season." Zehar scanned the enormous mulberries, plucked out one the size of a cow's eye, and handed it to me. The berries bled deep purple nectar as we watched; a full quart of their fresh juice cost a quarter.

"Not the season?" I wanted to do the whole circuit, see every raisin. Stay here in this happy clamour, safe and a million miles from those steel-jawed horses and their insatiable Rider.

"This is only the beginning." Zehar shook his head and popped a raspberry into his mouth. "The fruit season begins next month. Then you will see watermelons!"

My treat saturated my mouth; I couldn't speak for joy.

"Shall we buy?"

We took a half-kilo of mulberries for fifty cents. The woman vendor was judicious to the point of balancing one more berry on the heap, to make an exact count. Behind us the Niagara of fruit and nuts and cheeses and spices and noodles flowed and eddied, under the watchful eyes of Zehar's people, these Uzbeks who were smart enough to recognize that an earthquake was the sign of the end of an era.

Is this to be a book about women? About Russian women? It would seem so, for their striking and startling presence, out walking everywhere in this irrigated, flat Mars-scape of a country, demands investigation, demands my vinyl clipboard and photo ID. What are they doing here, strolling about Tashkent Town, midday in thirty-degree heat, in their miniskirts, spindly high heels, and carefully madeup faces? *Clip clup clip* past the legions of squatting, kerchiefed local women, past the solitary Muslim-capped men, stolid as woodstoves in their square pill-box hats and antiquated dark suits. *Clip clup clip*. Where are these Russian women going? Where is there to go, now that it's all over?

My Uzbek guide, Larissa, appears in the two-star hotel lobby like an apparition, a glamorous interloper, Rondeau the Illusionist's forsaken assistant. The celebrated magician has forgotten his knives and gone back to Chicago, and here she is, left to spin the Wheel of Death on her own, without an act to follow. Pretty, and lost. Lost in her prettiness? Pretty lost? All of the above. Spin the great conjuror's wheel!

Larissa: twenty-seven, chestnut hair, extraordinary face, and the fine, straight nose of a nineteenth-century artist's model, dressed coolly today in a black linen-and-cotton suit, with the latest eye-poking Italian high heels in caramel lizardskin. Impossibly pointy, those shoes of hers. Self-composed, like she just stepped out of a vast fat novel. A novel yet to be written.

A first-class beauty, and why not?

"My mother is Russian, very beautiful. My father was Tajik, this is a Persian people."

"The same people as the Sakas," I nod, eager to show off my months of heavy reading. "The nomads who drove out the Scythians from Central Asia."

"Maybe you are right." She looks off into the street. "We will be leaving for Khiva by air tonight. I hope it is a big plane."

Khiva was one of the last redoubts of the locals against the Russian invaders, a fort-city of strange horror and skull-dressed walls, but who cares?

"It doesn't matter how big it is," I say, "as long as it gets you there."

She smiles at my mild innuendo, a flash of brilliant white teeth. Nature has taken good care of its hybridized love-child. In Milan or in Moscow, Larissa would be out shopping for fur coats in July, to beat out her rivals for the best selection; in London or New York, she would be checking out a Soho gallery, on the cellphone about tonight's opening, asking if Hugh was coming. And in my city she would be working overtime at the Agency, to pay for the lease on her silver Honda CRV and health-club dues, thinking about what brand of bottled water to get delivered to the condo.

In short, Larissa is an enigma wrapped in Guess and riddled with questions of unresolved identity. We must talk. About everything.

"Larissa? What is the point of it all?" I ask as soon as we board the plane, a jet that she assures me, after looking around, is a Boeing, not a Tupolev.

"You mean life?" She studies me, her eyes are brown verging on chestnut. There's a small, sharp scar on her right cheek.

"Yes, why are we here? Is history just a fire, burning us all to ashes? Or something else?"

"I ask myself this question all the time," she sighs. "Pushkin was the first to ask such questions in Russia. We ask such things in school, but we answer it with life."

She is taking me seriously, I crow. A two-hour flight alone with the Russian principessa who read Pushkin as a teenager! With pointy Milanese reptile pumps! Oh joy! Oh Woody Allen heaven! My eyes feast on her features as the plane ascends. We were soon conversing deeply, oblivious to our low passage westward over the fearsome Kyzylkum Desert, the Red Desert. Together with the even-more-terrible Karakum, the Black Desert, farther to the west, the Kyzylkum's scorching ferocity once framed and protected the ancient and doomed kingdom of Khorezm from would-be invaders, until Genghis Khan. The larger desert is in her eyes.

"I think we can learn from history, from our mistakes," she finally decides.

"Oh. An example?"

"Well, when Russia sold off Alaska to the Americans, that was a big mistake."

"Do you want it back?" I said, disappointed by this apparent show of the endless Russian craving for more land and lucre to misuse.

"No. It is just that some things are higher in value than money. But some people don't understand this."

From her tone I realized she was talking about her own life.

"So what are your dreams? What would you like to do?"

"I used to have dreams, before I got married . . . Now, I am a little lost."

"A little lost?"

"*Greatly* lost." She pronounced firmly, pressing her lips together.

"Greatly lost?" I repeated, the old shrinkster's trick.

"That is not the right expression, is it?"

"No, no," I hasten to get on with the conversation. "I like the way you say it, 'Greatly lost.' It is fresh, this expression. I like fresh."

She smiles again, and gives a sigh, staring now into the depths of her recent illusions, recanting them to a stranger flying over the blazing desert sands at thirty-one thousand feet.

"It was, I think, a mistake. I was twenty-two. I wanted to travel, to see the world."

She stares glumly at the passing sea of undulating pink sand, half-digested hills of old glue and broken plaster, a wasteland to anybody but my keen geologist friends, who would undoubtedly see Zelignite or Forbiddenite down there, in slag heaps of economically recoverable quantities.

"But isn't it ironic, though," I begin with an air of false cheer, for I can see she is falling into what the novels describe as the glum river of Slavic despondency. "Isn't it odd that I came here all the way from the West, to see this strange country? And you can't wait to leave it?"

"Yes." She waves her white hand carelessly. She's heard this all before. "It's what you call the Exotic. This is what you come for . . . As for me, I have a girlfriend, Jewish, she was lucky to emigrate to the U.S. as a refugee. I went twice to the American embassy, for a visa. But they rejected me."

"But, Larissa! It seems to me that life in the West is about shopping."

She waits for me to make my point.

"I mean, like, even in Moscow, it gets pointless after a while. A restaurant that serves crocodile *shaslyk*? What's the point of a life chasing such pleasures?"

"You have studied Buddhism, yes?" she says abruptly.

"Well . . . but . . . yes," I sputtered, thrown off guard by her deft reading of my closeted nuances. "Books, not practice."

"Well, when I was nineteen, before I was married, I was much interested. I studied with a Krishna ashram."

"*Krishna?* In Uzbekistan?"

In cartoons this is where the top of my head explodes, my exposed brain flying away on its own little white wings. "You mean the cult?"

"Yes," she said simply. "There were thirty of us, maybe. But some were quite crazy. And they kept wanting money from us, all our money. So I stopped and . . ."

"Krishna?" I shook my head.

She was the last person who would do such a thing, but she went on.

"So then I studied yoga, with a teacher."

"What kind of yoga? Tantric yoga?" I meant it as a joke.

"No, I *almost* did that. There was a swami in Philadelphia, Vernasu, who invited me to his ashram, but the visa people told me it was a sex cult and refused me to go, so it was lucky."

"So you've tried these things, marriage, eastern religion. And then . . . ?"

"First New Age, then marriage, and then I lose myself. They say here in Uzbekistan that the wife is the camel of the marriage." She was scornful, but it wasn't at the simile, it was at the naked truth of it. "The woman here must work, and she makes more money than the husband, yes. But she must do all the thinking, the planning of the family too. The man is of no help."

"I heard this complaint in Ukraine too. Exactly this. What is the cause? It can't be the death of so many men in the war. There are many boys now."

"Yes, *boys*," she said bitterly. "They don't understand the new economy."

"But it is not money, is it?" I studied her face intently, then changed tack and abruptly asked her, "Where did you get that?"

She told me the scar was from childhood. The third day of a new bicycle, she rode down a steep embankment and straight into the corner of a brick garage.

"Three stitches . . . I had a complex about it when I was a teenager."

"Everyone does, about something."

"I will tell you a secret," she suddenly announced, in a voice full of resolve.

"Go on," I nodded.

"I have a friend. He has asked me to go with him to Thailand . . . Have you been there?"

"Yes."

"What do you think?"

"About Thailand?"

"About this idea. I want to travel, see the world," she explained – as if she needed to – badly. Was she more hungry for travel, or for understanding? No mention of friends either.

"Let me tell you this story," I began. "This happened only a few months ago, a true story. A woman I know, good-looking, blonde, thirty-two, very white skin – the white skin is important," I added, and looked at Larissa's own long fingers fluttering over her tray as she sipped nervously at her coffee, awaiting my verdict, the man of experience. "One day she sees a man she knows and likes, Roger, in the street, and he invites her to Thailand also.

But as part of a tour group. He says the tickets are cheap, one left, and so she goes. Thinking she will have ten days to be with this man, in a foreign, exotic country. Yes?"

I wait for her to digest this preface, but she's ahead of me.

"She wants to catch this man, but it is a mistake?"

"Yes, a big mistake. They get to Thailand, which is filled with smooth brown girls in their early twenties; and this man, of course, Roger, he goes there to try something new. The exotic, right?"

"Yes," she nods sadly.

"And so this blonde woman, with her white skin, getting bright pink under the tropical sun, she sits at the hotel pool like a plate of unwanted spaghetti, wilting in the tropical heat —" It is a stupid simile, but Larissa appears entranced by the story nonetheless, and watches me intently now.

"When she should have stayed home, cool and cruel!"

"Cruel," Larissa repeated.

"Cruel. As cruel as you can be, without killing the man. This is what they love. Men."

"I think you are right," she nodded soberly.

"But now what? What does Larissa do now?"

"You are also right about the shopping."

"But I like your purse anyway. And your shoes! I will take special picture of your shoes, okay?" I was reaching for flippancy in the aftermath of the cautionary tale. It might have been her one dream of escape, kept buried in her Italian-made bag.

She shook her head. A deep breath of resolution.

"I mean, there is a tour agency from Paris, they specialize in special events. Once, they closed a whole street down in Paris, and they had chairs tied in red satin bows, and a fantastic lunch, it cost three million dollars for their rich guests. But it was a stupid idea, completely."

"So what are you left with?"

"I don't know." She studied the desert below, and from time to time I studied the details of her ensemble and carriage. The way her hands fluttered in the air, a delicate moth trapped behind window-glass. The way she pushed her glossy hair back behind her ears, and then pushed it forward again; the way she raised and lowered her sunglasses, as if to vary the unrelenting image of the desolation below her in the only way possible.

The black corrugation in the west was our destination. The Amu Darya River, what the Greeks under Alexander the Great called Khorezm, and the Persians called Djahkhun, the Crazy River, crazy because it changes its entire course without warning, suddenly abandoning all those who depended on its furious waters and depositing them at the doorstep of an implacable furnace. Where they would vainly cry out for a sip of water. Just a sip.

Chapter 16

Pavhalan Makhmud: Poet, Champion Wrestler, and Occasional Hat-Maker

Six hundred kilometres west of Tashkent, near the border of Turkmenistan, sits the old slave-market garrison town of Khiva. It's an infamous place, the subject of numerous Russian Romantic paintings, its khans' cruel sport with their victims providing graphic detail for mind-boggling tales, most of them true. This is the city of fabled caravans, of lurid and fantastic harems, the heart of a supremely capricious Orient, which captivated the West's poetic imagination for more than three centuries with its opium images of decay and splendid silks, gibbering madness and high-erotic sheen, the feverish Asia of Thomas De Quincey, Sir Richard Burton, who translated *Thousand and One Nights*, and the doomed poet Shelley, who must have been thinking of Khiva when he wrote "Ozymandias," "Two vast and trunkless legs of stone . . ."

Khiva is a rampart of serrated brown-mud walls, walls originally festooned with the gashed bodies of the week's unwilling visitors. Khiva is a mad granny's collection of impossibly tilted, blue turquoise domes reaching for the perfection of the uncaring sky. Khiva is the ancestral home of legendary khans, renowned for their addiction to slave-mongering and idle decapitation over trifles. Khiva is where I sit alone this afternoon, in a

176

blazing courtyard, watching the yellow sun streak through its gates and portals, an uneasy colour, and entirely lightless.

The nineteenth-century Russian painter Sererov built his whole career around the depiction of Khiva's excesses and fiendish barbarities. In his monumental work, *The Count*, he shows a group of Khivan deputies tallying a heap of fresh European heads, while the warriors who lopped them off wait patiently for their payment. Three heads for a silk robe, twelve heads for a full broadcoat with gold thread, according to my guide.

The old city within the ramparts is commanding, almost the size of the Kremlin in Moscow, eighteen hectares, and empty but for a handful of souvenir hawkers, who wait in the narrowing shade with their sun-bleached offerings of fur hats and glazed, blurry pottery.

The western sky is harshly pristine, and the mud walls of the fortress appear all the more futile and vengeful for being at such a remove from the uttermost precincts of heaven. The once-dominant Zoroastrians – whose many temples hereabouts were dedicated to pale fire for the worship of Al-Zhemani, temples which were supplanted by Islamic mosques in the eighth century (just as the pagan temples to Artemis were converted to Christian basilicas in Crimea) – survive only in India. The Zoroastrians believed that the earth was a clean element and refused to defile it with corpses, so they initiated the custom of entombment in above-ground sarcophagi.

Then, with the arrival of Mohammed, the Third and Last Messenger of the Divine Word, these Zoroastrian temples were rededicated to the glory of water; and the central ablutionary vessel, along with fine carpets, a minaret, the *mikhrab*, or prayer alcove facing Mecca, and the *minibar*, or pulpit, together constituted the five essential elements of a proper mosque. Khiva's central mosque, the Djuma, or Friday Mosque, dates to the tenth century A.D.; unlike the rest of the city it survived Genghis Khan's calculated incendiaries in 1228 because his troops stabled their horses in its barnlike interior. Genghis was a tribal shamanist, a believer in nature spirits and wild Luck. The northern Mogols must have felt wholly comfortable ensconced in this mosque; its forest of bare timbers was described by the great Arab traveller Yakut as a remarkable structure of wooden pillars, almost alive, an anomaly in a civilization devoted to works in stone and tile. The Djuma's carved beams of elmwood still stand intact after a thousand years, suspended in the desert air, a mysterious portent. Like other sites of great natural power – Clovis's palace in Paris or Knossos in Crete – Djuma exudes a strange, hypnotic force, something these Asian sects each sought to claim for themselves.

The ever-pragmatic, wholly-intuitive Genghis must have felt it too.

"My father was an Uzbek," Marena Allotarova, my guide through the ruins, tells me as we begin our preliminary stroll. "My mother was Russian . . . well, not pure Russian. Her mother was Volga Russian and her father was a Kuban Cossack."

"And your husband?" I was curious to see if she'd married a local; she was twenty-nine and airily confident after completing her long studies in history, English, and German.

"Half-Jewish, half-Korean. Would you believe such a mixture?"

"No. Was he, uh, European in his outlook? Or Asian?"

"His mentality was Soviet. He was faithless."

We had retired to the shade of a café, where a grinning youth served us sweet, syrupy Cokes and played a tape of trilling love songs, just for us.

"Faithless?" I glanced at her ring finger. It was bare.

"I mean he had no faith . . . the other too." She looked away. "Well, I was twenty-two, you know. All the girls in my time, they married at nineteen, so I was an old maid. I vowed to get married to the next man, and that's what such a stupid vow gets you."

"Does it confuse you? All this mishmash of peoples, and types. Can you make a life?"

"Well, since September 11, it's not so easy. Tourism is down here. Bad."

"Really?" I had no idea; it hadn't occurred to me that I was walking all alone through the most fantastic jade-tile palaces and staggering fortifications and eye-popping harems. All alone, for good reason. My echoing footsteps proceeded everywhere in egocentric pomp: no one else was here.

Instead of feeling happy with this entirely sound explanation, I now became uneasy. I had not seen a newspaper in more than a month. I watched Marena sip at her Coke bottle. Was she holding it to her lips like the talisman of the modern world, due to disappear at any minute? I could feel it, all right. Her unease. She took a wheezing breath.

"Yes. Tourism is down more than 50 per cent this year."

"I guess I should have realized," I began. "Getting tickets was so easy, and the hotel is nearly empty."

"No Americans. We are too close to the Afghan border."

"Ah." A light went on. Earlier I had tried making conversation with various Americans, both in Moscow and here in Uzbekistan. Most were uncharacteristically quiet and, despite my efforts at raillery, stayed that way. A whole agricultural team from Idaho had brushed me off. *They were afraid.* They were keeping a low profile and, more importantly, it was almost certain that the State Department or some other government agency had instructed them to do so. What would be the impact on international aid – and investment – in such countries as Uzbekistan if this reticence and anxiety continued? Some Europeans – like Jakob, a Swiss lawyer from Zurich whom I had met earlier in the week – had even told me

instructive tales of recent joint-ventures in Russia, in which the local partners took over the Westerners' half at the point of a gun. "Leave or we kill
you. Don't ask for money."

Where was growth and expansion going to come from, without a *Pax
Americana* of some kind, if a third of the world's resources was ruled by
gangsters and the dead hand of fear? I had asked legal counsellor Jakob
what the business prospects were, here in Uzbekistan.

"Dead and getting deader," he answered laconically. "What really
bothers me is to see the Russian thugs in Spain and Italy, where they are
busy setting up organized-crime rings."

"Well, you know it's bad when even the Swiss stop shaving." I made my
little joke, chaffing him about his unconvincing beard, the artful wisp of
the adventurer-traveller. But I wanted to cool the talk off. Similarly with
Mario, a management-studies professor from Rome.

I had met Mario in my Khiva hotel, the only other guest about that day.
He was travelling with a blonde local woman.

"Moscow is not a good place," Mario said, grimacing. "It's still ten years
later, waiting breathlessly for the counter-revolution. Nobody believes
what happened really happened. I gave lectures to the academicians last
year, and even the most basic things, simple book-keeping, the calculation
of a profit, even the recording of a transaction, was completely beyond
them. No, they didn't want to learn these things. They are fifty, on low
salaries, stuck on theories of central planning, Marx and Engels. They are
waiting for the return of Truth. It is hell."

"Hell?" I asked, making sure I heard him right.

"Oh yes, hell. Look at my friend here." He patted the bare shoulder of
his statuesque blonde companion. Raissa was wearing the tightest dress
possible, so that I had grave trouble deciding where to look, without feeling
implicated by her flesh. "It's impossible for the Russians in such places as
this, Uzbekistan. The rise of nationalism leaves them stranded. Russia says,
you are Uzbek, stay there. The locals look upon them as invaders, which of
course they were."

"They seem free to live, nobody bothers them." I was thinking about the
miniskirted women, walking freely in the blasted plazas of Tashkent City,
clip clup clip.

"Exactly. We were talking about this last night." Mario's eyes brightened, glittered, while his girlfriend's eyes looked off into the middle distance. "There has been no settling of accounts, not like in Vietnam or Africa. Why? Because even though it is ten years later, they are – how do you say it – waiting for the other shoe to drop?"

Now here I sat in an empty plaza with my Russian-Uzbek guide, Marena, hypnotized by the preposterous artifice of her Manchu acrylic nails. We were alone in the Khan's silent fortress city. The swallows careened overhead, disappeared and reappeared in the acceletron of the growing darkness. The Coke was barely chilled.

Over lunch the next day Marena tells me a story about how the local silk got its shimmer. *Princely* silk, it's called, *Khan-Atlas*.

"The Khan said to the weaver you will be beheaded unless you come up with a new design by sunrise tomorrow. The poor artisan's mind went blank, nothing came. He went at sunset to the Amur River, thinking to drown himself, when he saw the red of the setting sun, the white of the clouds, the blue of the river, all blending together, and staying separate."

Indeed, the bolt of silk I bought in the market that morning had a red sheen that showed through the black and white obverse, but it was nothing of itself compared to the extraordinary ensembles of the local people. Marena had an account for that brilliant fashion, as well.

"The evil eye makes us dress this way," she explained. "The first look is the evil eye's look, so it must be distracted by something else, and led away from one's own eyes."

I glanced at her spectacular nail-work again, then studied her clothing statement. European dress is founded on radically different principles of construction than Asian. It's all anatomical zones and sections. Setting up a dramatic opposition between the body and its coverings is the point of the Western exercise. In the middle of Khiva, this somnambulant dustbowl, twice-removed from nowhere and in the middle of nothing's backyard, Marena had announced herself in a pair of skin-tight jeans, Gloria Vanderbilt knock-offs, with an oversized zipper fly, a tight Polo shirt in white cotton, a gold heart necklace, chunky vinyl sandals in pale green, a rusty orange lipstick, specks of which had congealed under her lower lip and sat there throughout the meal, ready to flake off at any moment. It was fascinating; we were speaking English, eating our meal, and I was obliged to pat her damp knuckles a few times to check if she were really there, or a figment of my overheated imagination, a hologram beamed from a department-store window, circa 1992. In case you're ever there, this is what we had for lunch, me and the girl from Three Styles Ago, at the Khiva Madrassah Hotel:

A dish of dry red berries called *jida*, said to regulate blood pressure, from a bush that grows along the riverbanks and that tastes like our own Saskatoon berries; apricot seeds, covered in fine white ash, *kostashsky* in Russian; a thin, blanched sunflower seed called *semechki*, which Marena ate by the handful, ignoring everything else; pouty green grapes of a variety locally known as ladyfingers; sugar-roasted peanuts, *paravavda* in Uzbek; fantastically flavourful black raisins called *kishmish*, a Hindi word; *nun*, the Uzbek flat bread that was about an inch-and-a-half thick and embossed with a kind of seal in the middle of its glazed crust; an extremely sweet plum the colour of congealed blood, variety *Renclaud*, originally from France; a dish of both semi-sweet and semi-sour green apples, for balance; fresh cucumbers sliced lengthwise and served with stalks of coriander; fat, glossy tomatoes with dill; *chimchi*, the Korean salad of chopped red carrots, vinegar, dill, and cucumber in a hot sauce called *adjuka*, said to be a Georgian word; a plate of *kolbassui gur*, "sausage cheese," buttery soft and only a week old; a big pot of green tea from China, and for those who wanted it, a ceramic pitcher of cold *keffir*, a yoghurt drink.

That's the appetizers. Automatically brought to the table at lunchtime, with the menu. For the main course, we began with: *tohum barak*, the national dish, a large pastry filled with egg, butter, and milk, and served cold; then the soup, a lamb broth with carrots . . .

You see where this is going? Of course it's one reason why Marena is stuffed into her Gloria Vanderbilts, it's too easy to sit around the divan waiting for the next caravan of tourists to pop by and help yourself to a few pounds of sunflowers and maybe some *roulet*, the apricot cake-roll imported from Turkey; maybe it's the reason why Marena and her semi-stateless kin find it so hard to leave Uzbekistan. Not only does Russia not want them, but just look at these irreplaceable holy madrigals of food. The loaded saucers swim before my eyes, and I haven't even begun to describe what this stuff actually *tastes* like, have I? You want to go back to the Motherland's pale dill pickles and suspect tinned mackerel? This heap of mulberries: Should I try to wash them or simply die happy, the bloody juices leaking out the sides of my crimsoned Joker lips? I am becoming a gourmet-harpy, a fiend of fresh fruit, a dilettante at the Goblin Market.

Someone said, dismissively – was it Jakob, the Swiss lawyer, or that Englishwoman with the tattoo who complained about her room's air-conditioner bursting into flames at three in the morning? Whoever it was, they rejected out of hand the idea of a Central Asian civilization:

"They didn't invent anything, *these* people. They just sat and waited for the caravans and taxed them to death as heavily as they could."

Maybe so, maybe so. But you should really try these violet grapes.

Larissa of the pointy shoes has organized an invitation for me to dinner with one of Uzbekistan's state poets, Madrakhimor Erkin, sixty-five, secretary of the Writers' Union, author of thirty books of poetry and fiction. We meet in the grand city house of linguist Bahadur Hamraev, in the centre of Urgench, a town thirty kilometres north of Khiva, for a formal supper in the high-ceilinged dining room, done up with heavy red Bokhara carpets and heavier dark furniture. Erkin is white-haired, steady as a short rock, Spencer Tracy with Asian eyes set at soft focus.

"The poems are only about love," he tells me. "My novels are about real life. I write for people of all ages, because love can appear at any age, to anyone."

I shoot a glance at Larissa, who keeps translating despite a flash of indignation, but she keeps a lid on it.

"I understand you write long-form poems too. Dedicatory epistles." I watch her struggle with that last line now. This is fun.

"Yes," the poet-elder nods. "The *rubai*, the long poems, are dedicated to the people of the Khorezm."

I understand him to mean the classical name for the immediate region. It is equivalent to a Boston writer dedicating his opus to the Mayflower Colony; but is it a stylistic flourish or a political act? Erkin went on:

"Fifty long poems, to builders, architects, and workers. For example, 'Tamer of the Jahun.' The Jahun is a wild river. It's three thousand lines long, typically only fragments are printed. Then I did one to Iskander Dosor, a Hero of Labour, a cotton-picker who worked very hard."

"And your love poems, how do they sound?"

He motioned to our host, who placed a cassette in a large boom-box on the cabinet and translated the plaintive quaverings of the male singer.

> *There is no rest for me:*
> *Let's enter the beautiful garden*
> *Let's walk around the sweet places,*
> *Let's talk from the heart,*
> *Remember:*
> *You promised me eloquent truth.*
>
> *And she answered me:*
> *"I walked this garden so many times,*
> *I know my way around it, too well*
> *Let me now have the Peace of the Night."*

Six hundred of Erkin's love songs have been recorded. Small Uzbek migrant-worker enclaves in distant Saudi Arabia pass his cassette tapes around, and also write him to say they take his poetry books on hajji, the pilgrimage to Mecca. Whom does he admire? Of course the great Pahlavan Makhmud, the Khorezm poet (1247–1326), a kind of Robin Hood who wrestled for a living and occasionally made hats as well, giving the money to the poor. Makhmud penned a famous line, "Much easier to dye the sky red than to explain the Eternal to a stupid man." But Erkin also lists the Caucasus poet Rasul Gamzatov, Arab writers like Ali Sherha, and, among the Europeans, "Pushkin, of course. Lermontov – and Goethe, for his tragedies and comedies."

"It's all the same thing in German. Tragedy, comedy," I interject.

Larissa gives me a sidelong glance and doesn't translate it.

"Now I am working on a love poem from the heart of an eighteen-year-old girl, 'The Sweetness of the World Is Gathered on Her Lips.'"

My translator blinks heavily at this conceit, but she dutifully carries on, and I am about to pursue the issue of authentic voice when our host, Bahadur, rushes into the room and tells us to drop our forks, we must come outside immediately.

Fearing another eco-catastrophe, I rush out with the others into the back garden.

"The flowers are opening! The flowers are opening!"

The rear courtyard can barely contain these clashing armies of red roses and tall yellow trumpet-flowers, thousands of blossoms. The hot-yellow blooms are popping open one by one, trembling violently as the dusk descends, like teenagers having sex for the first time; hundreds of honeybees drone, robot vacuum cleaners lost in sweet amber. Nocturnal blushery, not crimson clarity, wins the battle.

Erkin the poet and Bahadur our host giggle like schoolboys as they wander through the quivering rows. All further talk is suspended as the desert air unfurls its gaudy new perfume.

Chapter 17

Three Girls Named Star

Five hours to Bokhara from Khiva through the Red Desert, rocketing along at 150 kilometres an hour. Straight road, but bashed up. The highway has never seen better days; it will only get worse.

Timur, our driver and Larissa's husband, is judicious about the use of his car's brakes. He prefers to go around objects on the road, rather than slow for them. There's nothing in sight but dumptrucked sand dunes and, sitting atop each one, a single sayal bush. An angry, spiky little flag. The camel's thorn bush.

"Do camels eat this thorn bush?" I ask querulously, though I don't care. Nobody replies.

We sit in the car like three nuclear-test dummies, immobile in the unchanging landscape. The desert continues to throw tentative objects on our path. Something large seems to have burrowed under the asphalt at several junctures. Is it the *zimzim*, the desert crocodile, seeking a new den for its hungry brood?

Speaking of brooding, I am sitting in the back, Timur is driving, and Larissa holds the cellphone with the two-foot aerial and makes obscure calls consisting of monosyllabic *das* and *nyets*, with more passionate intonation to them than the dialogue from the Uzbek soap opera I saw this morning. There is not much room back here; the Daewoo car is designed for Kamchitki doll-people. I throw my legs this way and that, telling myself I should be grateful for the air conditioning. It's forty degrees Celsius out there at ten in the morning, and only thirty-five or so in here. What movie are we doing? *The Sheltering Sky?* I can't remember what happens. Three people, driving in the desert, but then what? Well of course they all die, but in *what order?* I feel like Dennis Hopper back here, or maybe Lee Van Cleef. Whatever happened to old Lee? That diamond-back rattler smile of his. Perfect smile for this heat-mad desert. Okay, in this movie we crash, or I kill Timur. Semi-accidentally, of course; then I flee/survive/kidnap leggy Larissa. She has nice legs; I can see a good cross-section of them from back here. Will she come willingly to old snake eyes, or must he force her? Hang on, another *zimzim* road-shudder. Blasted animals, I thought they were mythical!

We lurch, the tires shriek. A small animal bounds across the shoulder to safety.

"What was that?"

"Polecat." Larissa says laconically.

"A polecat?" Incredulous tone.

She refers to her dictionary.

"Sorry, no. A ground squirrel."

"Ah."

Satisfied, I lean back. At least there is some kind of life out there in this desert.

I mean to ask her if the only difference between this bleached-out aridity and the lush lands behind us is *water*, but my throat is getting dryer with each passing moment, so I must go back to my movie.

Hopper Lee smiles his big crazy killer-smile at leggy young Natalie Wood, reborn as a tourist guide in Uzbekistan, and despite herself she grows faint, or maybe it's the pulsating heat, we don't know yet. Suspense builds . . .

Five after ten, only four hours and fifty-five minutes to go. Hopper Lee smiles, a world-weary addict's smile, this thrill-seeking, this drug-masked, hyperventilating user, who would have his way with women, *for his own pleasure*, but his heart is not pounding. (Well it is, but only with the heat.) What's wrong, trusty old sex-pirate? Oh, oh. He misses his wife. Five thousand beautiful women since landing at Kiev airport, and she's the only one to turn his crank? He must be really sick or something.... Except, of course, for that art-curator back in the sex-rabbit gallery, but that was only some kind of ethno-genetic, bio-programmed manic outburst, not the unholy, lusty heaving of an eye-popping hallucination in three dimensions.

No, it's not good, this; this full-faced lack of erotic affect, this desert stupification. Think of something intelligent to think about, there's the lad! Get the brain working. The rest will tag along. Here's something:

Last night, when we drove back to the hotel from the poetical dinner party, I had asked Larissa about her reaction to the voice issue, how she felt about a sixty-five-year-old man taking on the voice of an eighteen-year-old girl.

"Well, of course, it is just poetry." She said this tentatively. "So it doesn't mean much."

"Just poetry?"

"I mean that such love poetry is all a fiction. It has nothing to do with real life."

Stoutly now.

"You've decided that, or are you unsure on that point?"

"Almost decided on it."

"Almost decided?"

"Practically for sure, decided."

"Mmm."

What did that mean? Was I making too much of this issue? Had Flaubert fleshed it out for all time in *Madame Bovary*, the bored housewife who courts disaster with a smooth stranger? Or was this a rejected chapter from *Anna Karenina*? Did Uzbeks entertain such dilemmas? To go or to stay; to run or to hide; to shrink or to bloom, even for one night of luxury? Of course this was the central concern of the European novel, the Drama of Recognition, but where did that come from? Not exclusively from the artists' plot-box, surely. Dreiser got his plot for *An American Tragedy* straight and intact from a newspaper clipping. The hero drowns his inconveniently pregnant working-class girlfriend for a crack at the rich one. The long odds of love! People do crazy things for love in our society; whether they got it or not, was another question. I thought about my wife, her background. Some kind of crypto-Teuton, Danube-Schwabian river horde, who took a wrong turn in the eighteenth century and ended up in

Yugoslavia. I once found a newspaper article that suggested the Danubians were remnants of primitive Goths who had settled among the hill Slavs in the seventh century, and they still chopped heads and held raunchy human pole-sacrifices long after everyone else began holding cocktail parties and smiling politely at bad jokes.

"So you think you're a Goth, maybe?" I asked her, after reading a choice selection aloud.

"I'll cut your head off, and then we'll see."

I didn't exactly miss her; it was more like I missed the sense of our close-quarters *engagement*. A line like, "I'll cut your head off, and then we'll see," was good for at least two hours of hard practice while I worked on my comeback. Although, by the time I got something cooking, she might have already left for yoga. Then it would be five hours later, when I would brightly announce, "If you do, it will make me shorter than you!" while she shushed me away like an unwalked dog, away from the TV set and her show, *The West Wing* or something.

Five hours. No, four hours and thirty-nine minutes.

I tried to imagine Genghis Khan's troops riding over this five-hundred-mile wasteland in the 1220s. A billion thorn bushes, one dead fly. No water. Did they travel at night? They were so violently destructive that the oasis kingdom of Khorezm never really recovered from their attack. It was probably this last fatal hour of heat that did it to them.

We reach Bokhara at dusk. The hotel has a cool, shaded courtyard, and at the back is an *eidivan*, a twenty-four-foot-high veranda, with carved pillars of cypresswood and strange floral designs worked into the rear walls. Lines from the designer Rennie Mackintosh, a lucid, improbable admixture of colours – turquoise, seagrass, pumpkin, and acid blue. The house once belonged to a Jewish merchant, rich. The Jewish quarter in Bokhara dates back to the eighth century A.D. The building has the black-and-white exits, two of them leading from the cellar storage, a feature all Jewish houses had traditionally.

More phantasmagoric minarets, more *medrassahs*, the Islamic teaching halls. Bokhara was a university town until the Bolsheviks arrived in 1920.

Now there's a sense of quiet suspension. No muezzins. The kids laugh in the great square, playing soccer. They are kicking a saggy ball around with staged bravado, making a great show of their individual stylishness, great Pelé histrionics despite the flatulent trajectories, flashing smiles of victory at a well-placed kick that ends in a two-foot fart. They know how to play, even if the ball doesn't. I begin humming the theme from *Lawrence of Arabia*, walking through the near-empty plaza, as close to home as the exile can feel, and then an eight-year-old picks up the tune, and pretty soon half of the kids are humming it at the top of their lungs.

A trio of young girls approaches me and ask my name. They have the extra-large eyes of the Tajiks, the Persians who founded the Sogdian Empire in 100 B.C., long before the Arabs' arrival in A.D. 700. Their original religion was Zoroastrian. The four sacred elements, the battle between good and evil.

"And what do you do in Canada?"

"Married?"

"You wife wanted to come too, so why didn't you let her?"

The questions were hilarious and astute. I was facing an Inquisition of twelve-year-olds, conducted before a medieval minaret, with Venus rising in the west over their heads, bright as a pearl on the scanty necklace of the night.

"And what are your names?" I realize this is the first real conversation I have had for weeks, soft with uncontrived mutual interest, and their answers are:

"Star."

"My name is Star too."

"Mine also, but Beautiful Star."

"Three stars!" I ask. "Hollywood stars?"

"No, Bokhara stars!"

They look at me with their huge Persian eyes, and it hits me like a thunderbolt that all the Persian miniatures were drawn from life, precisely this life, and these big doe eyes that see the world from the side and from the front at the same time are now looking at me. Three pairs, curious as gazelles, stellar travellers disguised as omniscient street children.

◇

Every day in Bokhara becomes more dreamlike. The past proposes its special occasions in small signs, subtle gestures. In the *hammas*, the eighteenth-century baths, now publicly open again after decades of official censure, I lie on a marble slab and stare at the tiny dome-hole high above, and the bluest iris of the sky stares right back. The different parts of my body are rousing themselves, one by one, breathing freely again, and all the lumps and aches, ignored for so long, bestir themselves and submit their plaints to the great gouts of steam descending like a cloak of brotherhood on us all. Here are the other bodies: an old thin man who yells in Uzbek, then growls *da-da-da* in Slavic affirmation of his continued existence; a pale pink tourist who has plunked his naked two-year-old son down into a red plastic bucket and is lavishly scrubbing him, squeezing the wet rag over his little cropped head as the boy demands.

"*Kak te?*" He says to me in Russian.

"Ka-*na*-da," I reply, carefully emphasizing the second syllable in the local fashion, so he will understand me.

"Ah. Ka*na*da!" He gives me his free hand, pumps it in joy, and introduces me to his wide-eyed son.

The expert massage follows, hot-heaven's sign that we are loved by the Creator equally (sometimes). All rubbery joy now, I join another Westerner in the carpeted anteroom for the green tea. His name is René and he's from Rotterdam, and he has come to Central Asia solely because, in his job as a software programmer, he has "met" a girl on the Internet. Nadia lives in the much rougher country next door to us, Kazakhstan.

"Is she Russian?"

"Yes. Twenty-six. She's a law professor." He is quick to add.

"Law professor? And how old are you?"

"Thirty-two. So it's not so bad, this age difference."

"And were you happy when you actually met her?"

"Yes, she looked something like her picture, at least. So I was satisfied. I took a chance to come here and it was good. I had a nice time."

"Yes, but what is wrong with Dutch girls? If I can play your mother for the moment."

I am lying naked on a bench to one side of the long table, sipping the valorous tea, and I can see that René is what girls usually dismiss as a nice guy. Hard-working, sexually harmless, not a jot of dangerous energy.

"I never find one who likes me," he says simply.

"Oh, sure, ah," I sputter, grappling with the blade in my guts, knowing this is the terrible answer that will rule his life, and maybe hurt him more than he has already been hurt. "But, but, this girl. What do you know about her?"

He decides to tell me; no, he is eager to tell me. Who else is he going to tell? His laughing co-workers back at the software studio? Those groovers dressed in black, in the latest square-toed shoes, rolling their eyes at pink-faced René, who still hopes for a democracy of love?

"She is very serious. She doesn't get my jokes."

"Jokes? Give me an example." I pretend now to be a psychiatrist, taking invisible notes, and he appreciates my comic routine.

"She wanted the change from something I bought, for a taxi, and I said, 'Oh, you're going to bankrupt me.' And she said, 'Keep your stupid money!' And she got really mad."

"What else?" I could tell he was only getting warmed up.

"She spends *hours* putting on her face. She's completely painted. It's, well, ridiculous."

"So what are you going to do?"

"Of course she wants to come to Holland, but it's hard for the visa."

"And you, how do you feel?"

"It's great. I told myself I would come out here and have a good time. And I did! So what happens next doesn't matter."

The barber poked his head through the curtain. It was time for my haircut and shave. Another hour of bliss. I could have stayed there until nightfall, as I slowly came to realize that this is what we needed in the West, to regain our humanity. The confessional of the body, these steamy portals of deep introspection and ablution, the physical atonements of wet flesh on the slick slabs of marble.

"What movie are we in, then?" I ask Larissa. We are sitting, the three of us, under a restaurant portico in the late afternoon, eating from an enormous platter of freshly sliced watermelon. The ancient elmwood shutter creaks on its cast-iron hinges. We are quite alone. The courtyard is like a setting from a cinematic mood-piece. *The Red Sky*, or maybe something by Bertolucci that was never released.

"Who are we, then?" she asks quite seriously.

"Well, you of course are Natalie Wood. Do you know who that is?"

"She was Russian, yes?"

"I think so."

"And Timur?"

"He's Brad Pitt. No, maybe Tom Cruise."

"Tom is the name of a cat, like Tom and Jerry," Timur protests. He speaks in Russian, but I understand his objection without translation. She shushes him.

"And you?"

"I'm Dennis Hopper. Crazy wild-card dude. Do you know him?"

"I think so," she says doubtfully. "So, do you like folkloric show tonight? Or would you like to go to disco, maybe?"

"See? There it is again, the Choice: Shopping or the Exotic. Neither."

"Neether?"

"Neether. I want to make a movie instead," I pout. "Great sets, great cast. No script."

"Too bad."

"Yes, isn't it." I stare off.

The three-hundred-year-old shutter creaks by itself, stealing the scene.

Well, I am making a movie, except it's a book. And the book is sniffing around this Zoroaster thing, this ancient war between the forces of good and evil, a hair's breadth of advantage between them. It turns out that Larissa is knowledgeable about this lost religion as well.

"So the Avesta, the sacred book of the Zoroastrians. When was it written?"

"In the seventh century." She knowingly adds, "B.C."

"I see." She is right, of course. Zoroaster damned the violent steppe nomads of his time as people of the Lie, followers of Ahriman, ruler of chaos. Zoroaster, an historical figure, was taken up by Nietzsche as Zarathustra, the first prophet of early Modernism. "And the name of their supreme god, and their symbols?"

Ahura Mazda, she tells me, and explains the meaning of their chief symbols, a triangle and a double triangle, joined in the middle by a bar.

"Sun, air, ground, and water."

She draws it on a slip of paper ripped from Timur's cigarette pack.

"I saw this sign on the old mosque here in Bokhara, this morning."

"Yes, that is because it dates from the ninth century A.D. It was one of the two mosques that survived Genghis Khan, and they were both Zoroastrian before the Arabs came."

"How did these two temples survive?"

I could feel the power emanating from both of them on my tour this morning, the Ismail Samani Mausoleum and the Magoki Attory, the Cave of Spices.

"You see, both were covered with earth by the people to protect them. The Magoki Attory was already half-buried in the ground, because it was deliberately sunken to protect it from the desert winds."

A few hundred paces from the spice cave is the Kalon Minaret, once the tallest structure in Central Asia. The Mongols did not destroy the Kalon Minaret, because it is forty-seven metres high, and gave Genghis's sentries a commanding view of their conquest, but is fascinating to note that here in Bokhara also, like Khiva's Friday Mosque, local people risked themselves to save the Zoroastrian sites, and only them.

"Let's go look at this Zoroastrian temple again," I said, meaning the Samani Mausoleum. I watched a fly alight on the last pieces of our decaying watermelon, a close-up to signal the end of a pregnant scene.

I came out of my room at three in the morning and silently descended the plank steps to sit on the *eidivan*, the colonnaded porch, to look at the desert stars. Sleep won't come, something keeps me awake; perhaps it's the paper bag crammed with the rich spice tea I bought in the bazaar. The room is dense with the heart-pounding pungency of cloves, cinnamon, cardamom, and whole fresh nutmeg. I stare at the constellation of Orion, working it out. A fresh breeze laps against my face; distant roosters anticipate the false dawn.

I came here looking for the new nomads of Central Asia, thinking that these Tajiks and Uzbeks and Sogdian Persians and others would be on the move again, cut loose from the bounds of the old Regime. But they were grounded, utterly self-reliant, socially solvent, and bounded to the flood-plane's procreative power and the ancient traditions of their great southern rural culture.

What was this seventy-year-old regime of self-appointed bosses and crumbling two-storey party buildings to them? These people who had seen whole civilizations come and go over the course of the last five thousand years. Over green tea earlier that day, my local Bokhara guide, Nagira, forty-six, had complained only about how stupid the Soviets were.

"Rich people are not bad people, like they tried to tell us. They are clever, hard-working, that is all. Even our greatest poet, Abu Rudaki, tells us an example of this. A rich man was drowning, and the people could not save him, because they kept calling out, 'Give us your hand, give us your hand!' So Abu cried out instead, 'Take my hand!' and the rich man did so at once, because the rich are so used to taking things, not giving. But they are still worth saving, these people!"

"So what is going to happen to the Russian people here?" I had asked her. We were alone in the dark, cavernous *medressah*, an Islamic college given over to silk handicraft manufacture.

"I lived in East Germany for more than four years, when it was under the Soviets," Nagira told me, her expression stiffening. "Forty kilometres east of Berlin. My first chance to live with foreigners. My husband is a concert musician. And I can say this, the Germans are very good people!" She raised a thumb of appreciation. "But the Russians, they never invite you in, they are very cold, selfish. They only take things, never satisfied, always looking to push the other down. Even their children today, they kill each other in the schoolyard over toys, just like their fathers do in business."

"But you get along with Russians here," I pointed out. Nagira had said hello to at least thirty people that day, half of whom were ethnic Russians, without changing her demeanour.

"Of course, these people grew up with *us*," she said, looking at the tea in her bowl, swirling the amber liquid around the few leaves floating on top.

The Tajiks and the Uzbeks in the local countryside might not get along at some point, she explained, but then such internecine situations might simply be ploys in a foreign power's interference and, more, the subversive product of such a power play. Nagira told me how she spoke to her daughter in Russian (because she was in university), her husband in Tajik, and her son, who worked for the government, in Uzbek. "No problem," she smiled. "I have a good ear for languages." Delicately boned, with large black eyes, she was the sort of woman who would find a place for herself in any village or cosmopolitan city with equal aplomb, and I could see I was not her only admirer, for the bazaar was filled with her well wishers.

At the end of the tour I had tried to give Nagira a tip, for we had gone well beyond our appointed hour, but she refused it. It was Friday, holy day, a day for alms, so I was able to press some notes on her by asking her to pass them on to the poor as she liked, the blind and the crippled who sat uncomplaining outside the mosques.

It was becoming clear that it was not these great tribal peoples who were on the move again, but their former masters and bosses. History had cut them loose, millions of European, would-be settlers had been abandoned by Modernism and its claims for the world solution. Restless and uprooted, it was for the Russians to decide who they were now, and where to go.

And when.

Chapter 18

At the Sign of the Blue Tongue

It is the morning of our departure to Samarkand, the hometown of Larissa and Timur. They exhibit the usual signs of hopeful anticipation, mixed with the casual dread of parental homecoming. They must enjoy these escapist blitz-tours around the sunny southwest.

"Larissa? What's with Uzbek women and their single eyebrows?"

The young woman at the bus stop sports a large, dark mono-brow, and she is looking at me expectantly, as if I am supposed to whistle a hearty *hubba hubba* at her.

"Yes, it's true. They have this special lotion, called umas. It looks like sorrel. They paint it between the brows and it makes thick hair grow there."

"Do they use it anywhere else?" I am thinking about a new product line for our tattoo parlours. Crops of hairy tattoos sprouting everywhere from the body.

"I don't know," she says. "You don't look so good. Did you sleep okay?"

"Not much," I equivocate. A twinge of guilt after last night's revelation; my book is secretly about them now, the Russians. And the half-Russians like her. Not the others.

She sighs. "Maybe it's time to see a doctor."

I watch a donkey pull a cart with an enormous bale of hay. It's exactly how I feel.

"Sure. Are there any here?"

"In Samarkand. We'll make the necessary doctorial interview."

"Doctorial interview? What will be our thesis?"

"This is not the right word?"

"You could say visit. Or appointment."

"I am sorry. Sometimes I'm not sure, from my English studies, what is the correct usage."

"No, no. I'll just add it to my list."

"List?"

"Yes, I love these expressions of yours. I'm making a list: *Snobistically*, *greatly enheartened*, and my favourite, *lame* juice: 'Greatly enheartened by his successful doctorial interview, he snobistically ordered a fresh-squeezed lame juice from the bartender.'"

Timur said something in Russian. He had heard the word *juice* in all this.

"He asks if you want something to drink, before we go to Samarkand."

"Do we drive through the desert?"

"A kind of *green* desert," she answered.

And so it turned out. Cotton fields as far as the horizon, flattened mega-plantations in every direction, a monoculture feeding the textile industry, and set between the shiny rows of flat puffy-plants were mulberry bushes, millions of rows, all painted white with lime to a height of four feet.

"Why do they do this?"

"There is a kind of large black beetle. It kills the tree if they do not."

The economy of Uzbekistan had been given its large direction by Central Planners in the 1960s, when the Soviets began exporting cotton on a massive scale to the mills of Liverpool and other Western countries for hard currency. How much of the nation's attendant social grief is the result of the mall-world's insatiable demand for blue denim? The new Uzbek Republic was as addicted to its commodity trade as was Brazil or Ceylon, and with equally disastrous results European – not least of which was the evaporation of the Aral Sea.

There was nothing more to see for the next three hours: cotton fields, mulberry trees, and the slow rise of the Pamir Mountains in the southeast, the first beginnings of the great Asian Plateau. A brown series of terrific dents that marked the end of all five-year plans for a brighter future in the applied rules of plate tectonics.

We pulled up to a pretty little town, with green parks, spouting fountains, and avenues of white-painted poplar trees. We were nodding with car-boredom, traffic buzzy-busy all around us. Samarkand was a university town, and it was plugged into the wider world, judging from the Internet cafés, places called The Blues Seen and Moka Spot. Kids with backpacks. Up a side street a whitewashed building had a single word stencilled in black in large Roman letters: DOKTOR.

"This is it."

We entered the modest clinic. There were two or three pregnant women sitting there, and a young student who looked as if he wasn't enjoying his courses. An Asian woman in a white lab coat led us immediately into a dinky back office, illuminated only by a small desktop lamp.

She is Chinese or maybe Korean, about twenty-seven, and she has one of those round mirror-forehead things with the Cyclops-hole cut in the middle of it, something we last used in black-and-white B movies like *The Snake Pit*. Two vials sit on her desk, a blue one and a brown one. A metal ruler. Nothing else. One light in the room. A medicinal smell, vaguely familiar from my childhood.

Larissa and the doctor engage in a lengthy conversation in Russian, looking speculatively at me from time to time whenever they run out of long words.

"What are you telling her?" I manage to interject finally.

"That you are sick."

"Oh."

The doctor bids me sit in her chair, pulls the table lamp to my chin, and puts the Cyclops mirror over her face.

"Open your mouth and say *ahh*," Larissa translates quite unnecessarily, for the doctor is already prying my jaw open with her metal ruler.

"Ah."

"AHHH!" The doctor instructs me with serious force.

"Ahhh."

She says something to Larissa, satisfied, and turns to scribble a note on a pad of rough brown paper. It appears to have been made from leftover stalks of the cotton harvest.

"She says you have no tonsils."

"That's what they did to all the kids in my country. Why, is it time for a big class-action suit?"

Larissa knows my snobistical tone, especially when she hears these rhetorical questions. The doctor meanwhile has opened the blue jar and is dipping a cotton ball attached to the long metal ruler into what appears to be Waterman's No. 2 fountain-pen ink. I think she is using it to swab the instrument before talking a blood sample or something. But no, she has other plans.

"Open your mouth. Wide," Larissa instructs firmly.

The doctor has placed the blue-dripping cotton ball on the end of the ruler-thing, and from her stance it seems she proposes to insert the thing into my mouth.

"I say, I —"

"Say AHHH."

"Aw . . . *owwww!*"

The doctor has gone mad. She's risen from her seat and has thrust the bloody thing down my throat, like a toreador making the final coup. She's killing me!

"*Ah! Ah! Ah!*" I manage to wrest myself away, almost falling backwards in my chair.

"Did she get it in?" Larissa asks from somewhere within a pink fog.

"Bloody hell! It went right into my gut!" I sputter and froth. The stuff doesn't taste like anything, except maybe school ink. Cold.

I see Larissa and the doctor exchange surreptitious glances.

"Did she *finish?*" I ask very specifically.

"Sure, sure." Larissa says encouragingly as the doctor advances, her enamel Oriental eyes flashing with the matador's final assertion, and plunges the rod into my gullet before I have a chance to jump off the chair.

"Ahhh-GAA!" I desperately tug at her arm, but the little broad is tougher than she looks; her arm twists around like a piece of coiled steel, she will not relent this time.

"AHH-*GAAA!*" Down it goes, down into the lower depths. I see Timur and Larissa floating like lesser deities around the wrathful Cyclops Queen as I gag and sputter and hot tears spurt out.

A distant voice. "It's over. She got it this time."

"Great," I am able to mumble.

"You know, we are used to these procedures," Larissa says to me as we proceed out to the receptionist to pay the bill. "We have them since childhood. Here, clean your lips. They're blue."

"You are being snobistic, don't deny it. And what was that stuff?"

I wipe my mouth with the proffered tissue. It comes away dark blue.

"Iodina."

She says it like some fat Russian girl's name.

"Io*dine*?"

"Yes."

"Jesus." I am afraid to ask her any more. The receptionist says something.

"How much is my bill?"

"Fifteen hundred *sum*. A dollar-fifty."

"A dollar-fifty?" I count out the bills as manfully as I can, the unruly child escorted out of the doctor's office by his parents with promises of watermelon and ice cream.

"Then, after lunch, we can see the walls where Alexander the Great attacked in 325 B.C."

"Okay." I turn away to wipe my eyes.

"And how do you feel?"

"Fine. Really fine."

"Timur says for you to look at your tongue." Larissa hands me her compact.

"Good God." It's completely blue, bright blue.

Blue like the Violator in *Spawn*, the French-kissing clown of death.

"I could get a gig with KISS," I bluster, not sure if Gene Simmons was two or three acts before their time, but they laugh anyway.

I am quartered in a private cream-stuccoed house in the centre of old Samarkand city, the original residence, according to a bronze plaque affixed to the wall, of the Tajik journalist Rajab, killed in 1960 for "speaking the truth," by the authorities, as his fourteen-year-old grandson, also named Rajab, is proud to tell me over tea. The boy has bright-blue, inquisitive eyes and is tall and coltish; he speaks English, Tajik, Uzbek, and Russian, and he plans to work in the tourist business. Why?

"I like it. The people."

"Foreigners?"

"Yes." He smiles happily. "They are funny."

The house is a series of enormous empty rooms, with machine-made red "oriental" carpets laid everywhere, and the odd piece of heavy dark furniture meditating off in its own courtyard, as it were. Two vicious little lapdogs try to bite me through the glass panes whenever I try to see the rose garden in the rear, so I confine myself to what I call the "living room," only because it has no beds. The houses of the neighbourhood are set around courtyards, all accessed through a main iron gate. The women sit on benches in their red or dark-blue shifts, gossiping easily as they take turns hanging clothes from lines stretched between the whitewashed poplar trees. It's summer, and everyone is outside, sitting in their gardens with trays of tea and fruit.

Rajab, the murdered journalist, must have been happy living here, with the morning doves and the incontestable truth of roses to help him face the hour he surely knew was coming.

So what shall I call my movie? At dusk we went to the Shahr-i-Zindar, the tomb of the Living King, where the cousin of the Prophet Muhammad is interred. He was beheaded by Zoroastrians in the seventh century A.D., as the local defenders fiercely resisted the epochal Arab attack. It is said Zindar simply picked his head up from the battlefield, put it back on his neck, and descended into an underground paradise, a place that one can visit in this lifetime by climbing into the caverns through his crypt – but only at the cost of being instantly blinded by the astounding sight. Was this a Muslim story, or Zoroastrian?

"It seems to me that this story is very symbolic," I say to Larissa as we sit down in a outdoor café surrounded by froggy green canals. Night descends around the bower of huge trees. Bats come sputtering out. She has ordered watermelon and chocolate ice cream, and takes a tentative taste of each, careful not to spill any on her smart linen suit.

"Yes, the Zoroastrians, they had many such symbolic stories and tales. They had three main gods, according to their prophet Zarathustra. The supreme god, the dark one, and Mithra."

"Who was Mithra, exactly?"

"He was the warrior god, always shown with the bow and arrow. He fought the forces of darkness. You see, in the Zoroaster religion, you choose: good or evil, it's up to you."

"Is there any symbolism to your watermelon and chocolate ice cream?"

"I don't know." She looked at her platter with surmise. "When I was in university, we discussed such things, but I did not study them myself." Sadness overcame her.

"Did you ever have those dreams, where you get a call from the teacher, years later? And they say you must come back, write the examination again, there was a mistake?"

"All the time," she nodded and shook her head simultaneously, and quite forgot the spoon of ice cream in her hand. "But it is always secondary school, not university."

"Me too. Ah, high school." I was astonished that the hard psychic currency of this motif had made its way through the collective dreams of the entire world. How did this work? I too was always back in high school, sweating over some test I hadn't studied for, and never would.

"It's anxiety, yes?"

The ice cream melted away by itself; she was looking at me for the answer.

"Something like that. How about the dream where you go to school, only to find yourself in your underwear, walking in the street?"

"Yes, except that I am naked."

"No kidding. Completely?"

"Yes. Not a stitch."

"My God . . . Do you have any *recurrent* dreams? Like, I often dream of riding in a car that goes down a sloping road, faster and faster, and I must turn the wheel this way and that, to avoid these stupid freight trucks."

"Yes, in my dream, I am alone in a car, with no seats, no steering wheel, sitting in the middle on the empty floor, and there are only two things in this car. One is a gear shift, yes?" She pulls at an imaginary device to illustrate. "The other is this pair of strange brakes."

"Strange? How strange?"

"They are weak, far apart, stick up in the air, not much use."

"And the gear shift, it is big, strong?"

"Yes. *Very* strong."

"It has a *knob* on the end" I raise my eyebrows meaningfully.

"Yes, of course . . . Oh!"

She looks down at her melted dessert; the light has gone on. I proceed.

"And these brakes, they stick up, open wide apart. Can't say no?"

"That's right."

I can see from her eyes I've got it right.

"The job of the brake is to say *no*. The shift says yes, more, yes! It changes the upper speed, the momentum of your life. Who does this to you, at this time?"

"My father . . . ," she says with liquid astonishment. "He wants me to go to this new travel school, and so on. But why is there no steering wheel in my dream?"

"Because the dream is about *yes* and *no*. Fast and faster, male and female. Very economical, like all dreams."

A wretched street beggar shuffled into the café, and as the waiters gently shooed him off like a stray cat, I realize that he is the first "homeless" person I have seen, apart from the handful of polite mendicants at the mosque in Bokhara. The bats come and go, large and unnoticed by the diners.

I am thinking about the irruption of the mechanical world and its arcane rules, into the subterranean group-mind of the West. All those clever Hitchcock devices of ticking clocks, violently skewed perspectives, omnipotent paternal locomotives; and above all else, *cars*, the keenest and richest signs of the Self, the running *I* fleeing from its own experience, fending off other, half-submerged industrial threats to its own existence, plummeting headlong down some wild road that follows the palpitating rhythms of its laboured heart and lungs. And always leading back to the empty House. The place where you can put your sliced head back on, and learn to smile again, in a novel fashion.

What did it mean, this tale of decapitation?

What layers of truth are hidden by the dust of destructive conquerors, hidden or forgotten completely? When these tour guides tell us things, such as the fact that the old yellow mosque bricks were made from no less than one hundred ingredients, including egg albumin, but that the ancient recipe is now lost, are we supposed to look back at history as a series of unique mountaintops? Forbidden heights, never to be scaled again? Yes, the cruel Asian rulers always beheaded their greatest architects, so they would never dilute their glory. That's the story. Was this theme really a lament for lost civilizations, a requiem for their perfect order, their lost magical power over nature? Or was it a prayer offered for the very ordeal of civilization? That it *must* lose its head, and will go away forever at the day's end? There's your ongoing horror, that a headless man must always live down in the basement. The Sogdian Empire of the Indo-European Sakas was centred on Samarkand, the Khorezm Empire was centred on Bokhara. Lost empires, one country now. The country's existence, of itself, proves nothing; like a house filled with ghosts, its fresh coat of paint deceives the casual eye into thinking it has solid foundations. Scrape a little and there's all manner of ghosts awaiting the latest arrival – Buddhist, Zoroaster, Muslim, Tsarist Orthodox, and finally "Soviet Period" ghosts.

And what was this psychotic, last bloody episode of Soviet rule but a sustained effort to end History at once and flush out these ghosts for all time? Now it was the turn of Tamerlane Nationalism, an ideology firmly bent on developing its own forms of creaky spookiness, with his giant iron horse-statues erected in every town, and billboards announcing the president's climactic edict in large Roman letters: THE FUTURE OF UZBEKISTAN IS ASSUREDLY GREAT!

"'Assuredly great,' is that how you would translate that big sign on the highway?"

I withdrew from my flight of thought and saw that Larissa was similarly preoccupied.

Her dish of watermelon lay untouched.

"Perhaps . . . You mean that 'greatly assured' is not proper?"

Dark eyes were brooding over something.

"*Nycheho.*" I hastened to reassure her. "It's nothing. What are you thinking about so deeply?"

"Another dream."

"Another dream? Recurrent Dream?"

"Yes. Recurrent."

"So, go ahead. Tell me."

I lean back, always the professional. I should set up shop here, charge a buck-fifty a visit.

"It's about this man, not such a nice man. Bad, in fact. He comes to our house, and he wants to put me in his leather bag and take me away. And he asks permission from my parents, and of course they say okay."

"Of course."

"So he carries me off to his house, a strange, terrible house, and puts me up in the ceiling, and skins me, after taking my clothes away."

"*Skins* you?"

"Yes, how do you say it? He takes my skin off. Completely."

"Good God. How *old* were you?"

"Five."

"Five? Was your home life terrible at this time?"

"Not at all. I had an extremely happy childhood."

"Mm. Go on."

"Some neighbours came. They saw me, and rescued me from this man and took me down from the ceiling."

"A man and a woman?"

"Yes. I knew them slightly. They were friends of my parents."

"I see."

"So. What do you think?" She waited patiently for my analysis.

I drank some more clear pear juice, examining the label, stalling. It said all natural, no additives. Nothing but pears. Pears, but what buttocks! It was one thing to talk about going naked to high school, another to enter that hidden central vault where childhood begins and ends in screams against the unassailable knife.

"I don't know. Of course 'the neighbours' are your parents. You realize after your ordeal that they are social beings, constrained like everyone else, and must be placated like everyone else, socially. Huge shock, this."

I take a sip.

"Then who is the man? Who takes my skin off?"

"Well, it's *you*, of course. All these people are you. But who are you, in him? I cannot say."

She nodded, taking it all in. Around us sat a happy family of middle-class Uzbeks. Their long table was groaning with untouched delicacies of the season. They were making ready for a group camera portrait with their sumptuous meal. The photographer was good, he managed to get the three tots to look at him each time he snapped one off. I envied him; I had missed four close-ups of the snarling Pekinese in my guest house so far today.

"What do you think?" I said, trying to shift the subject to a new plane. "Do you think Uzbeks have such dreams as ours?"

"I don't believe they ever talk about such things, or even think about them at all."

"Really? They just dream about sheep? Bigger sheep?"

"Perhaps," she smiled wanly.

"Do Uzbeks dream of acoustic sheep?" I shook my head at the wonder of it, the possibility of their endlessly extended pastoral innocence.

Night falls over Samarkand, the city that has seen Tamerlane, Genghis Khan, and Alexander the Great, and yet risen, and risen again. In the dark sky outside my window, I can make out a handful of stars, scattered around the black shapes of the subtropical maple trees that huddle together in the courtyard, far from their native land, and all the more splendid for their remove.

Only a few stars, but enough to illuminate my thoughts. I saw with absolute clarity that the headless saint, the Living Prince who dwells within the foundations of the Shahr-i-Zindar, is none other than the living spirit of the great city itself.

So what shall I call my movie? The question follows me from place to place, will not leave me alone, or let me sleep (except in the morning when it abandons me to the doves and quarrelling finches). I have discovered late in life that the problem of history is the problem of good and evil, and that the meaning of history is the continued work of distinguishing hourly which is which; hourly, and in its smallest detections. I come out of the Shahr-i-Zindar, the mausoleum complex, half cakey ruin, half eye-splattering blue kaleidoscope, and I am at peace, staring at the scruffy weeds growing from the turquoise domes with droll amusement. Then two gypsy children approach from behind a broken wall smelling of urine. They stroke my arms and push too close to my wallet and camera, and my good mood is ruined in an instant; a few more grovelling gropes and I want to strike them down for the pollution of their touch, and the cultural fixity of their bad intentions. How can there be peace, when others can incite us so easily to the point of murder?

We are driving to the great Samarkand Market, and for the fifth time in as many days the police stop our vehicle, asking to see the registration. Timur is gone a long time. It's hot; we'll be late for lunch.

"You said you paid twenty thousand sum a year in road bribes," I turned to Larissa. "That's an average worker's monthly wage. But I didn't ask you how much time you spend on this nonsense."

"Time? In a year? Maybe ten hours."

"Ten hours! What a waste! And is it getting better, I suppose?"

I had read in *Lonely Planet* that Uzbekistan's president had ordered the police to lay off.

"No, it's getting worse. More time, more bribes, each year. Maybe 10 per cent more, each year."

"It's stupid shit."

"You don't have such things in your country?" She was serious.

"All these police would be in jail, in my country," I bitterly mutter, refusing to turn around, lest the green-uniformed copper decides to ask for my passport, which I forgot back at my guest house.

In the local *hamman*, the temperature is not so hot-hot, but the massage is expert, deft. I seem to be bending more with each visit. Perhaps I can get a job as The Human Pretzel by the end of this trip, assuming there are more such steamhouses to the east. My man is woggling my head this way and that, and I can see through the rising sheets of vapour that a half-dozen fellows reclining on the marble benches are following his moves with great interest. Now the masseur is putting his delicate foot on the small of my back and pulling hard at my slick shoulders, arching me like a compound bow and sending a gut-arrow of internal anguish skittering off into the drain.

Still, despite these holistic efforts, I am filled with the usual traveller's ogreish rants. The flatness of the country is making me surly. Or maybe it's the old scars, ancient rages, the flashburns of various traumatic inflections coming to life again in the ease of the South, flaring up like a gas blowout in the otherwise empty spiritual desert. At tea, I must make my choice between fresh figs the size of fists or buttery smooth apricots, dripping with nectar, accepting the gifts of the earth as my plain due now, small recompense for too many hard choices, and not enough right ones.

Lunch at Larissa's parents'. I feel I am courting her, which in a sense I am. I am courting her as a character in a book, an actor in my film. I want a performance from her, a great performance. She has the power, the talent, the technical skill. But do I, as the director?

"Please excuse this." She apologizes for the apartment lobby, which is pitch dark, cryptlike. We splash through pools of water on the tile floor, heavy dripping sounds. A pipe has burst somewhere above.

"Soviet, just like Moscow!" I say cheerfully, and then stumble on a loose tile.

Her mother and father, each fifty, greet us at the door, and usher us into the dining room, where the table is already set with dishes of prepared mixed salads.

"Uh!" Larissa's three-year-old daughter pouts from around the corner. She's a pretty little girl, with curly brushed bangs, and the pale face of the overprotected housebound. The stranger has upset her equilibrium. She stares at me, then runs off, crying now because I dared take her picture.

"Excuse me, she is not well. She has a cold." Larissa rubs her hands together.

"No friends her age? No daycare?"

"No, we have not such things in Samarkand." Larissa says, biting her lip, torn between her daughter's insistence on complete attention and her role as the international hostess.

"And no friends. Alone."

"You are right. How do you know this?" A trace of embarrassment.

"It's obvious. . . . And where is your room?"

She leads me to a small bedroom off the kitchen. Old school books on the shelf, a small battered desk, a square bed with a dark frame and a blue satin coverlet.

"It's the same as when I left, almost," she tells me from the middle of the room. I stay at the doorway, readying my camera.

This is where it all begins, I say to myself. This is where History and one's life first meet.

In the child's bedroom, at an hour when no one else is watching, in a place where no one else can do anything.

Chapter 19

Who Was Natalie Wood?

It is impossible not to become fascinated with Central Asian carpets. A daunting prospect. In Samarkand, there are any number of rug dealers, and the famed Bokhara carpet is one of many on offer. You must be able to distinguish at a glance whether the carpet is machine- or handmade, pure wool or mixed with cotton, from a sheep or camel, with natural or artificial dyes, all just to be able to sit down and look with any degree of competence.

Then there are the regional variations. This afternoon I am looking at a fine collection of small carpets from Turkmenistan, red and black mostly, with geometric rather than floral patterns, and as each one is unfurled, the two dealers take turns announcing its provenance:

"Tekin . . . Yakmut . . . Charjou . . ."

Tribal regions. The list is interminable.

Despite the cheap prices, a hundred dollars for something that took a village woman three months or more to weave, I am reduced to the defensive posture of the idiot tourist, who must grin, *Ah very nice, very nice,* as I try to remember where exactly it was that we came into this dark, echoing hall of burgeoning Ali Baba treasures, and from which we must now seek as graceful an exit as possible. Do I know what I like? Of course I do.

But the weight of my ignorance grows with each visit to the bazaar. At the end I am brought to the grim determination of the newly blind, anxious to make it to the end of the day without mishap or commercial disaster.

I have looked at many books about carpets, and drunk more cups of weak tea while they were lugged out before me. But I think the problem is that there are two orders of experience that have never met in me, and remain far apart: I have never seen a real carpet that is also represented in a book, open at its exact page in my hand. The books are always about other carpets, and the carpets I like care nothing for books. And more, each carpet seems so unique, so individual, it feels like a mistake to impose a bookish connection based on a few details of apparent similarity.

The world of real carpets defeats the order of Linnaeus: that all things are siblings perched in a symmetrical family tree. No, on the contrary, every carpet is its own pretty monster; it must be approached on its own terms, with circumspection and a good strong light in hand. In other words, buy, risk. Plunge. Don't look over your shoulder – for comparisons, or for comfort.

I can see the addiction in it: your collection can never be complete. Look at these Afghans here. Indigo dye, fantastic colour, the deepest cobalt hue of vast time itself. It's not the carpets I am afraid of, but their incessant demands for more blank walls. ("And the old carpet cried, we need more walls, more walls!") How many huge homes have been built, whose sole function it is to keep the owner's carpets happy at night, and sufficiently separate so that one can fully appreciate their finely turned borders, and the active play of their encrypted designs?

The tourism business in Uzbekistan is down 80 per cent as a result of the events of September 11. In the Samarkand Market, I strike up a conversation with a man in a ruined trench coat selling Soviet war medals and the memorabilia of other regimes – Tsarist banknotes, ancient arrowheads, cosmonaut medallions – out of a homemade wheelbarrow. Arcane treasures. A professor of linguistics, of course. I ask the Russian how he thinks the local economy will do in the next decade, and he tells me I am greatly mistaken to ask such a question.

"There is no economy! So how can there be any growth or decline? Zero is zero!"

I mention the gas pipelines, the fuel the West wants, pumped through to Turkey, and he remains sublimely indifferent to Uzbek's assuredly great future as the twentieth-first century's Saudi Arabia.

"Too many borders! No seaports! Landlocked! Who will control the pipelines? Three countries? Five? And what will *we* get out of it, at one end of a long line of greedy hands?"

I understood. Uzbek's economic history was always about brokerage, accommodating the flow of goods from China to the West and back again. Its recent Soviet-camp role as a commodity producer of raw cotton (sixty thousand square kilometres in the region, under irrigation) was proving ecologically disastrous and financially crushing; and whoever was making the real money on the trade was living far from here. It would be the same with petroleum; the cash was at the tap between the producer and the consumer, not at the dirty well-heads where only more disasters lurked.

The tables had been turned on Uzbeks. Now they would produce, and someone else would tell them how much, and exactly what they would have to pay to get their sweat-goods to market.

I am relatively alone in Samarkand, as far as other tourists go. I believe I spotted two American women in the Registan, hiking through the great square between the two blue sixteenth-century mosques. The Registan's mosques are famed for their portrayals of mosaic animals – in contravention of Islam's injunction against representations from natural life. Cartoon leopards glow in the sunset, mythical deer swoon coyly.

But I can't be sure; some of the local women dress in denim and sport backpacks too; and they would pass unremarked in our world, provided they did not replace all their natural teeth with solid gold ones, as more than a few people here have done. One was a stout woman about forty, who stopped me in the Central Market and asked if I were French.

"*Mais non. Canadien.*"

"*Canadien? Anglais Canadien?*"

"*Oui. Et vous?*"

"De Samarkand, bien sur! Aimez-vous notre ville?"

"Je l'adore!"

I wanted to ask her about this curious convention: *"Pourquois vous avez les dents d'or?"* but after pumping my arm up and down and giving me her best twenty-four-carat smile, she sailed off into a crowd of sellers of *chap-chap*, the flat local bread with roasted sesame seeds on top. I chewed away on one, left to imagine that this was the safest way the locals had of dealing with their national economy. And socially, the gold-mouths were quite fetching in the bright light of the market square; or, so I wager, in the candle-lit boudoir. (What other surprises would night's embrace reveal?)

I am thinking about my heroine, Larissa, who stepped out of a fat Russian novel, the biggest novel yet to be written. Thinking of antecedents, thinking of Natalie Wood. Everyone knows who Natalie Wood was – well, not really. They know she was the dark-eyed, high-strung luminous beauty who starred opposite a young Warren Beatty in *Splendour in the Grass*, the Armenian-American director Elia Kazan's first studio picture. And probably they know she drowned in strange circumstances in 1981, falling from a family yacht moored off Catalina Island.

What they don't know is that her career as a bona fide Hollywood actress is the subject of an intense, international, cultlike fascination on the part of Ukrainians and Russians, who both claim her as their own natural daughter. She was born Natasha Nikolaevna Zacharenko in San Francisco in 1938, and after a successful career as a child actor she made her first big appearance in *Rebel Without a Cause* with James Dean. To watch her performances almost fifty years later is to shudder anew at the complex layers of meaning she gives every scene. In a deliberately black-and-white production like *Splendour in the Grass* by an immigrant artist who choose William Inge's screenplay for what it said about America's social impermeability, we come to understand the impact of Modernism on the individual; we learn, with the overwrought heroine, the acute and bitter truth, that Parents Can't Help. Natalie Wood burns like a torch in the bathtub scene, where her mother tries to douse her newfound sexual passion with a dripping sponge and careful solicitude. But it's not about being boy-crazy, is it? It's more than sex she wants, it's the whole thing, life, *everything*; it's got her number now, and won't let go until she's exhausted.

She's playing a *Russian* character, a *Slavic* heroine. (As Kazan undoubtedly knew well, and needed.) She makes the limp baby-dolls of *Dr. Zhivago* and *Anouchka* appear all the more forgettable by comparison, the dolly-blanks of Anglo-American manufacture they were all along. Kazan knew exactly what he wanted; David Lean wouldn't know a real Russian woman if she bit him on the nose – he's all *eye*, no voice. Watch our Natalie trill before they send her off to the psychiatric clinic, incandescent with her unrealized being, a caged bird with nowhere to fly. This is who her fans adore, what Kazan knew he had in Wood, this girl-woman who is too beautiful, too smart, too talented, for our earth's mean precincts. She will either learn to make the accommodation in an act of spiritual humiliation or die young.

When groups of expat Ukrainians get together, as they did in the dacha near Kiev, the subject of Natalie Wood invariably comes up, a talisman for their edgy mood.

"So did you know Natalie Wood was really Ukrainian?" one of them will say, and the others will nod silently, pondering her fate and its intersection with their own troubled trajectories. A sodium flare that arced high overhead and briefly illuminated the broken world for all that it was. What choice does Larissa have? What choice do any of us have? It's simple: to burn, or not to burn.

My last night in Samarkand, and they want me to go to the folkloric show.

"There are no discos or nightclubs here, really," Larissa implored.

"What about the Pink Floyd Club? I saw it when we drove to the hotel yesterday."

"It's not so good."

"Club Afrodite?"

"Well . . . if you really want to go to such places."

Such places. What did that mean? Ten-dollar hookers and rotten kiosk vodka? This was a college town. Where were all the students, singing along to *We Are the World*? . . . Okay, the folkloric show.

We return to the Registan. The setting sun has burnished the leopard mosques in a glittering pastiche of copper and mica, and streaked them in afterglows of burnt cinnamon. We enter an enormous jewel box, and an echoing plaza filled with bedazzled pigeons appears like an ocean of desire through the archway. A round, wooden stage, forty empty tables, have been set up in the inner courtyard. In the background, the mosque's blue-tiled walls catch the last of the sun's splendour, while swallows perform their twilight tricks faster than a human eye can follow.

I choose a chair in the middle.

"What time is the performance?"

"About now."

"Where's the rest of the audience?"

"I think we are it."

The three of us sit down. The sound of our chairs scraping fills the amphitheatre. Silence. A distant door opens, a man comes forward, reverently carrying something precious in his outstretched hands. The light of truth? He brings it over to us. A platter of tea and nuts.

More silence.

There are three of us, and then some local street kids arrive, who have crawled in from the back entrance. Three fake-bearded musicians appear, one with *tamburas*, the other two with the *dombra*, the Uzbek horsehair-stringed instrument. I sit like a pasha in the middle of the blue-tiled expanse, as eight or nine harem dancers of different hues and sizes come out of another doorway. Clash of cymbals, ringing music envelopes us. Each girl does her routine, volcanically staring at me sitting there, a mere fifteen steps away. Shall it be the tall dark one with the quirky hand gestures, or this hot little brunette with the crimson headdress and the flawless complexion? I indulge myself in the fantasy of the seraglio on offer; yes, they invite me, with their crook'd hips, and sidelong glances that are longer than strictly necessary for the needs of dramatic engagement.

The one in the canary-yellow ensemble leaves the platform, comes to me, and takes my hand, bidding me to dance at the generic tribal wedding they are now celebrating. I've got my black silk shirt on tonight, open almost to the navel on account of the buttons popping off, button by dozy button, and I easily find the beat and get to it, dancing my head off in the middle of the costumed chorus line.

Boom-boom boom ba ba, Boomp,
Boom-boom boom ba ba, Boomp!

My shirt tails are flying; I've got the music now, and I am not about to let go.

I sit down, flushed and exhilarated. Larissa reminds me that this is my last night here.

Tomorrow I am off to Kyrgyzstan, the original homeland of the Scythians, their cousins the Sakas, and the probable birthplace of nomadic horse-culture itself. Kyrgyzstan, immediately to the east of Uzbekistan, is mountainous and underpopulated, a country that is reverting to pastoral nomadism after the collapse of its local Soviet regime.

"I hope you are okay there." She sighs.

"Why wouldn't I be? I am having a good time now. I feel much better."

I eye the dancer with the red headdress. She's outfitted like some caravan princess-bride on whose person the whole fate of an empire hangs. I can't get enough of these people, my greedy eyes devour their haughty postures, their falcon eyes, their musical, adroit little fingers.

"Well, you know. Your tour operator there had tourists kidnapped."

"Japanese? I read about it."

"No, the Americans."

"When was this?"

"Last year. They were kept prisoner in a village for fifteen days. Finally they let them go, and the Uzbek air force bombed the village completely with the permission of the Kyrgyz government."

"Last year? I don't think this story was in my guidebook."

Back at the hotel I was about to fall asleep when I remembered about the Americans.

I got up, turned on the light again, and pulled out the book I bought brand new, only a few months ago. No mention of kidnappings. I checked the publication date: 2000.

The book was two years out of date.

Chapter 20

Notes from the Underground

"**D**on't worry, it's an Aleusyshev. Good airplane. We will land."

"In one piece or two?"

Midnight at Tashkent Airport. We passengers are walking across the tarmac in a light, foggy rain towards a two-propeller plane, with the original silver body and odd dents of a vintage relic from the Second World War. Except we are going to fly it into the Pamir Mountains, not admire its provenance. To high Kyrgyzstan, under hard sheets of rain, in a chromed collector's item. The tarmac is ringed with such technical oddments; they probably cannibalize the old buses for spare parts.

"It's like the last scene of *Casablanca*," I say to Marcus as I test the first rung of the slick, rickety ladder that snakes up into the craft.

"It could be the start of a beautiful friendship," he laughs, throwing his head back to catch a face full of heaven's cold loose change. He's so happy to be heading off into his favourite place in Central Asia, as he has repeatedly told me in the dim waiting room. We take our seats, which are laughing too, loose tongues that won't lie still, and we haven't left the ground yet. The seats flop like cloth bags. I twist around to show him the chewed end of my useless seatbelt.

Marcus laughs again.

"What's this red lever here?" I point at the device by my head.

"Open it if you want to bail out quickly." He laughs and laughs. "Everything's mechanical. Not electronic, so it works. Don't worry."

Marcus Bensmann is a thirty-three-year-old literature and philosophy grad student from Dusseldorf who was so profoundly affected by doing his doctorial thesis in mystical St. Petersburg that he ended up here, playing Rick in the untamed hills. St. Petersburg uprooted him, seduced him, left him in the care of the wild boys of Central Asia.

"It was the best! The *demi-monde*, the white nights of northern summer. I heard a hundred ghost stories while I lived there, every one true. Everybody has their favourite phantom. The city is built on the graves of thousands of workers, and their ghosts swarm through the streets after nightfall. Particularly in summer."

Marcus has a long shock of curly, uncontrollable hair, Baltic blue eyes, droopy lashes, altogether the air of a footloose nineteenth-century student of Pushkin. *Vandervolken*. Free and easy, carelessly smoking a cigarette, dipping into a long story, untroubled by the need to finish it before starting another one, coming back to it with one last puff of his amorous cigarette. It seems that he didn't come to St. Petersburg as much as the fabled lagoon-city came to him, waking him at psychological midnight to a fantastic inner vision of life that stayed long past dawn. Now the philosophy student was an itinerant journalist.

"I came here in 1994. It was a complete blank then," he smiles happily. "Then, last year, bin Laden." More smiles. "Now there is trouble down in the south, fighting." His eyes sparkle, chuckles of narrow escapes.

"You mean Afghanistan?" I peer anxiously out of the little porthole.

The right wing is still intact. No view. Only night clouds. Do they have radar?

"No, Osh, the second biggest city in Kyrgyzstan. In the south. I will be going there in a couple of days. War."

"War?" I examine the red lever, try to decide what to do if the door should suddenly swing open. Grab the seat? It is so flimsy.

"Yes," he closes his eyes dreamily. "I will go down there, maybe tomorrow if I can arrange it. I have a good source. I'll ask him his advice on the stories, and he'll tell me how to get through the official security down there."

"I haven't heard any news in a month," I say. "What's happening?"

"They killed the deputy prime minister of Afghanistan two days ago."

"Who did?"

He shrugs. "Warlords, layers of intrigue. I was here when there was a power vacuum after 1991. Karate was banned here in Kyrgyzstan, but some teachers taught courses, and their students became their supporters, and now the karate teachers run the country from Bishkek."

"They saw their opportunity?"

"It is very interesting to see how power works: it collects and grows from such small beginnings. I saw it happen myself, in Kyrgyzstan."

"What about Russia? How do you explain the Soviet phenomenon?"

"Soviet power was always against the aesthetic of life. For example, since the idea is that everything is perfect or will be, under the equalization program of communism, there is no need for psychology, psychotherapy, and sociology, except in gross material terms. So, all they have are pills and shock treatments. No self-awareness develops, a complete left turn from Dostoevsky."

"I was surprised to see the writers favoured here in the former Soviet countries are always Pushkin and Lermontov, early nineteenth century. Not the moderns like Dostoevsky or Turgenev."

"The classics, yes. Safe, romantic. But there is the fundamental *private* space, nonetheless, that the average Russian maintains against the public sphere. And this hidden Russian chooses who or what he is, in this private persona."

"Sounds a bit schizophrenic," I mumble as I look around at the lumpy Russians half-snoring, nostrils all agrog in a cloud of stale vodka fumes. The flight is full of them, the new carpetbaggers of Central Asia, on the lookout for a spare tire factory or an export concession that fell off a truck. "It's just that there is no historical comparison for the scale of this Soviet-made devastation. How many Russians died in their 1930s purges? Ten million? Even Genghis Khan didn't kill his own people."

"Yes, the Soviets kill everybody, including themselves. Especially themselves. This is the great experiment, to perfect the human race. Only the Russians would attempt such an experiment on such a scale, and it is right out of *Crime and Punishment,* or *The Brothers Karamazov.* They didn't read Dostoevsky, no, they *applied* it."

"And Genghis Khan? What was the impact of the nomads' attacks on their culture?"

Marcus looked like he wanted a cigarette. He pursed his red lips.

"Two things. Of course, Peter the Great is a Khan who pushed his armies to the ocean, which the others did not do. But the Tartars left the churches alone, and so they became the storehouses for the wealth of the Russians. The rest of the gold the Mongols took out of circulation; so while the rest of Europe was developing trade and commerce after the Renaissance, Eastern Europe was reduced to barter. The legacy of Genghis Khan lives on today, in the barter economy after the 1989 financial collapse."

"They seem to have lots of cash in Moscow, judging from the price of crocodile *shaslyk*."

"The problem in Russia is that the people who were the pillars of society in the West – doctors, professors, teachers, scientists – are impoverished. Only the gangsters have power, through money, and the decent classes struggle away in their tiny apartments."

We banked sharply and began a steep screamer-descent, which the Russian pilots always did military style, dropping abruptly to avoid unnecessary exposure to the theoretical groundfire. Why change a good thing to coddle a few queasy passengers?

We landed, as Martin had promised. A potbellied Asian guy in a white acrylic shirt swayed over the seat and jammed a cigarette in my mouth as we disembarked.

"Smoke dis," he slurred at me, "and shud up!"

I spat the cigarette out of my mouth and threw it on the floor at him, ready for a fight.

"You too noisy!" He swayed on his feet, blinking.

The other passengers gasped in alarm, wide-eyed, as he tottered in the aisle and almost fell over. His briefcase was stencilled in English, *Ministry of Irrigation*.

"He's really irrigated," Marcus grinned.

WELCOME TO KYRGYZSTAN, said the illuminated sign outside the plane.

It was still raining. Inside the glass bunker, the guards in their big green caps watched us descend the rickety aluminum steps and enter their mountain realm.

At two in the morning, my tour driver had still not appeared at Arrivals, and the crowds were thinning out. I accepted Marcus's offer of an overnight place to stay; he rented a flat from a Tatar family, and he told me something of them, as the father and son drove us into the heady alpine heights of Bishkek City, through a long road, dead straight, lined with full pine trees towering above us. The clouds had lifted; stars gathered around the treetops and the air was clean, cool, and scented. No buildings, only trees on the airport road.

"It really is an amazing thing. These two men, father and son, went off to Germany to buy this car."

"Second-hand?"

The black Fiat looked in good condition. The twenty-year-old son drove easily, while Yakmat, the father, spoke to us in Russian of recent local events.

"Yes, they bought it for seven thousand dollars. And then they drive it all the way back to Kyrgyzstan. I wrote a story about their journey. It was a modern Tatar odyssey, a great adventure."

"Except here the father goes with the son. Not leaves him at home with mom."

"That is there their strength, very clannish. Yakmat is the leader of the clan, the family, because he is the most successful, resourceful."

I studied Yakmat's family when we reached his apartment, another Soviet-style high-rise facing an inner courtyard. His wife sported a bright dyed-red beehive, and joked and laughed with us as she served the *solanka*, the ham soup, and fat cabbage rolls with tomato salad. She was a Tatar too, but apart from their coal-black eyes and pronounced cheekbones, the couple looked more European than Asian. Or maybe it was the way they laughed, bantered, welcoming Marcus (and me by extension) as the returning scion of the always-far-flung clan. Later in the week, Yakmat's family was due to attend a wedding in Kazakhstan, a three-thousand-kilometre round-trip. Another epic. I went into my appointed bedroom and left them drinking black tea and chattering away, perhaps deciding who was going to Scylla and who would be off to Charybdis later that month.

I began to rearrange my bag, removing the heavy clothes from the bottom and stuffing away the shorts and sandals I would no longer need in this alpine clime. Then I crawled under a mound of goose-down comforters. Fresh linen, God bless Mrs. Yakmat. It was cool here, in both senses of the word, like an alternative Katmandu, *circa* 1962. Just replace the English freaks with Tatar car dealers and there you go. Ribald sport in the hall of the mountain kings. Marcus had confirmed my dark suspicions about one thing, though, in passing: the Scene was dead.

By the Scene, I mean that Bohemian circus that had once traipsed through these parts in the 1970s, running from London and Amsterdam through Kabul, ending in the silk-lined hippie-dens of Nepal and India. The Hash Highway, the violet loop that began decades ago somewhere in Morocco or Paris, and then randomly touched down in Ibiza, Crete, and, the last I'd heard, Phukat in Thailand and Goa in India.

"No, the Internet killed it off," Marcus spelled it out. "The Scene is over. Now you must make your own scene."

I closed my eyes, still wondering at the sustained, near-ecstatic joy in his voice.

The princesses, I must not forget the princesses. I met them on my last night back in Tashkent, when Larissa took me for a farewell dinner at the Russian restaurant with the oleander courtyard.

To begin with, there are three of them, sisters. Lena was the oldest at thirty, then Marusha, and the youngest, Deva. Okay, what about them? Three sisters, pretty of course, sitting by a cherry tree in the late-afternoon light. I saw them for the first time in the courtyard of the little restaurant in Tashkent, together at a rough, painted wooden table, taking their dinner outside. I would see them again in my mind, fixated on recalling each gesture, each utterance. I could not take my eyes off them. I insisted we go to this restaurant when I learned from my guides that Lena ran it. I willingly became their faithful servant, their secret admirer, the writer of this epitaph for their class.

The three sisters were something I had read about, but never dreamed still existed and walked the earth every day – especially there in that dusty provincial town of Tashkent, far from Moscow and St. Petersburg: White Russians.

Yes, these three Russian sisters were variations on a theme of charm made visible, the reality of superior breeding and all that class implies. Each of them grew more elegant, sophisticated, and polished every time you looked. Each gesture rang truer than true, a faultless sonnet in every one of those tapered white fingertips.

Flawless complexions. Rosebud lips, perfect ears. Changelings.

"Tell them I must speak to them. Say I want to take their picture," I instructed Larissa. "Publicity for their restaurant, whatever."

Unlike the common beauties walking Tashkent town, they had scarcely glanced in my direction, despite my eager, over-tipping custom and array of chrome cameras.

Of course I knew who they were, although I had never seen such people in my life before. Not in real life, at least. A sufficiency of nineteenth-century novels had taught me to recognize the Russian aristocracy when I saw it; that white finger curled delicately around the porcelain teacup said it all. The sight of them, taking tea by the cherry tree in a whitewashed courtyard in suburban Tashkent, was unbearably affecting. This was a last remnant of the *boyarskii* class who had ruled real Russia – rural, village Russia – for over a thousand years; who had produced Pushkin and Lermontov and Tolstoy in the first place. The very last remnant. Now they were almost extinct, a distinct, fabulous race, killed by the Bolsheviks for their pretty hands and lyrical eyes.

"Our grandfather came here from Siberia," Lena told us after we made our introductions. "He was very rich but lost his property, but not his life, here in Tashkent. We are related to the Romanovs."

I glanced at Larissa when Lena said this. What thoughts had my modern, angst-ridden urban beauty about these hereditary, near-mythical beings? Her alternate heroines? Their very language was another species of Russian entirely, soft and modulated, even a foreigner could distinguish it at once from today's industrial Russian by a few phrases. Lena told us why she was here every night with her sisters.

"I bought this restaurant only last month. I need to get it in order," she smiled sweetly. "I am a children's doctor, but today that is not enough."

Her smile grew sad. How she must have loved her little patients! The name of her restaurant was Lise. Their sole and louche waiter also hailed from the nineteenth century, Misha, a sleepy young dolt whom Timur sharply corrected for his every transgression, and there were many during the meal. But the food was worth it, the long wait and forgotten drinks: it was elevated above the mundane sense-life of our century, as ethereal as its fairy-tale proprietors.

Here's the explanation for the Revolution you won't find in George Kennan or Robert Conquest: race war. A rabid, biologically driven aristocide, a drive to extinguish at one blow and for all time the Whites, the refined, naturally superior class that every civilization will succeed in producing over time. Somehow (was it the shock of recognition in those famously unsparing novels of Dostoevsky?) the soup-slurpers became so conscious of their rank inferiority that it became impossible for them to live in the same world any more. Marxist *resentiment* and cheap machine guns did the rest. What choice did the Reds really have? It was either kill the mirrors of their own worthlessness or live as slaves to the pathological, unfulfilled rages of Dostoevsky's slovenly street-characters. But then the bully-boys could never rise to the level of humane intelligence and art themselves – as three generations that have produced nothing but toxic squalor and brutal chicanery have proved, beyond all argument.

My two Bishkek City guides, Slava and Farida, apologized for not showing up at the airport, saying Ground Control gave them the wrong time by almost two hours. Another sign that all is not well with Kyrgyzstan, this starkly beautiful country of ice-cream mountains and pine forests and wildflower meadows. I can see them all, these natural attractions, glowing like an alpine mirage beyond the city limits.

"*Official* unemployment is 40 per cent," Slava, my tardy driver, remarked as we drove by the deserted, cracked streets of downtown Bishkek, all overgrown with hearty weeds. Small sellers sat at the broken traffic lights, their pathetic wares nearly invisible, some occupying a square foot or less. A harried thirtyish woman escorted a drunken man across the frost-broken paving, propping him up with her elbow. He was too old to be anything but her miserable father.

"What's the real rate, then?"

We drove past a statue of Lenin, "The Father of Our City," as Slava told me. The black figure was still intact too.

"Much higher." He shook his head and adjusted his oversized sunglasses.

What could be higher than almost half the population, and still function?

"And you, Farida," I turned to my interpreter-guide in the back seat of the Toyota. "What's your background?'

"My father was Tartar, and my mother Cossack and Ukrainian."

"So that makes her Russian!" Slava joked. "When you mix all the colours, my grandmother used to say, you get Russian!"

"Shall we go into the mountains now?" Farida asked me as our morning city tour deteriorated into a unsightly medley of unkempt parks, boarded-up government buildings, and broken fields that had once been manicured lawns. A new word, the *ruinurb*s.

"Sure," I answered. We were soon winging our way down a country highway between a double row of whitewashed trees, streaking through a magical tunnel of green filtered light. After fifteen minutes, I asked them to pull over. I wanted to breath this mountain air directly.

"Oh, look at this."

Slava pointed to a shiny, toothy bush growing happily at the side of the road.

"Good God, is it wild?"

The marijuana plant sat there, healthy as only a high-altitude crop could be.

"Yes, everything grows here," he replied cheerfully as I stroked its leaves like a favourite pet. "Poppies, all kinds of things."

We are following the natural banks of the Chu River, and the olive foothills soon give way to snow-capped mountains. Under the high-altitude sun these peaks gleamed, iridescent as a speckled trout pulled dripping from a stream. I kept reaching for my sunglasses, forgetting I already had them on.

"We had much rain this year." Slava looked from one side of the road to the other. "No tourists, but healthy weather at least."

"Why no tourists?" Herds of scrawny mountain horses bounded freely over the mossy turf. There were no cars, no trucks. No road signs. A green veldt, broken with odd stonework.

"Well, for one thing," Farida spoke up, "there was an accident in this river by a Canadian gold-mining company. A truck filled with cyanide fell into the river, and so the tourists don't come here rafting any more."

"Yes," Slava joined in. "Even though everyone knows cyanide only lasts a few days before it's decomposed by the elements. It's highly unstable."

On cue they stopped talking at this juncture, waiting for my reaction to their disclosure. Okay, so their world was breaking down. What was I going to say? That *cyanide* was one of those words tourists never like to hear, in any context. Along with *pickpocket, market bomb,* and *typhus*?

"That's too bad," I mumbled, peering into the swirling depths of the tannin-stained river. The vegetation along its banks had clearly survived, despite the catastrophe. It was jammed with every kind of herb and flower, a vast parking lot for bees and butterflies. Tall stalks of fragrant giant lavender waved at us in passing. Along with the hilariously rotten, meat-carcass smell of the wormwood, it competed to steal its way into the interior of our car. A neon-orange plant parasite sprouted everywhere, a fungus as curiously hieroglyphic as sprayed graffiti. Two or three varieties of buttercups, red poppies, tiny perfect daisies, and a short waxy bush with bright apricot berries all shoved each other around like bullies.

"Ephedra," Slava pronounced as he pulled the Mitsubishi wagon over to the gravel shoulder and jumped out. "The berries are edible."

He popped a few into his mouth as I joined him. They had a nutty, curious texture.

"Ephedra, ephedra." I took a few steps into the glowing field, looking for something else exotic to taste. "What's that in English, again?"

"The same. They make ephedrine from this plant."

"Ah, ephedrine!" I paused in thought as I gobbled a few more. Where had I seen that name before? I was quite cheerful and animated as we drove off, and it eventually occurred to me, from the glibness of our conversation, that this was the active ingredient of diet pills and other patented speed-demons.

"No, no! A handful of these buds is nothing!" Slava frantically waved his hands over a landscape littered with natural hallucinogens of every sort. "It's the altitude! It can make you quite crazy!"

"Just how crazy-high are we now?" I turned to Farida, for she held the map.

"Maybe 2,600 metres. Almost 8,000 feet. But we are going much higher today."

The road continued to climb, mounting a series of dun and green hills shaved bare by the prancing herds. Now we passed cattle, horses, and occasional flocks of large goats, who were charged with keeping this landscape as trim as a five-thousand-hole golf course. No other traffic at all. Every twenty minutes or so we saw another vehicle, perhaps a truck sagging with metal scrap, bound for China to the east, or an overloaded Lada with farmer-families headed out for a rural wedding, the men's characteristic white-felt top hats perched casually on their heads like brimless Stetsons. Their hats were so tall they jammed up against the roofs of their vehicles; or maybe they helped keep the roofs up, for their cars were so laden with roped bales of cargo that they could barely make the steeper grades, and often had to pull over to the side just to let their steaming motors cool off.

"Would you like to visit the ancient tower? It is on the way to Sonkul."

"Sure, why not?" Sonkul was a lake, sacred to the nomads, high up on the approach to the Tien Shan Range. "What's the history behind it?'

"We don't know much about it. It's maybe sixteenth century A.D., or Bronze Age. Never been excavated."

"That's quite a spread of dates."

The unsung site appeared soon enough in the middle of a stony plain, mute and indifferent to our argument. First, a great sandy earthwork rose out of a thistle field, its ramparts ten metres tall. Nearby stood the Muslim minaret, and beside it a small cottage museum; and in a field buzzing with bees, a collection of stone babas, roly-poly carved stone figures, a metre in height, obscure in gender. What was this tower doing out here in a grassy waste? Nothing in the little museum explained anything; the labels confined themselves to self-evident declarations like "arrow heads" and "piece of temple decoration."

"Who lived here before? In ancient times, I mean?"

"The Sakas, the Scythians," Farida said. "They mixed with the Chinese people, and become the original Kyrgyz people."

This was not what the history texts stated. Scholars claimed the Sakas, like other Indo-European peoples, were driven out from the Central Asian steppes by Turkic tribes over the centuries, then finally and permanently by Attila's Huns in A.D. 400. Perhaps Farida's account was her socially acceptable way of announcing or justifying the existence of a new, proto-Russian blend, by creating old antecedents for a continuing tradition of racial hybridization.

It was getting late. Slava said we had a choice. We could ascend to the summer camp of the nomads by Lake Son, another three hours' drive away, or we could stay at a sanitarium at the base of the mountains. "Whichever you prefer."

"A sanitarium? What kind of sanitarium?"

"A salt mine. For people with breathing problems."

"Let's go then."

"Excellent!" Slava clapped his hands with satisfaction, did a U-turn, and headed up a bumpy track to a nearby hillside hamlet that clutched fast to a gravel wash, the whole positioned just below a grey, snowy ridge. The discoloured snow turned out to be an exposed vein of coarse salt, naturally – a great raw wave that followed the line of the knoll and then scattered itself over the landscape in loose pieces like dirty laundry. How it got there, what geology had left it exposed like that, no one could say. Slava and Farida went off to bargain for a room. I was left alone with my speculations. There were about fifty people staying here in the convalescent spa village, mostly well-off Kyrgyz women (judging from their heavy gold jewellery and smart city shoes), a handful of Russians, and a few ethnic Koreans. The village was brand new, on the theme of rustic alpine. The entrepreneur who built it had provided many unnecessary doors that skinned your knuckles when you opened them, bathroom light switches in highly improbable locations, and wildly uneven wooden steps. The place was clearly built for Martians with multiple heat-seeking tentacles. I, as the destiny-favoured Westerner, had to pay four times the going rate for my interplanetary splendour. My double room sported a green Soviet refrigerator, a clear glass table that shot straight for my knees as I walked in, and two scrimpy beds from the set of *Snow White*. Who needed drugs in a place like this? It was already trippy. The beds were so Alice-short I would have slept better standing up like a dairy cow. After a dinner of chopped-up pieces of this, a mashed pile of that, and a lugubrious red and green sauce of whatever ("How do you like the food?" "Fancy, real fancy!"), we proceeded at once to the salt mine.

The entrance lay through a small outbuilding decorated with a hand-tinted photo of the President of the Country. His rosy cheeks were something to behold; the pastel artist must have worked in the mortuary trade as well. A silent security guard in a pasty-green uniform directed us with a careless wave to a flapping wooden door, from which a cold, abysmal breeze steadily blew. The salt mine, its main shaft. I took a deep breath and pushed the door open.

It was instantly colder. They said it was eight degrees Celsius in there, but it felt like zero Retrograde. Large maroon air vents snaked their way above the passages, and battered crystal chandeliers hung from the rough wood mining beams in a hopeless attempt at festive illumination. The flickering lights worked off a generator, and only served to emphasize the tunnels' funereal atmosphere. One could make out small groups and single individuals, walking slowly in the distant gloom, taking their measured steps in a dutiful re-enactment of Dante's third circle of despair. Which deadly sin did it serve to punish? Stupidity? Torpidity?

"Where are they going?"

"Nowhere. They just walk. You can do the same. Or you can sit down. Most people stay the whole night, breathing in the air, deep."

"It has thirteen chemical elements," Slava added, already looking back at the exit. "Iodine, sulphur, chlorine . . ."

"Yes, yes. I'll go for a tour, maybe do some writing. Thanks."

I let them go, and proceeded without hesitation into the twilight depths, imitating the careful pacings of the other pilgrims, these dim resident pedestrians of a wholly invented Hades. This was their idea of a health cure. An extended visit to their favourite theme park, the Next World. I passed entire staterooms cut from the living walls of salt, furnished with curtained beds, blankets, and quilts, everything one would need for an extended sojourn in this sunless labyrinth. Here was a pool room and, beyond that, a cavern festooned with strings of red-and-green Christmas lights, and the word *BAP*, "bar," a perfect spot for chatting up that hot invalid from the crypt down the hall. A young Kyrgyz fellow appeared from nowhere and turned on the mirrored-ball lights for me.

"Disco," he said hopefully, and began fussing with the bottles of ancient mineral water that sat gathering salty dust on the stained tin counter.

"*Muzika?*" He pointed to an old-fashioned stereo system.

"No, no. I go write." I said in Russian, "*Spivo.*" I showed him my notebook, as my voice thudded, sounding unnaturally flat in this crystal oblivion.

He grinned, a sad knot of jumbled teeth, and helped himself to a tot.

Continuing my perambulations through the caverns, I came upon a cluster of people closely examining a dark patch on a sheer wall of white salt.

"Hey! See, Mister?"

An older man tugged at a clump of thick black hair sticking out from the rock wall.

"This is from bear, long ago."

He plucked our a few coarse hairs and showed them to me.

"Never go bad, like pickles."

Indeed it did appear to be a black bear's hide, but what geology had transported the beast here, under thirty or forty metres of sea salt, I cannot say. Some ancient and mysterious cataclysm had passed by over our heads – and more than once, for now the old man led his group down the passageway to another curiosity.

Here was some flap of textile, also sticking out of the salt wall.

"Felt, Mister. Please, touch."

I was confounded. The scrap was man-made, but again it had only been exposed by these postwar mining excavations, and how one could explain a climate that suddenly created thirty feet of rock salt above a human settlement of recent Halocene vintage was beyond my powers of invention. A glacier of minerals that moved fast enough to trap bears and nomadic tents was clearly the culprit, yes. But what was its genesis?

I soon found myself in a private rock-chamber furnished with a picnic table, whereupon I sat down and wrote, making these notes from the beginning. Forgive me if they seem dull, and distant from the sunny hours they aim to describe; they are recollected in a dark cell ten paces wide, superbly cold, and shot throughout with acid whiffs of sulphur and iodine, and punctuated every twenty minutes or so by the restless stomping of my fellow pilgrims, these penitents making their appointed rounds in the artless tunnels without.

Chapter 21

To the Summer Pastures

More flowers, blossoms of every kind and description, runts and giants both. A mountain hothouse of loopy white dog roses, sheets of creamy edelweiss thick as the Duke of Argyle's Persian carpets, greasy mutton buttercups, and great startling masses of blue forget-me-nots, the whole endless garden bed flashing brilliantly as we ascend to the three-thousand-metre mark and the charged light grows intense, shifting to ultraviolet, the celestial side of the spectrum.

The blue hurts, it's that bright. Magenta snapdragons nod off sleepily, overseen by a fat, sinister plant with five or six ground-hugging, spiky leaves, sitting upright by the roadside like a spiteful schoolmarm with arms crossly folded. *Marmot-flower*, Slava calls it: the thick trunk turns brown as a fur wrap in autumn. Another insidious plant he calls *mother-stepmother*; the sunny side of its slender leaves are smooth and yielding to the touch, while its undersides are rough and "cruel."

Slava brakes for birds, scattering little black-and-white finches, outraged kestrels, even a flock of crows. He more than brakes – he toots his horn at them from a goodly distance. It would kill him to injure one of these tiny creatures. His bland, square face, hacked up with the remains of adolescent acne or worse, is awash in joyful contemplation as he spots a new plant, a purple ball perched on a tall green pipe, a whole quiverful of them, proud target arrows waving from the banks flushed with pink clover.

"Wild garlic," he intones like a prayer. "Let's take one."

He gives me the stalk to chew, and I nod, agreeing no, it's not bitter. More like powerful, like all these high-alpine plants. Robust, potent, but never mean.

We ascend higher.

The air grows noticeably cooler. The great green range of the Mulda-Toh foothills fold themselves into rumpled bundles, the soaked laundry of the gods. Not a tree. Not a whiff of smoke either. Thin strands of sheep and horses, tiny dots high up on the distant slopes. One tumble and they're gone, lost forever. Lower down, clusters of camels and yaks. I get dizzy when I jump out of the car, stumbling over the mossy rocks, dazzled by the bright-orange lichens. The *etazalamid*, the high-altitude pill, should have kicked in by now, but who knows? You can get altitude sickness at 2,500 metres, or at 5,000. We're at 3,300 metres, so anything can happen.

We arrive at a huge plain, an enormous bowl-shaped depression, and we find the white pill-boxes of the nomads' yurts sheltered off in the far corners of the horizon, tucking themselves under the roof of the sky. Iron-clad storms roll over the distant, glinting lake, beating at the peaks with their fists, while Lake Sonkul shows itself as a steel blade that slashes and disappears between the mists and the low-slung, freighted clouds.

"It's pretty cold up here," I say, staring at the red-cheeked Kyrgyz children whipping up their horses and tugging at tent-ropes. Despite my scrutiny, their whole pastoral gadget system of leather cinches and gaiters and braided cordwork is beyond me. Slava sees the nomad encampment he is looking for, and we fishtail over the cropped turf to ask about the camping. It's the middle of July, and this mercurial mountain weather has dropped decisively from 25 to 8 degrees Celsius in a half-hour. Slava gets out of the car and approaches the white yurts. I dig through my pack for my coat, wishing I had one of those white elf-hats, the felt crowns the Kyrgyz men wear. Slava returns from the palaver.

"They say they are not ready. There was much grass this year in the valley below, lots of rain. So everything is late. They only came up here a week ago."

"I see. Okay, let's go." Thunder rolls like a drunk clearing his throat.

"You don't want to see the lake?"

"I've seen it, haven't I?"

"I think so." Slava looks at Farida.

I can tell he is relieved. He doesn't like the look of the weather any more than I do. They do not fancy driving through the coming storm or, worse, trying to negotiate these roads after the rain has washed out the passages on the way down. We want to beat this black-eyed gale, but which way? A quick look at the map again and we immediately head off for the steep exit on the western side of the plateau. It's a smart move. The windward range is green, fantastically alive, and bristling with knotty pine trees and the verdant luxury of a juiced-up undergrowth. Canyon groves, jutting boulders, sinuous waterfalls, it's a different world down here, sylvan and crisp. A northern Gothic landscape fantasy plunked down in the middle of Asia. There's ample opportunity to see it all, for the road consists of a series of narrow switchbacks that bring us right up to the faces of tremendous overhangs and perpendicular limestone buttresses. An excellent place for a stronghold, tilted at ninety degrees, warlock-proof. All we need now is an auburn-haired princess named Gwenythel, plaiting her virginal locks in a stony keep.

"Shall we have lunch?"

Farida has lined up pickles and smoked ham in a cardboard box, along with fresh discs of local bread and imported chicken pâté.

"Not yet," Slava says, eyeing a stream's overflow that trickles lazily across the road. It's just the beginning; soon the dripping will become a torrent. "Let's get down first."

The western descent proves steeper than the eastern ascent, steeper and more problematic. The switchbacks are so tight the steering wheel shrieks in protest, gouts have washed out already, my ears are popping, but we're happy, the water in the stream racing down beside us is clear, trout-cold, and the lushness of the flowers on its banks testifies to the purity of the land. We drop a thousand feet in as many seconds and enter a new country, heavily treed and mossy.

We park the car beside a spooky tree littered with Muslim prayer-letters and set up on a patch of grass as spongy as a flophouse mattress. No flies, no bugs. A chocolate butterfly careens madly over our jar of wild blackberry jam, drunk on its sugary fumes. Slava must tell us his story about American trekkers, one of whom made the strategic mistake of feeding a shepherd's half-wild dog with a scrap of dry bread.

"The Kyrgyz shepherds never feed their dogs," he recounts. "The animals must steal what they can, or kill marmots. So this American woman feeds one dog, and four or five dogs all betray their owners and follow the trekkers off into the hills. The trekkers can't get rid of them. One day, two days, three days. The dogs stand guard at their camp every night. On the fourth day, the trekkers tie the dogs up, to make them stay, but a few hours later, the dogs came, bounding happily over the empty fields. They had broken their ropes, and were so glad to see their friends again. So the trekkers were stuck with these dogs the whole trip, right to the airport."

"That's loyalty for you."

I loaded another biscuit with blackberry jam and popped it into my mouth, savouring the flavour and mix of textures, as the cocoa butterfly waffled between my eyebrows, deciding whether to come in for an emergency landing on my nose. Alone above the sheer canyon walls, an eagle drifted on the updraughts. A rumble of thunder broke behind us.

A white pellet hit the teapot with a *ping*.

Hail.

"Let's go."

In two minutes we were packed and heading down into the Narin Valley, where fertile grain farms lined the brown river as far as the horizon. The swollen flood had captured isles of emerald trees between its banks. So much rain; the land was green, the cows fat, the horses didn't know what to do with themselves. I was happy again.

Who knows such rural splendour? Bright-yellow fields of canola and, behind them, a mountain backdrop painted in blue, purple, banana, orange, and rose, with a topping of glittery white at their icy peaks. We stop for a picture, and discover that these same fields are alive with songbirds and honeybees. Everything is alive, intense. More arrogance of flowers, a hundred scents packed tight in the single breeze. Slava falls to the ground, pulls tenderly at a fuzzy grey leaf, and holds it up for my admiration.

"A kind of mint," he says dreamily.

In truth I don't know what it is, and neither does he; and what's more, we enjoy this loose tramping about, the secret complicity of the naturally lazy and happily ignorant, three travellers weary of indexed books and the rectitude of proper labels. We'll invent our own if we have to, drifting around in the mountain steppes. And it soon comes to that: *pistachio flower*, on account of the bright-green stem, and *dog-ear thorn* for the other. Slava likes this game; he tells me he prefers the English names to the Russian ones, the former are so expressive.

"Forget-me-*not*," he repeats aloud to himself. "Forget-me-*never*."

I spot a fantastic ledge of pale lunar sandstone, changing colour in the afternoon. I admit aloud to a major failure of language. It's hopeless, this irreducible beauty.

"How can I begin to describe all this landscape?" I shake my head. "It defeats me."

A few minutes later Slava looks at me and says, "It stood out like a great reef, a proud peninsula lost to a green sea."

A great reef: there's the Russian soul for you. Generous, dreamy, and always aware of what is truly important in life. Knowing where you are, in the long voyage of the heart.

We pulled into the sprawling rural town of Narin, and the nut-brown faces of the valley's farmers and herders greeted us at every turn. The men were squatting at the sidewalks, in deep conversation, or riding scrawny horses *cloppity-clop* through the streets, and pushing hard at ancient and battered Ladas – in an effort, I suppose, to get them started, except that I saw this procedure re-enacted so often I concluded they merely used the defunct vehicles as pushcarts or sledges for transporting raw field goods to market. There was no gas at the pumps; they were bone-empty. There were no cafés or stores either; it was a city of eighty thousand people only in the fourteenth-century meaning of the word. I thought my guides were joking when they said we would be staying in a yurt here in town for the night. They were serious. The hotels were "no good." The owner of the urban yurt-camp had four white felt tents on offer. They were clean and airy, and I was glad of it. The dusty airless apartments in Kiev and Moscow had come close to finishing me off. I could see the clean sky through the smoke-hole of my assigned quarters.

Supper was served in the main house by the owner's twenty-year-old daughter, who, like many of her peers, had studied English in a conscious effort to become more "international," as she put it. Slava was cheerful at the dinner table, whereas Farida became correspondingly moody. I was getting tired of this tag-team replication; I had witnessed too many simplistic emotional pairs-games already, and so I turned my attention solely to Slava and told him about Mario, the Italian management professor back in Tashkent.

"He was travelling through Uzbekistan with a good-looking, blonde Russian woman. She was about thirty, single mother with one child, and he told me he was undecided about her, after a week travelling together. Too moody, he said."

I shot a quick look at Farida at this point. Yes, I was vexed by moody guides, and now feeling good enough to kick back a little.

Slava understood exactly what I meant.

"Mario, you say? Not Caesar? That is funny. For we know an Italian business expert who came here to Kyrgyzstan, a man who also has a blonde Russian girlfriend with a child. Same story."

"Same story? Wait! I haven't told you the story yet, Slava! I actually saw this Mario twice. Once, back in Samarkand, with his sexy girlfriend, where he seemed to want to talk a lot for a guy on a heavy date. Then again at the airport, just a few minutes before he was leaving her. He looked relieved."

"Relieved, what does this mean?" Slava turned to Farida.

"Relaxed, comfortable again." She was paying close attention to this story too.

"So anyway we got into a discussion of the Russian character, Mario and me, at the airport in Tashkent. Of the women, at any rate. Mario said that they had no self-awareness at the level we take for granted in the West, after our decades of pop psychology and psychotherapy. That they were instinctually blind. Highly rational in their professions but unable to articulate their feelings, even to themselves. Mario was relieved, he also said, because he was exhausted by her incoherent moods after only one week."

"That's the story?" Slava drummed impatiently on the table, ignoring his cheese blintz.

"Just one more thing. At some point a German joined us, Marcus, a journalist. He disagreed with this analysis completely. In his view, the Russians had one face turned to the world, public, and another, a private person, whom they kept to themselves. And this divide, he said, was intentional, conscious. . . . So what do *you* think?"

I looked patently again only to Slava, punishing Farida for her low temper.

Slava was decisive.

"My friend Caesar? He said the same thing exactly as your friend Mario, that his girlfriend was moody, irrational. She broke it off."

"What, their relationship?"

"Yes, and Caesar took it badly. Very badly. He asked me to find him a psychologist, and I did, a nice woman. Before I met her, I believe completely that this was a false profession, like fortune-telling, but when I listened to her discuss his problems, my respect grew total."

"*Listened?* Where were *you* in all this?"

"Translating. The psychologist was here in Bishkek. Caesar really needed her."

"And did he get better?"

"What he did was write a book, *Caesar and Alisha*. In English, then translated into Russian."

"About their relationship? It was published?"

"Six copies on a computer. And he handed out extra copies to his friends so they could read about his difficult romance."

"And did this book help him?"

"Yes and no. He met another girl, also Russian, also blonde, also with a child. Actually, she was a classmate of the psychologist. Now he fights with her also."

"Who? The psychologist or the new girlfriend?"

"Both, I think."

"Time for another book."

I turned to Farida in uneasy triumph. To see how she was responding to this.

She nodded quickly. She'd been waiting for the opportunity to defend herself.

"Well, *of course* I am moody sometimes, and I do not know why. And I would like my man to guess and ask me why. But there is always another side to the story, and I know these people you are talking about."

"And?" I was fascinated.

A regular little hothouse of suppressed passions, in steamy old Kyrgyzstan.

"They are not so one-sided," she sniffed. "The woman knows something is wrong. She may not be able to say why, exactly. But this does not mean things are okay. And Caesar!"

She shook her head as if it was beyond bearing.

"Yes," Slava joins in. "This is true. Lots of things in Caesar's book are not true. He has no understanding of what Alisha means, when she says or does something. It's all him. Him, him, him. You know, there's this Chechnya policeman who works in this country? Every night when he comes home, no matter how late, he honks the horn for his wife to get out of bed and open the gate for him. Although he could easily do it himself. And she is Russian, I must say. But not all Russian women are so moody, and passive. Svetlana and the others in our tour office, they are great. Confident, capable, no madeup problems."

I drained the last dregs from my bowl of black tea and went outside to my yurt. The stars were materializing over the mountains, little grey chickens were clucking through the wet grass. I lay down on my felt mat and closed my eyes to the sound of raindrops hitting the soft roof, and soon floated downstream in a dream-sea of sweet mountain air.

In the Narin bazaar I managed to buy two cassettes of Russian music I'd heard snatches from, on the local radio. One was a collection of Slavic retro-cool tunes, with full accordion and echo-chamber in the style of Johnny Mathis, and the other, the unbelievably hot Anna Pugachev. From the first note she made the hair on your neck stick out. ("Pugachev? You never heard of Pugachev?" They looked at me as if I were a feral dog, attracted to the light of civilization.)

Farida and Slava sang along to each tune, the day was sunny and the road good, and we finally found a gas station that sold petrol for twenty-five cents a litre, supposedly eighty-five octane. We were headed east towards the caravan *serai*, the travellers' way-station that marked the beginning of the great Silk Road itself, after it exited the bleak hinterlands of China and spilled out on the plain, aiming haphazardly towards distant Persia. It was the Silk Road that gave nomad culture all its glamour and lucre, for command of a goodly section gave the local Khan his stipend, until Portuguese merchantmen found an alternative route around Africa in the sixteenth century, and the Asian animal caravan went into sharp decline thereafter.

"Would you like to see old fortifications? It's on the way."

"Old? How old?"

"We're not sure. Some say sixteenth century, some, Bronze Age. It's not excavated."

"You said exactly the same thing about the last place."

"No one knows anything much here. Perhaps you'd like to come and dig?"

"Give me a shovel."

It was maddening. Here were the two Kyrgyzstans; the women with bright-red dresses and kerchiefs and the men in their elf-hats lived in the first. With their high cheekbones and noble bearing, they were an attractive people, especially when they were out riding, and all the features of nomadic life became visible in a blur of romantic excess. How much was a good sheep fetching at the market? Three thousand sum, about seventy-five dollars. A good horse, twice as much or more.

But the past? The second Kyrgyzstan, a past that had once ruled and shaped us all? The Russian empire had faded to the point where all the schoolchildren were learning English now, and no one remembered anything.

"A few years ago they threw stones at our tour vehicles." Slava shook his head. "Now they wave and pose for pictures. They recognize that tourist dollars are their money."

The material remains of the Soviet regime were quickly reducing themselves to a few rusting iron sculptures set up on pillars at the local crossroads – eagles, ibexes, buxom mountain maidens. Garden ornaments, an amusement park of badly painted gnomes. This was how the Soviets had evidently conceived of this land, a kind of Disneyesque theme park, holiday camp for loyal apparatchiks, and the Kyrgyz people had largely left their souvenir baubles alone, left them standing without destruction or defacement, melting in the rain like old jam-cakes. Even the ubiquitous road portraits of Lenin had been subtly altered, as they now depicted the clean-shaven current president. History was fading fast, history was retreating quickly from the cities and the grip of its administrators, and those who needed its symbols and slogans would have to look elsewhere for their comfort.

We came to the battlement. A high, sandy wall enclosed a rectangle we paced out to about two hundred metres by three hundred metres. You could see where the old moat had been dug, and it was still filled with water from the spring's heavy rain. Serious natural bounty now filled its ditches. A million bees hovered over the mud foundations; perhaps they were responsible for diminishing its fatal grandeur in the first place. How many grains of sand did a single bee carry off to the hive-works in the distant hills, over its entire working life? There was your scientific formula: you could date these ruins by using statistical beeology.

"So who built this, and why?"

Shrugs all around. Even the bees were shrugging, millions of them. I looked up to the Pamir sun; no answers from it either. I took a few pictures. History plus honeybees equals the picturesque, a short and coyly brutal truth. Of course someone could dig it up, but how was such science going to change anything? Next year the weather would be different, the cattle fatter or leaner, their owners' lives better or harder, prayers to the ancestors answered or not. There was something more important lying at the bottom of their souls, and something more interesting for these people than mere history.

By mid-afternoon we had left the last of the big wheat farms far below us; we were once again ascending into the summer pastures of the upland plateaus, whose smooth green hills knew only herd animals and the occasional yurt, and were otherwise free of all imposition from the lower world. The green hills showed little inclination to become mountains either, for, apart from a few jagged ridges of broken granite teeth, they rounded themselves off nicely, a mild and easy parkland that stretched out forever in a trekker's delight of easy tramping and infinite sightlines. A singular world. The grass grew, the tiny horses ate it, as did even-tinier sheep; the laws of gravity suspended themselves so that the beasts could reach the richest fodder growing high on the perpendicular molars without tumbling off.

The goal of today's trip was what my guides called the *caravan serai*, a hotel for the traders using the Silk Route dating to the sixteenth century. It was thirty kilometres from the Chinese border, and it was said to contain a secret tunnel that ran directly under the mountains, ending at length in a stone belly in Turkestan into which a hoard of gold and other precious cargo had been deposited.

About five o'clock we turned off the main road and followed a dirt track that ended in a broken bridge. Slava told me the permanent disrepair of the bridge was used by guides to dissuade tourists from going farther, those who had no sense of the constraints that dictated travel in the mountains: "Oh, too bad. The bridge is down." The Torugart Pass awaited, the main land route from Kyrgyzstan into Chinese Turkestan, with a short window of opportunity that closed for stragglers and fools.

Without stopping the car, Slava plunged straight down into the river and proceeded to shoot across several shallow channels in great violent splashes before mounting the grassy bank on the other side. The valley we

came to was exceptionally well watered and lively. We were up around 3,500 metres, more than 10,000 feet, and the air was the purest I had breathed. A collection of yurts sat framed against the snow-capped range to the east. I half-expected an actor from *Lost Horizon* to come out and greet me by name, bidding me to enter the carpeted mystery within.

We parked the vehicle on the front lawn that ran on for miles, got out, and stared at the canyon walls that framed this valley. Under the walls a mile away sat the abandoned stone *caravan serai*, brooding on its place in history. Herd animals brayed and neighed around us. Despite their apparent familiarity with the place, I could see that my guides were just as awestruck. They grew silent. Slava giggled at the sight of a marmot slithering across the meadow.

"Look how fat his behind is."

We were all happy. There was nothing for us to do but drink warm bowls of milk offered by the yurt-camp owner, and stroll over the hills, to watch our lengthening shadows stretch themselves out after a long day. The dinner consisted of mutton dumplings and fried bread, then I was shown to my yurt, a sixty-two-stick yurt, as opposed to the ninety-two-stick yurt in which we had taken our common meal. The yurt's smoke-hole provides a satisfying light that changes constantly, rather like a campfire; it's a common element of North American teepees as well, and creates a different sort of consciousness than the window of a hut or cabin. Here, the central dome-eye, with its attendant stick-ends, must impress itself on the minds of nomadic people from the earliest age; that, and the shamanist free-floating shapes they stitch into their wool felt carpets, creates a mood that is inescapably mysterious and sky-connected. I felt I was at home in this sur-realistic circus, the suggestive and hypnotic symbols surrounding me emanated from Scythian times, and the wobbly abstractions of eagles and wolves easily insinuated themselves into the candid show of dancing shadows and candlelight. The oldest wool carpet in the world had been found in the region north of here, in the Pazyryk tomb-hoard, dating to the third century B.C., when the local Scythian horsemen were at the height of their powers, and showing what looked like large-nosed warriors atop their decorated steeds. These grasslands might have been the original homeland of the Indo-European people, whose early association with cattle-breeding is reflected in their diverse languages and their social structures. The colour-ful animated designs on the *shyrdaks*, the felt panels hanging in my tent, quieted down as soon as darkness fell, and I studied my breathing instead.

It was growing cold. I heaped a pile of sheepskins and cotton coverlets into a massive assembly, then tunnelled into it, after blowing out all but the last candle. The night grew so cold that, by ten o'clock, I was obliged to use my own sleeping bag as a kind of face blanket, and I decided to keep the Kyrgyz elf-hat that I'd finally bought for a couple of dollars on my head, where it so richly belonged.

When all was ready, I half-crawled out of the woolly mound and snuffed out the last candle. The darkness was profound. A horse snorted, close by. A cow passed gas. A dog barked. The tethered camel groaned. The women tittered in their Turkic tongue, still working away in the dark.

Then it began all over again, starting with the horse. Somewhere in this stereo production I joined in, with my own damp and tuneful snores.

Slava believes that, if you make yourself a belt of dog hair, it will cure your backache. Also, if you have an unaccountably bad feeling in the middle of the day, you should telephone all your relatives immediately, for one of them could be suddenly ailing or worse.

We are ambling over the alpine meadow, and, spotting another marmot, he regrets we did not bring bread.

"You should see them come out, nose first, big eyes. Terrified but greedy for this treasure." He laughs.

He tells me that, after a stint in the Soviet Army in Mongolia ("We sold our supplies for vodka and leather coats, but the customs police found them and burned everything"), he got a good job at Lake Issy-Kul, the biggest lake in Kyrgyzstan, in what he was told was a toy factory.

"Then we see this big thing like a bomb, and I say to myself, This is not a toy."

It was an atomic torpedo. The Soviets used the lake as a top-secret test site. Several complementary uranium mines, also top secret, had graced the neighbourhood. They began life in the 1960s, and everyone connected with them had been well paid, and now the sites were all ghost towns.

"I got work as a tailor. I work on my machine all day, very hard, in Bishkek. My wife gets mad at me, and tells me to go out."

"So you're divorced."

"No, I am successful. Since I was single, I had more time. I make résumé on computer, I get this job at the travel agency. After two or three months, my wife pray me to come back."

"Begs you?"

"Yes, begs. You see, before I was passive. I don't like to fight, to argue. Then she sees that I am okay guy, I don't need her to tell me what to do every day, to survive. It's okay."

"Does she work?"

"She breeds dogs. Big Caucasian dogs. The biggest." He shows me a scarred hand.

"They bit you?" The Caucasian dogs were giants of the canine world, as far as their tempers and teeth went anyway.

"Yes, unfortunately. I was the same with the dogs, as with the marriage. I do nothing at first when the biggest dog growls at me. Then he roars at me, and still I do nothing. Then he bites me. I must act, to save my life.

When they stand on their back legs they are as tall as me. I hit him with a metal bar. You can't be lazy with these animals; I learned you must punish them for nothing or they will try to conquer you, like certain people in former Soviet Union, the Chechens and so on."

"Why do you have such animals in the first place? It seems like a lot of work."

"For breeding. We have seven dogs, all very big. A good puppy brings in almost two hundred dollars."

"So the Chechens look for trouble?"

"Americans know nothing of these people. They are good as single people, as individuals, the best. But you put a whole group together, and they start fighting immediately, with themselves, or their neighbours. You don't know, do you, that they cut off the heads of the New Zealanders, and laid them on the road, after the government refused to pay ransom?"

"New Zealanders? When was this?"

"You see! Everyone from America never hears this story! It happened five years ago! They do it only for money. You must face such things, not hide from them or pretend it's okay. Because then it only gets worse."

Slava: a Russian who begins adulthood by selling off army property and unconcernedly building atomic weapons, first learning how to conquer the world's fiercest dogs and his marriage, then himself. Learns to stare down the slavering beasts of havoc and ruin, while sparing the tiniest of God's creatures without blinking.

Slava, who honks for birds and sidesteps the edelweiss.

Chapter 22

Lonely Penitent's *Guide to the*
World's Worst Trips

I should have flown to Kashgar, the provincial town of the Turkic Uighur people in Tien Shan, Chinese Turkestan. I would have saved myself hours of pesky officialdom, and a full day's worth of choking road dust, with nothing to look at but a slag heap of indifferently raw hillocks, rivers gone dry, the poorest mud houses this side of Bangladesh, and the back of my Chinese driver's scrawny neck, as he swallowed and wheezed, his Adam's apple bulging up and down like a bad set of truck shocks.

"Kyrgyzstan's primo trip" is how the guidebook hooked me into spending close to twelve hundred dollars on a road trip it warned readers would be "plagued with uncertainties . . . but absorbing and grandly beautiful." Flying would have cost me a third of that, and I might have seen something besides a concrete border gate that looked like the side entrance to a bankrupt suburban mall and an endless grey horizon lost even from itself. Up to this point, the book had been reasonably accurate, and on the whole provided useful advice. Here, however, five full pages devoted to this border crossing suggested something more moody than logistical planning behind all the spilled ink. An unexamined enthusiasm for noisy hobbling, a Houdini's zeal for escaping self-made shackles.

But that's today's travel guidebooks for you. They can make a fetish of discomfort and pointless aggravation, as if anyone is actually going to take the fifteen-cent bus from Geekapoo to Ugarama that only leaves on Thursdays, at three o'clock in the morning, from the signless petrol station with the broken air pump. A prideful call to the Elect, that's what many of these books are up to, at bottom, loudly shilling for a religious sentiment that should have become extinct with *The Scarlet Letter*. When what our touristic age really needs now is a new Nathaniel Hawthorne, to expose the spiritual hazards such dogmatic enthusiasm for public mortification always brings.

You're right: I've got nothing better to do than sit around and deconstruct my guidebook. I've sunk that low. Sitting here in my underwear and stale socks in my malfunctioning hotel room located down in this lower intestine of Asia, listening to the sand-filled wind howling outside. I am not a *real* traveller, no. The self-inflicted disciplines of the smugly real traveller, who must trek rather than hike, and who will wear those Velcro sports sandals through thorn bushes and icy blizzards alike, these announce a new Protestant ethic, just when you thought it was safe to go out and have some fun again.

"It's not for everyone," *Lonely Penitent* promises its eager acolytes about such bad trips. A New Zealand woman I met once, cycling by herself across the Rockies, complained bitterly to me about another highly lauded day-trip that proved to be eighty unwarranted kilometres long. The others at the hostel thought her a whinge, despite the fact she made the trip by midnight. And so they come (or at least buy into it) in droves. Cant for the creed.

What can I say? My day at the Torugart Pass began well enough, with a crystalline sky, a dry road, good all the way to the first Kyrgyz checkpoint. A bit of business, this. The officer who is examining my passport with the aid of a computer drops it on the counter and mumbles "Later" to me in Russian, although he has just processed six other people in about two minutes each.

It's the shift change, my luck. I stand in the little red box marked out on the grubby floor, afraid to move. A large lineup forms behind me, border-dwellers, women with dribbling babies, dark-faced trader-boys. Pashtuns mostly, up from Afghanistan. I am feeling vulnerable in my red outlined box at Counter Number One, but there is nothing to do but stand and wait. I try not to stroke my money-pouch, which is tied around my neck.

I am carrying a wad of U.S. cash, because they don't take anything here but Benjamins for the next two thousand kilometres. We had passed the first checkpoint an hour ago, sailing through; this high-security station is the one my guidebook, *Lonely Parmesan*, said would be the toughest, and the rest of them, no-brainers. The replacement officer comes, stamps, yells, tells me to go. I can't find our car. It's okay, the car is sitting in the customs garage, and from their looks it seems Farida and Slava have been searched as thoroughly as it has, but I don't dare ask. I am about to get in when another officer asks for my passport. He seems to be illiterate, asking Farida to tell him where I am from, despite the gold lettering on its cover. She tells him. We go.

This is not the real border. We soon get to the real border, a high stone arch set on a rocky promontory, with the Red Chinese star on top. The scenery has been nothing special, not for the last hour or so, as Slava has warned me. Hugs goodbye. I take my bags, as required by local law, and physically walk them across the dusty frontier under the eyes of two sturdy Chinese lads with machine guns and big green caps. My Chinese driver and guide are waiting patiently behind another designated line in the dust, an invisible-but-famous line in trekker circles. I turn and wave back at my Russian friends like a kid on his first day of school. They appear proud of me, and urge me onwards.

I get in the four-wheel-drive Toyota Land Cruiser and we're off.

Now the fiasco begins in earnest. For eighty kilometres down the pocky gravel road we see nothing but fiercely impassive rocks, severe washouts, bleak gravel slides, and yawning potholes. A large building rises out of the flying grit and baked alluvium. Chinese customs. Two fellows take my passport and disappear, reappear, and ask me to open my bags. I pull open the main zipper,

"No. All this ones," the officer demands testily.

He wants all the zippers opened by me personally, every one, and the bag pulled open, according to his demonstration. It's hot in the parking lot, the acrid dust blows freely around us.

"Ah!" His eyes seize on something tucked away.

They take my copy of last week's *Central Asia Times*.

"No newspapers!"

We're up around 3,500 metres. It feels like the sun is sitting only a mile over our heads.

Now he pulls out my *Lonely Pinhead* books, flipping through each one as if he's speedreading the damn thing. ("You can take the fifteen-cent bus from Geekapoo to Ugarama that only leaves on Thursdays, but remember it leaves by three o'clock in the morning, from the signless petrol station on Wallagooga Road. Look for the broken air pump.") It's clear that Chinese don't like books, at least not glossy imported ones with detailed maps. He tosses them back at me with contempt. We drive away finally, and I am relieved but sorry. I should have torn out that article in the *Central Asian Times* I wanted to save, but I had no warning they would be so paranoid. *The Lonely Paranoid* said nothing about this, for obvious reasons. ("*What* obvious reasons?" "*You* know.") Another half-hour of tortuous driving, now the road grime has turned positively filthy, and it's still a moonscape out there. I want to take a quick snap of this lunar perversity, but my guide barks at me.

"No stops permitted!"

"Oh. Sorry."

I forget her name. It is either Mrs. Loo or Mrs. Poo.

The driver is Mr. Kong or Mr. Wong. Silence.

I decide to make some light conversation, to while the hours away.

"So, Mrs. ? Are you married?"

"Yes. Husband."

"What work he do?"

"He, geography."

"Ah, geography! And children. You have child?"

"Gold, oil. Explore."

This is not going swimmingly well. I decide to go for the basics.

"Uighurs? We see Uighurs?"

"Not now. We see later."

I survey the dead landscape, struggling to find common ground.

Four days with these people.

I knew nothing of the local inhabitants, tribal Muslims ruled by Beijing. Try again.

"What language do Uighurs speak?"

"Uighur. They speak."

"Ah."

Okay, let's drop it down another notch.

"Mrs. ? What time is it now?"

"Ehh?"

"Time. O'clock?" I point to my wrist.

"Ah. Beijing time, almost six o'clock."

"Beijing time? What time is it *here*?"

"Here?" She looks at me as if I am a moron.

There *is* no here; we're in some kind of blasted bowl of gut-wrenching effluvium. *Lonely Plodder* calls it differently, of course. ("Kyrgyzstan's primo trip. It's not for everyone, sometimes cold, uncomfortable, plagued by uncertainties and not all that cheap, but . . .")

"Local time, local time!"

I raise my voice, tasting the crud of the road on my cracked lips, despite the sealed windows and the sputtering, tepid air conditioner. "*Kashgar* time!"

"Ah. Local time in Kashigar? Is almost four o'clock. Two-hour difference!"

I pull out my watch and realize it's the same as Kyrgyz time, except that somebody might have simply told me that, instead of me having to pull these teeth.

And what was this Kashigar? The same as Kashgar? Or another place, miles away?

"What's that?" A big white building with a red-tiled roof appeared on our right.

"Immigration. Chinese Republic.

"*Another* checkpoint?"

"We must wait. They rest now."

We stopped the truck at the gate and watched a guard fiddle with a child's school desk for twenty minutes, positioning it just perfectly on its concrete base. Then he waved us forward.

"That's it?" I was incredulous.

"No. We go in building. Take your bags."

I counted no less than six booths in a row to which I was required to take my passport; there may have been more. At the last two booths, a pretty and spoiled little girl of eight, obviously the daughter of some high official, snatched my passport out of the hands of Officer Number Five and ran it over to Officer Number Six. Then she pulled out a huge magnifying glass from the latter's drawer and examined me with it, while the two men did their best to grin delightedly at her theatrical antics. In the next room I filled out an "Entry Form," and presented it to the adjacent booth.

"What you?"

"Canadian."

"Nationality?"

"Canadian."

"Ah! Go there."

I went to the next booth.

"What you?"

Eventually they accepted my signed declaration that I had no STDs, coughs, mental diseases, or political literature, and stamped my passport.

"Now take bags here," Mrs. Woo pointed to a large X-ray machine.

That they had already rummaged through my bag at customs was of no concern. My things were immigrating too. Into the machine they went, and a deep male voice from the inner office shouted out,

"Books! You have books!"

I pulled out the *Lonely Pillory*s again, praying he would confiscate them so I could get my money back, and the officer immediately demanded if there was anything about China in them.

"No, just Central Asia."

I pulled my things together and shut the bag, and looked to the Toyota. Two more guards asked to see my passport before we made it to the exit door.

"Is that it?" I turned to Mrs. Woo, my face caked with dust and sweat.

"Border is big problem now," she shrugged.

We drove another half-hour through a bleak sandstorm; a grey film blanketed the truck. The only relief for the eyes was the occasional grove of transplanted saplings sitting morosely in the middle of each slag heap.

"Ah, see that tree?"

"Yes?" I raised my head hopefully.

"That is poplar!"

"I see."

"And this one? This is willow!"

"Very interesting."

"Would you like bread?"

She offered a dry-looking bagel that had seen better days. I had been travelling since eight-thirty that morning. It was now almost six.

"When do we get to Kashgar?"

"Less than one hour more."

"Is there water in hotel?"

The road grew steadily worse, a constant riff of construction detritus and scummy natural sand swirled around us. It was difficult to see the giant slug-holes in the road, for the crews had been excavating deep channels for water mains, and their random excavations were unmarked and innumerable. We passed cakey red-mud houses, each with its own plot of dust-coated poplar trees, while a steady stream of erratic motorcycles and wallowing fuel trucks competed for the one free track the road crews had left open to traffic. It was growing dark, miserably cold. Bleet of horns, constant wail of sirens. This administrative settlement was a cacophonic mess, a disjointed human overspill in the middle of nowhere, void of use or purpose.

"Okay, we stop here."

"*Another* checkpoint, Mrs. Woo?"

I was ready to bite her head off.

"Give me your passport, please."

We took our places in a queue in the middle of a mangy street, while the guards inside the hut took their sweet time spelling out the foreign letters in Chinese characters. I turned to the two young English businessmen behind me, cheerful fellows I had first noticed in the original border checkpoint, hours earlier.

"Long day, huh?"

"Oh, yeah."

"Is it worth it?"

"So far, no."

Mrs. Woo tapped me on the shoulder. We could go now.

Go where? I wanted to scream. Back to the rampant dust clouds and the bone-jarring root canals? With Mr. Goo or whatever his name was, exclaiming at each spine-crunching landing "Hawchh!" or "Heeoch!"

depending on its severity, and nothing to look at except tiny, desperate children holding up their tin platters of dusty apricots for sale, and tumble-down lean-tos filled with gritty watermelons? Was this environmental degradation, or incredible human pluck, this clinging to a sort of life in hell? I didn't know and, more, I didn't care. This was the place my parents warned me about, the alternative to eating my cauliflower and beets. I had been suckered in by the *Lonely Panderer*. But unlike the customers of the King and the Duke's soldout road show in *Huckleberry Finn*, who had paid good money to see the Duke romp around butt-naked on the creaky stage, and then refused to admit to their envious friends that they had been suckered, I was not going to wait a minute before I got out my rotten tomatoes.

This one's for you, Tony Wheeler . . . *WHOMP!*

The silver TV in the hotel room doesn't work; neither does the electric hair dryer, despite the pretensions to virtualized modernity stencilled in red on the walls: *E-mail: Neisd@163Net.* Nor do two of the three table lamps (yes, they are duly plugged in, and the bulbs work), and there is a heap of coarse gravel sitting on the bottom of the tub after each shower. The magnetic key-lock doubles as a room-switch to power all the lights, but the maid must first show me how to jam a piece of cardboard in the electric sleeve to get it to work. A triple-sized bed, two of everything, shower caps, apricot hand-soap in such tight shrinkwrap I must pick it off with tweezers. This is your standard ersatz luxury, the bleak elegance of the simple-minded, with all the coyness of a dollar-store bowl full of wax fruit. The tipoff is the toilet telephone. Who's going to call when you're on the pot, the Duke? It's the flip side of the above experience, the inherently egregious struggle to redeem oneself through the false economies of low-budget travel.

This suite is real travelling's direct complement, this pampering yourself; and in these silly little rooms we are pampered, relieved of any duty to stay upright so we can be fed a diet of room-service goodies and cabled erotica. You need never go out, why bother? Everything's at your apricot-cream-lotioned fingertips.

It's your due, this heedless splurging after our daily self-mortification. There you were, so self-disciplined, seeking a rough autonomy as instructed. You wanted to know the back roads, you wanted to be free of the mad touristic crush. You too don't like those "cellphone types," who provide our *Lonely Party* readers with their two minutes of sheep-headed Goldbergs; even though it is only through their efforts that the plane that brought us here landed in one piece. No, we're eco-snobs, and there's nothing horribly wrong with that, we're harmless enough (as long as there's still a platter of jumbo shrimps left on the all-you-can-eat buffet when you arrive, freshly showered and famished *from the field*). But such practice depends largely on self-delusion, the tightly held fantasy that, by creating these artificial problems of rural logistics and primitive transport and risky medical crises, you'll somehow learn to conquer our own, more deep-seated, problems. For the record, I've met a lot of people who have travelled a long time, who are dull as rug bricks, far more boring than the ones who stayed closer to home. But we're not talking about boring me (always an easy task). We're talking about the wasted possibilities in travelling.

What I've noticed is how personal issues get obscured by these fake catastrophes, the train schedules that change without warning, the meals that should have stayed on their plates instead of rattling around Albanian Air's floppy Piper Cub. Ask such a traveller what they have seen, thought, experienced, and it's inevitably a dull, nodding moan, punctuated by a reference to some recent cataclysm involving American Express or their ten-pound Nikons. But don't take too long, for such people are always looking over their shoulder at something that is determined to pursue them all across Asia, something that won't be dissuaded by this vain creed of petty martyrdom urged on them by their guidebooks.

There was more to say on the subject, but the power in my three-star hotel suddenly went out. I eased over and flopped across the bare acre of king-sized mattress, feeling around for its metal frame like a man blinded by technology, wishing I was back in my yurt with no hard edges. Where you always came back to where you started, to a friendly lullaby of sighing beasts.

Chapter 23

Welcome to Kashgar City, Big Noses

When Mrs. Woo told me to meet her at nine-thirty in the morning at the hotel lobby, of course she meant Beijing time. She even pulled out her watch from her smart little bag to show me the obviousness of it all.

"So sorry," I said, rubbing my eyes.

It was just after 7:30, the sky was overcast with grey muck, and it was impossible to judge the hour from the birds. I picked at my breakfast of scrambled eggs, steamed buns, a cakey bread, and various unpleasantly orange pickled dishes. The non-view outside the café belonged to Kashgar, still a busy local trading centre two thousand years after it began as an oasis on the route from China to the West. But what did it trade now, with the Silk Route gone forever?

"Where are we going today?"

"Id Kah Mosque. Abakh Tomb. Traditional Minority Handicraft Factory."

"Right."

Mosque, tomb, handicrafts, the triptych of acceptable tribal Muslim folk-culture, with officially still-communist China running the show over the local Uighurs, rather than the ex-Soviet party bosses who had performed the same function over the border. These Uighurs, who have lived here since Turkic tribes began moving out of southern Siberia in the fifth century A.D., are nowhere in evidence in the hotel, despite their population of seven million in Xinjiang Province.

Even the short drive along the main road, a busy strip of Chinese commercial offices and high-tech outlets punctuated by a large iron Mao festooned with red-and-green pennants, revealed the essentially schizo-phrenic nature of this last Western outpost of the Chinese empire.

Here, against the backdrop of a new virtual Great Wall consisting of glitzy neon lights and cellphone links, one could see the last remnants of the Uighur civilization. Hand-crafted wooden houses and crumbling outbuildings were roofed with woven crooked sticks, a sore donkey or mule stood tied to a pole, skull-capped men walked with ornate sticks. The disparity between the Chinese in their smart new cars and motorbikes, and the Uighurs with their pushcarts, showed the local culture's essential estrangement from our modern imagination. There was no connection; the two worlds merely overlapped and fought for space, the technical one apparently stronger, or at least far noisier and more colourful. The low open doorways of the Uighur dwellings afforded glimpses of ancient carpets and rough-hewn benches, with no artificial lighting. The Uighurs pushed their solitary handcarts filled with straw or brass cooking pots, the Chinese drove smoked-windowed cars or rode bicycles in large platoons, wheeling in unison around obstacles. If they rode at all, the Uighurs seemed to favour the solitary motorcycle, equivalent of the footloose horse. Some of their women rode motorbikes too – through heavy traffic, the wind whipping away at their headscarves.

We passed the odd woman hiding her face behind a face cloth, but for the most part the minority people looked remarkably urbane, especially the young. The teenaged boys dressed like British street thugs, the girls might have dropped in from Palermo or Lisbon. There was far more genetic diversity than in neighbouring Kyrgyzstan too, with large noses, hazel eyes, and creamy complexions in evidence. These were Turks who had turned east in the sixth century A.D., but they could have passed for contemporary residents of Istanbul, despite fifteen hundred years of total separation. But this was not Anatolia, this was Xinjiang – "bow, land, field, border," in the Chinese. Why did they come here and stay in such an arid territory?

Perhaps life here was better then. The *China Times*, the official English-language paper, reported today that desertification continued to plague the country, growing at a rate of 8 per cent per year. Another story described an aerial attack on locusts that were gobbling up some northern province. But then why had the Han, the Yellow Valley Chinese, come, and far more recently too? I asked Mrs. Woo about the smart Chinese ladies we saw walking in the streets, bareheaded, carrying bright parasols for the sun.

"Han girl make good wife," she informed me. "Han man make good husband. Not like Uighur man."

"Why, what's the difference?"

"Han man help with child, do cleaning also. Kitchen. Uighur man not do these things. Even Uighur woman like to marry Han man."

"Really?"

"Yes." She closed her eyes and opened them. "But Han man not like to marry Uighur woman."

"Why not?"

"Because of religion. Religion is big problem. Cause fight. Me, I don't like religion, any religion, but especially I don't like Muslim."

"Why not?" I repeated stupidly.

"Because you see how they sleep at the mosque all day? Pray five times, never work? When they are sick they never go to doctor, they pray for God to help them. That is why they are poor." She shook her head violently.

"They have many children also?"

"They have to. Minority people."

This is what I had read, so I went on to ask her how many children she had.

"One."

"Would you have more?"

"Not allowed. Chinese can have only one children. What is law in your country?"

I blinked, flushed with shame. I had forgotten their famous law.

She had said minority people can have *two*.

"As many as we want," I answered carefully. "But most people have two, or none at all. So it comes to the same thing as here, almost. Birth rate is declining."

We strolled through the old town, an organic jumble of warm brown mud walls concealing courtyards from which tiny children peered out. Women in bright scarves looked up to catch a good glimpse of Mrs. Woo's hot-pink pantsuit and strapless chunky sandals.

Mrs. Woo has a short blunt-cut, professionally coloured. Her lipstick is the colour of good port, and she wears a polished stone bracelet of the same burnt red on her left wrist. These two competing standards of beauty, co-ordinated style and rural floridity, hold no dialogue here. The Uighur women are neither coy nor reserved; they regard us with direct interest, despite the fussiness of their costumes. The older woman are handsome, and the younger, poetic-dreamy. I watch a Uighur woman in a long dark-red dress with gold flecks sprinkled over it, bantering with the pot-sellers sitting on their little stools. She good-naturedly demolishes one, and then the other, with her sharp street wit, throwing back her shoulders in public triumph. A hearty physicality is their strong suit.

The Chinese women play at a much higher register than this. Ultra-sopranos, each has her own tuning fork, a not-so-deep place within them where they get all giddy, and volatile.

"Big problem in China, inland China," Mrs. Woo says abruptly. "Is marriage breakup. Reason is always the same."

"Money?"

"No, no. Money is okay. Each year get better. One or other finds some-body else."

"Ah."

"You have this in America too?"

"No. Big problem is, nobody finds anybody in America. All lost."

"You make joke." She grins at me.

I can see the tip of her pink tongue.

"Almost true," I protest.

"You funny man."

"I hope so."

But then she surprises me. Are all Chinese women full of surprises? We pass an outdoor café, a clutch of wooden tables, lamb turning on a spit, Uighur music pouring from loudspeakers.

"Hear that? Uighur music *very* strong." She demonstrates, beating out the rhythm with her hand. In time too.

"You like Uighur music?" I stop in my tracks.

"Yes, I like traditional music very much. I know some songs."

"Sing it for me," I prod, hoping for another show of her saucy tongue. But Mrs. Woo says okay, and begins to sing as we walk through the dusty, urine-rank streets, past creaky mule-carts and staggering, overloaded porters. Two full verses, pitch perfect to my ears. A nomad song with sudden shifts in metre and chord changes, it's a perfect lotus of music, fully realized and unbearably sweet.

I clap my hands, and she bows and says, "I would like to sing another one."

Now everything is forgotten, now the tawdriness of these grim alleys disappears in an instant. Only this song is darker, with strange counter rhythms that plunge us into a mood of tranquil sonority, heightened by staccato bursts, each coloured differently. I am entranced.

"That was Tajik song," she announces.

"When did you learn them? As a child?"

"No. Last year. I like learning foreign languages. Minority songs."

"Do you think you will stay in Kashgar?" A person like her, full of icy fire? How long would it continue to arouse her eclectic interests? I got the answer I expected.

"Big problem. My father goes Inland, to Shan-Tung Province. I don't think he comes back. He wants me to come too. Better for baby, but my husband disagree. No jobs for him, not easy to find. Must start again. But I think, is worth all this trouble."

"Mrs. Woo, tell me this: the sand that these street cleaners keep sweeping away, all day long. Is it getting worse?" I was thinking about the *China Times* article and that dreadful trip through the Torugart Pass, which between the two sets of drivers had cost me, I hated to admit, about the same as an entire week at a Club Med.

"Yes, every year worse. More dirty."

"Really?"

She raised her chin, nodding assent, and stared at me with woeful eyes, eyes finally stilled for a second or two.

The hotel porter brought my laundry at nine in the evening, and I am elated. I lie on the bed, draping my shirts one by one over my face, transported by the scent of simple starch and the clean lines of perfectly folded boxers. Their innocent fragrance recalls my childhood, when I was eight years old, passing Lee's Hand Laundry every day on my way home from Dewson Public School. Starched shirts are my madeleines. Forget about jade snuffboxes and Lao-Tse; let's acknowledge that these people helped build the railways that created our country in the first place, while feeding it properly and keeping us crisp from Elliott Lake to the Van. They introduced the idea of the exotic to us; without them we would still be scratching our armpits and sniffing over bowls of lumpy oatmeal. I can forgive the Chinese almost anything. If they are not clever enough to tackle the blight of desertification, God help us all.

The first rule of travel writing is that you don't give the game away. The second requires you to break the first. It demands, too, that you master a special code of artful camouflage, which will render even the most pointless travel excursion into something fit for public consumption. Some examples:

"A good base from which to explore . . ." i.e., worthless.

"In former days the seat of a forgotten dynasty . . ." i.e., worthless.

"The tomb, now largely reconstructed . . ." i.e., worthless.

And my personal favourite, the ultimate conundrum: "If you go early enough, before the tourists arrive, you will get a glimmer of the glory that was once . . ."

Of course you are a tourist, and not even a special kind. Oh, you can write (one hopes), but you could just as easily be doing this business scribbling about fashion shows or primary-school street gangs, and the cost and wear of travel is as taxing on you as it is on the other fellow in the next room, a traveller who doesn't need to start working at 10 p.m. every night There, he's already stopped kicking the wall in time to the White Snake playing on his Walkman and gone on to an untroubled sleep, while I am left still watching the green-and-red neon sign that has turned my room into a livid aquarium, an underwater set in which I am the luckless diver, sitting on my flashing coral seabed. Staring at my notepad.

So why do it? It seems to me that there are two compelling prospects travelling inevitably brings forth, something that hanging out with six-foot teenagers with high-definition cheekbones or J-Boy and his crew will never deliver, no matter how crisp one's insights into their social influence. Between the highs and the inevitable lows of travel (which taken together create an emotional pH factor that is slightly alkaline) lie great chunks of dead time. Their obduracy forces one to meditate – or to *brood*, as my mother called it.

The second factor is the opportunity to meet people, great characters; and while many of my fellow travellers will always prove shockingly dull, a few will be found who know what day it is – and, more, who can eat the local food without making faces.

Yes, the truth is, there is no relationship between distances travelled and intelligence gleaned. Today I visited the famed Kashgar market, in former days the site of a vast horse-and-cow bazaar, now largely relocated, and owing to my guide's insistence that she eat a hearty late breakfast before we departed, I was unable to get there before the tourists arrived. Two jolly Englishmen, with red cheeks and identical pork-pie hats and tummies full of good stout, hailed me from across the sea of steaming animal droppings. They were the ones I had last met at the Immigration Station a few days before.

"So what have you guys been up to? Anything special?"

"We just got these fantastic haircuts!" Tweedle crowed, lifting his hat to show me.

"I got them to throw in a shave and beard-trim for the price!" Twaddle added, thrilled.

"How much?"

"Forty yuan! For everything!"

Five dollars.

"You negotiated a joint haircut?"

"Aha! You've *got* to see this place. A whole street of barbers!"

"What else have you guys been doing?"

"The beer's good!"

"Yeah, the beer's great!"

"That big green bottle that they always bring you?"

"Yeah, I think so."

"I think so."

All around us the donkey carts charged up the hill and down the hill, bulls bellowed. Sheep muttered and refused to budge, tied together like furry fish on a string. Their owner was jerked forward and almost fell over, as they all pulled back, suddenly in unison. Herd animals, right? A black bull, a few minutes away from his own end, seizes one last opportunity and jumps on a passing heifer, almost ripping off the truck fender he's tied to, in the final great lunge. A few massive thrusts, a bellow of triumph; and they manage to pull him off, winded and spent, shuddering, and he looks to me with his great loopy, yellow eyes, as if to say, "God, what a day!"

You see?

Nine-thirty on a Sunday morning, and already I've found someone interesting.

The price of watermelon is dropping to unprecedented lows, according to the *China Times*. Because of "oversupply and trade from other regions," the wholesale price has gone from 3.2 yuan a kilo to 1.2 yuan, which is good news for me, because at 15 cents a kilo I can eat as much as I want in the restaurants Mrs. Woo insists on taking me to – this whether I am hungry or not.

"Why are those big men eating whole tomatoes?" I point to the table beside us. They are all crouching over their big red field tomatoes, like grizzly bars devouring a plate of dripping heads. It's something ritualistic, sociological, but Mrs. Woo scarcely glances at them.

"You notice everything, yes?"

"I notice you change your lipstick today."

"You are right!" She laughs.

"Yesterday it was darker, like your bracelet. Today, it is more pink."

"Aieee! You notice too much!"

"You won't tell me why they eat whole tomatoes like apples?"

"Maybe one man does this, and rest follow. Like sheep we saw at Sunday Market. Poor sheep."

"Poor sheep?"

"I ask one man, please don't hurt sheep. It makes me feel so bad to go to animal market always. Human beings so bad. They kill everything, eat everything."

I looked down at our lunchtime spread. Fish with fan mushrooms, tofu and chicken in red pepper sauce, egg and tomato omelette, salted dry beef slices; the only thing that had no animal products in it was the watermelon. Mrs. Woo, of course, was eating everything, as I was, but picking, while I was already enjoying the watermelon and waiting for her to finish.

"Yes, well, maybe the sheep goes up in next life, and sheep-beater goes down."

"Heh?"

She studies me over her chopsticks, pinching an assortment of plucked goodies.

"Karmic Wheel. Buddha."

"Ah! . . . Humans very bad. Even eat each other."

"That's the answer to the big world-problem. We must eat other people. You know, Mrs. Woo, you look really delicious . . ."

"Aieee!" She begins to laugh uncontrollably.

The big bear-men at the next table pause in their culinary havoc.

"Your arm, Mrs. Woo. Just one bite, please. Very small."

"Go away! Leave my arm . . . *alone!*" She gasps.

"Okay." I pick up a slice of watermelon instead.

And slowly bite into it, still looking bug-eyed at her arm.

"You know," she says, regaining her composure and speaking seriously, "my mother told me when I was little girl. In the old days, people were very poor. Had money, yes, but nothing to buy. No food. So they ate their own children. They did this thing in more than one province. Terrible."

"Old days? When was this?"

"Let me think." She looks to the left corner of her mind. "In 1962, I think."

"1962! They ate people in China in 1962?"

"Oh, yes. They were *very* hungry."

This story twigged my memory. I'd heard something like it earlier, in Ukraine or Russia? Maybe both. Dana had said something in Kiev, so had Lena in Moscow.

"In the last war? In Russia? The children would disappear one day, and the neighbours would ask, 'Where's little Ivan?' And the mother would point to some bones sticking out of the soup pot and say, 'He'll be ready in fifteen minutes.'"

"Brrr." Mrs. Woo shook herself; despite the beautiful clear day and a pleasant lunch under a thatched patio, and eight generous dishes of food, she was still shuddering with the late tremors of a huge aftershock that had broken half the world asunder before she was born.

The sign outside the busy Semen Restaurant & Bar in Kashgar says, WELCOME TO OUR RESTAURANT, BIG NOSES. It takes me a moment to decode this. I know of the common epithet *gai-lau*, pale ghosts; but really, this is the pot calling the kettle black.

The *Semen* Restaurant?

Chapter 24

The House of Stones and Earth

The night train from Kashgar to Urumchi in the eastern part of Xinjiang Province is half-empty on this Monday evening in late July. I have a soft-sleeper, the lower bunk of four, furnished with pinkish satin coverlets and hand-stitched linens, giving my cabin an uncanny resemblance to a funeral parlour dressed in full-service frippery. Either that, or I am over-tired and imaging it, lying comatose here on my stiff bier. Every Chinese who sticks his head into my death-bower has the same calculating look, a young Bela Lugosi on the prowl for fresh, throbbing life.

In a word, I'm spooked. Maybe it's the grifting deserts outside the streaked windows, the unloveliest deserts in the world, the foul end-product of a satanic mill running amok, determined to stifle the world under a blanket of dead ash and cinders. Turkestan is what the world will look like after we're finished with it. Drained of all resources, a pulverized nothing.

Or maybe it's the spirits lurking out there, zombies who don't like these straight steel tracks China Rail has laid out, cutting through their ancestral wastelands. Perhaps it's the vibes I got from Li-Po, a thirty-year-old guy who told me he was an unemployed machinist, in idiomatic English too good for his story to be true.

But first let me describe the Chinese train. I have a first-class seat; the compartment is about seven feet square, and the two bunks above me are unused. This is lucky, because I would have no place to put my bag otherwise, as it will not fit under the narrow bunk. My sole companion is an arthritic senior army officer with comically back-combed hair. The hair appears to be dyed as well. He's probably the only Chinese with this dual problem. What does he call his monthly treatment? Surely not Grecian Formula.

A number of other uniforms parade back and forth in the train's narrow corridors. Large young Chinese ladies in faded rose outfits are the most conspicuous. They greeted us at the start of our journey wrapped in festive crimson sashes with gold lettering, too many characters to simply announce the itinerary. They must have been spouting an exhortatory verse: "On Ribbons of Steel and Harmonious Travelling We Will All Arrive Safely in Our Nation's Glorious Future." Then there are the lean men in grey wool, with black caps and colour photo-badges. Another chap has a pinstriped uniform, a few other women wear pale-green serge and fore-shortened cowboy hats of loden green. What they variously do for the state's security, I cannot imagine. Only the pink ladies make eye contact. The greys might be rail-guards heading for their stations, since we passed a sentry at the mouth of an extended tunnel dressed in similar fashion. Highly militarized anyways, this hinterland.

Of the civilian passengers, less than a quarter are local Uighurs. Urbanized Han Chinese make up the bulk, smartly dressed and confident. They play cards, sit on the pull-down stools by the corridor windows, and read prodigiously. On the whole, they are quiet, civil. Many do isotonic exercises against the door frames in the morning. Others fiddle endlessly with their cellphones.

A tall, lean Chinese woman is reading a paperback out in the corridor, the only free seat is next to her. The book's in English, *Prayer and Fasting: The New Way* to something or other. Sixteen hours to go. The sand dunes are full of grit and broken clay. Do I chance it?

"So, is it working for you?" I ask.

"Sometimes." She looks up with intense eyes. Yes, she's fasting all right. Or at least removing herself as far as possible from this profane world and its oversweet nectars.

She tells me she is from Taiwan, that she and her female friend are now travelling to northern Xing-Shen after visiting the western region. They're ordinary tourists too.

"You find it different from Taiwan?"

"The people here are – how can I say this? – they seem to have bad thoughts." She looks around the passageway. "I don't know who to trust, if anybody."

She studied in an American university for three years; she says the Taiwanese are "traditional," and rich; they speak a more classic Mandarin than the mainland because the island, formerly known as Formosa, was the final redoubt of high-level Nationalist army and professional families. Families like hers. So it surprises me when she launches into classic evangelical Christian agitprop a few minutes into our conversation, killing it at once.

"Have you ever wondered what plans God has for you?"

"All the time," I answer unhesitatingly.

"If you read the Bible every day, and open your heart to Jesus, then you will find your answer."

"Do you read the Bible every day?"

I could go or stay at this point; but I plan to stick with it, take her seriously, get to the bottom of this one-sided delivery. There's no one else on the train to talk to either.

"Yes, Psalms. Song of Songs. Very beautiful."

"Now, let me ask you this. When you read the Bible, is it the stories that give you the message, or the poetry? Which is greater?"

Always the professional, I seek ways to improve my craft, and she resists, of course. I am but another species of Snake. More subtle than most, perhaps, but still writhing away in the old flesh-pot.

"It's the Word of God, speaking to me directly, telling me I am important, precious to him. This is what is so different from Asian religion."

"Asian religion?"

"Buddhism! They believe if you are bad, in the next life you will be animal."

"Or a hungry ghost."

That one always bothered me more. That big belly, the tiny mouth.

"But I have a soul. I'm unique. I'm not a dog." She was getting agitated.

"One Asian theologian, he wrote a book, *Water Buffalo Wisdom*. He said Buddhism was cool, but Christianity was hot, engaged, committed. Direct action."

"Buddhism tries to copy Christianity now. They give money for relief, they hold services like Christians too. But they collect money for rituals, from the people. And these rituals don't mean anything. They are empty."

"I thought that was the point . . . ," I began, but then she was called away by her friend, and left. Her book and glasses sat on the little table.

A fellow who was standing nonchalantly a dozen paces away immediately came forward and took her seat, moving her things off to one side. He was dressed in the classic casual summer business attire, a soft golf shirt, khaki chinos, good leather belt and requisite enamelled designer buckle, with the chrome sports watch, cellphone, and pager all providing points of distinction.

"I speak bad English," he breathed, smiling apologetically. "Can write, not speak."

He drew some imaginary letters on the table.

"Yes, yes." I nodded agreeably.

"Where you from, country?"

"Canada."

"Ah, Canada! Eric Lindros! Hockey!"

"Yes."

"Also, Wayne Gretzky!"

"Old, but great!"

"Very rich, ah!"

He contemplated me through his square-framed glasses with spastic joy.

"Big spaces! Open sky! So much trees! Céline Dion! Alanis Morissette! Bry-an Adams!"

"Ah, yes, Céline. Well, I don't know her personally, but —"

"Toronto, Edmonton, Ker-gerry." He rhymed off all the cities in the country, in rapid order, no hesitation. I said I was from Toronto. Some impulse made me ask what he did for a living.

"Ah. Machine." His voice suddenly became hesitant and awkward again.

"Machine?"

"Machin*ist*."

"I see. What company do you work for?" I smiled, ever the affable tourist.

"Oh, no job."

"No job?"

"No."

"Too bad," I nodded.

"I see you before," he changed the subject.

The bad feeling I was getting suddenly shot up a hundred degrees.

"Really?"

"Yes. In Kashgar. With a woman. Who was this woman?"

"That was no woman, that was my wife" was, of course, what I wanted to say. But he was now pressing hard, staring at me through his thick glasses, no time for jokes.

"The tour guide, of course," I said blandly.

"Ah." I could see his mind retract, recalibrate, go on to the next item.

"So how you like Kashgar? Very interesting, yes? Uighur people you like?"

"I don't see any. I ate good Chinese food, sleep. I am tired from my trip. I an writing book. Hard job." I smile apologetically.

"Book?" His eyes got wide. Over his shoulder I could see the Taiwanese woman frown. She picked up her glasses and self-help tract and left with a curt nod.

"She your friend?"

"No, I don't know her." I replied evenly. "I am writing a book about Genghis Khan."

"Uh?"

This took about ten minutes to communicate, as I knew it would. No one I had met in China, no matter how effective their English, could quite grasp this concept. It didn't matter how I pronounced his name, how many dates around 1240 I threw in, or whether I tossed the horse-warriors, Kublai Khan, and Mongolia into the pot. When they eventually did, they always said something like,

"Oh yes. Big King who unite ancient China and Europe."

This was how they viewed him, the Great Uniter of the Peoples, and if not purely Chinese, at least a kind of first cousin in whose successes the whole family could share.

"Writer? Huh. And you know Lai-Chang Xin? He live in *your* city!"

"No, who is he?"

"Fugitive from Chinese justice! He take millions in oil imports, no pay customs."

"Oh, I see. Never heard of him."

"Canadian government protect him! Why?"

He was furious now.

"I'm not sure. What did you say his name was again?"

"They say we *shoot* him. They do not shoot criminals *in Canada*!"

"Sorry, never heard of him."

After a few more side questions about my book, he left abruptly, as I knew he would. Was he a plainclothes police officer? Almost certainly. It was not just his inept play-acting, the way his poor English quickly evaporated as soon as he got rolling with his interrogations, or that he was an expert on the soft pop culture of my country, an old interrogator's trick that marked him as the trained professional. (What unemployed thirty-two-year-old Chinese machinist knew who Alanis Morissette was, or cared?) No, it was the predatory way he stared at my watch when I checked the time, forgetting for a brief moment that he was still in the role, and giving me a brief glimpse of the bully-boy in the backroom, the guy with the club who can do what he wants with his victim.

"What did this man want?"

The tall Taiwanese lady had returned, and looked after him.

"What I was doing here, everything. I think he was police."

"Really? He followed you on the train?"

"No, I think he just takes the opportunity to check on me. Why is there evil in the world?" I wanted to go back to our original conversation, find out why a Buddhist would become a born-again Christian.

"God let Satan have dominion over the earth," she answered simply, no thought at all.

"And bad spirits? They dwell here?"

"Everywhere, but especially in places where the people lose their values. If you accept Christ, he comes in and they flee. God will still be God after the world ends. You choose to be with Him in His House, or no place." She looked out at the intractable wasteland of gravel and dust, the broken distances of this old act of uncreation. The Apocalypse, from Car Fifteen.

I stared out moodily with her. An afterthought.

"What's your name?"

"Bee."

"Bee?"

"Bea ... Beatrice."

Her eyes were overlarge, luminous in the fading twilight. She had never heard of Dante, or *The Divine Comedy*. Nor did she have any interest in hearing about them

Her religion was much younger, and far more ancient, than all that.

"Where are we now?" The train lurched to a halt, and wheezed.

"Somewhere in Asia," my neighbour grimaced, looking out the grubby window. "And not the best part."

It appeared that Beatrice didn't like the western part of China. Or maybe she felt that she did not belong here. In the morning light the endless gravel pit outside was even more awful than at sunset, when the shadows at least covered its baked barrenness with a cloak of decency. This serial waste was once the initial leg of the Silk Route, the world's major commercial thoroughfare for a millennium. The only explanation for its existence was that the climate was a lot better here only a few hundred years ago.

The Chinese character for the word *gui-bi* signifies a house containing stones, built on earth. Thus, the house of stones and earth. Guibi, or Gobi as we call it, is not, strictly speaking, a proper name at all, but a kind of desert, which the Chinese distinguish from true desert, *som-mu*, the sand desert. I was not sure where this Gobi desert began or ended, but its cheerless vacancy began to attack me in my soul, and I retreated to my bunk and watched my cabin-mate, the three-star Chinese general, do his exercises to relieve what was obviously a bad case of rheumatoid arthritis.

I checked into the modern high-rise hotel in Urumchi, the capital of Chinese Turkestan, and left on my own to wander the city of two million, happy to be in urban civilization again for the first time since I left home.

Unlike Kiev or Moscow, this city felt real. Good food too, the best in Asia. A ferocious meal of hot chili lamb-skewers, cold garlicky pressed duck, a bowl of noodles as fat as your forefinger, a quart bottle of Tsingtao beer. The always-inventive Chinese have taken the possibilities of modern advertising to its logical limits; huge four-colour banners fall shimmering like open waterfalls from ten-storey buildings, streamlined buses are splashed in neon rainbows promoting nail creams and cellphones. A fantastic spectacle, this new Chinatown of the virtual age.

I went to sleep early, content, enjoying the kaleidoscope view of a busy city from my sixteenth-floor window, rising from the freely orbiting cranes and their brilliant scaffolds. The phone rang.

Amazingly, it was for me.

"You like massage, sir?" A female voice inquired.

"Uh, no." I hung up.

Did I just pass up an opportunity for a good story? Not to worry. The bed phone rang a total of twenty-eight times over the next two hours, in case I changed my mind. Finally I pulled the jack out.

I tried to imagine what she would look like, through the security peephole, whether she spoke any English, how clumsy or sublime our encounter could be. The phone rang again. What was this? The toilet phone? I had forgotten about it. I found the jack and pulled it out.

Now where was I?

Ah yes:

> So she came into my room, struggling to overcome a pair of tight white jeans and stacked high heels that could not disguise a certain graceless concavity to the calf, a girl from the provinces for whom I was this evening's big-nosed quarry. Perhaps her biggest nose yet.

Possibly as a reward for my sterling behaviour, I was visited by an erotic phantasm that same night. I cannot tell you her name because things proceeded very quickly from her unannounced arrival to a stunning finish, but she was definitely not Chinese. A pure brilliant blonde, perhaps the very same Nordic succubus whom those abject e-mail swains from Holland and Italy had been pursuing, all over Central Asia.

After the Lillith left me, I found myself in a group of thirty men with blackened faces, Vimy Ridge sappers or something. We had survived the Great War, and we were singing "Auld Lang Syne" to the tune of Handel's "Hallelujah Chorus," while laughing with tears of joyous deliverance and wretched sorrow for our lost comrades. The relief was visceral. Somewhere during the night I had passed a deep, psychological boundary marker.

Chapter 25

The Yellow King's Kids

Another day and night of languid train travel. We are heading east towards Beijing, following the south bank of the flood plain of the Yellow River, mother of Han civilization and original home of Wang-Tu, the Yellow King of myth and legend. This is the king who started the Chinese dynasties off, his reign lost in the mists of 2700 B.C., and credited with the invention of government and Taoism. The Yellow River got its name from the yellow sand that has charged its turbid raging waters with brass from prehistory to the present day. It's raining, and the river looks frightfully happy.

We have just left Lanzhou, China's heavy-industry city. On all sides are the pointy-cone mountains made famous by Chinese landscape art, mountains that cannot be found anywhere else in the world. It is remarkable how one assumes these painterly traditions are based on a formal artistic convention (the olive light of Tuscany, the massed skies of Constable), when it's just a regional reality, poking its snout out of the canvas. These misty gorges, this raging dragon-river, those irrepressible gnomic peaks, it's an enclosed dream-world twisting off into smoky geography. This is the well-spring of the Chinese imagination, not the other way around. The flood plain broadens after a few more river bends into narrow vegetable farms.

Carefully worked terraces of orange soil, strangely empty of people, are topped with an astonishingly blue patchwork of cold winter cabbages and acid-bright garlic. Even the plots of summer corn are elemental, gleaming like new metal in the preternatural northern river-light.

My eyes can't help themselves after the Gobi, they feast madly on the rows of giant radishes and broccoli. I stand by the windows of the train's passage-way, greedy for all the steamy green mist I can get – and the life it brings. I'll take it all, mystery, senses, renewal. I have been in a desert of one kind or another since I left home, months ago. Too long. But that's behind me now.

I've made myself a little nest in the upper bunk. It's comfortable; the Chinese train is easy. The other three beds are occupied by two men and a woman who play cards and generally ignore me, which turns out to be a good thing, because within a minute of stepping out into the corridor I am sur-rounded by cheerful people, eager to try their newly minted English on me.

They usually encourage the little kids to go first.

"Hello. My name is Chin-Chan Tan. I am in middle school. What is your name?"

"Lar-ree!"

"Ah!"

Delighted with the success of this preliminary exchange, the boy turns to his older companions for advice as to the next step. A brisk colloquy.

Hurry! Someone else may grab the foreigner! Ah, right.

"And *where* are you going?"

"To Beijing. And where are *you* going?"

"To Beijing also! And what is the purpose of your journey?"

"Secret police business. I am a spy." None of this registers, of course, so I say in a loud voice for everyone to hear, "Tourist holiday!"

"Ah, tourist." More consultation. Now this will go one of two ways. The speaker will either ask me to help him read his English lessons, which are printed on plastic reference cards, or he will ask to touch my nose. It's the latter this morning.

I bend down, perhaps growling like a bear when contact is made. This generally produces great hilarity, so I can leave now, clutching my bottle of sweet green tea and retire to my cosy aerie without further ado.

◆

We are slurping on slices of yellow melon, which my cabin-mates have supplied from an inexhaustible wooden crate full of fresh produce – little grapes and local watermelons, purple plums too. I am not slurping as loudly as they are, so I am probably enjoying it all marginally less. Still, it's a heavenly carcass that drips its myriad juices on the floor, and as we approach the outer precincts of the capital, I am thinking about the central government's one-child policy, now well beyond its twentieth year. This program, called the Planned Generation, began officially in the mid-1970s, but it was not strictly enforced for another decade. Anyone born after 1981 is likely to be an only child, and this social experiment is unparalleled in history – and it has unforeseen consequences both for China and the world. It's a future of sole children, no sibling rivalry, only friends. Unambiguous, this mono-kid culture.

And strange.

At the dining car this evening, a young girl said hello and promptly sat down beside me. No shyness here. I assumed she was fifteen at most, but I have made this same mistake before; teenagers in China look and act like eleven-year-olds. Polite, prepubescent, proper. She too looks like a kid, this Jennie. (It's her English name, which they are always free to choose for themselves and which they must think about first, as we might if we had to choose Chinese names for ourselves. I'd be Hung Fat.) Well, baby-faced Jennie is twenty.

"You look so young!"

"I am in university specializing in English."

"I'll apologize, but in my country, girls who are twenty wear makeup and have three or four earrings. In each ear, and at least one tattoo."

"Oh, I do not like these things!"

She speaks like a petulant ten-year-old, but without artifice. Is that the phrase I am looking for? Or is it without carnality? Maybe self-awareness?

"So, Jennie, you are an only child, yes? Are you lonely for this reason? Do you have many friends?"

"Yes, sometimes I am very lonely. But I have a lot of friends, many. I *would* like to have a foreign friend, but I don't."

"Am I the first foreigner you have ever talked to?"

"No, the third."

"Number Three, too bad."

I make a mock face of despair. She laughs.

Outside the dining car, the golden light pours in a riotous flood through a break in the showy green mountains. Fir trees cover the slopes with shivery opulence, the clatter in the restaurant car becomes deafening. The waiters hoist aloft jangly platters of wonton soup, winter melon and pork, beef and coriander, curried eggplant. Dishes bang about like mad at the next bend, sheer fell swoops of cutlery. Everyone is exceedingly happy. Good food, and Beijing in the morning!

"Who was your first?"

"He was Australian student. Young."

"Ah! The Australians are very strong."

"Not this one. He was tall, but . . . skinny."

"Skinny? I see. And did you like him very much?"

"No, not so very much. We did not become friends. So I must keep looking."

She wants me to write out my name, so I give her my business card. The card excites great interest, or least its reverse blank side does, which they seem to find more fascinating than its arty logos. Some would say they are spoiled, self-indulgent, even asocial. One kid whammed me on the back, hard as hell. I turned, and it was plain from his face that he was delighted to see me, but he had only the emotional dexterity of a toddler to express it. Now this first generation has reached adulthood.

One of the other kids, who may be fifteen but also looks ten, has dedicated a song to me on the train's interior broadcasting system. It's "Casablanca," by an English pop singer. He asks me if I like it. I look to his parents. They who have endured so much now stand silently and listen attentively a few feet away, careful not to intrude on his big moment. Their only child is conversing with a foreigner in a language they will never master. A whole parental generation has suddenly and voluntarily become immigrants in their own land, and in that distance of a few feet a huge and terrifying chasm makes itself visible, bigger and more permanent than anything we have traversed before. And the children, their brave children, now walk forward into this future, on their own, one step at a time.

One child! Only one child! A whole family's heart and soul, in one child! The child is everything, all the past, their sole chance for the future. What *not* to give this child? What pains not to be spared, to ensure this child has everything, the best possible chance?

And he or she is not merely the hope of the parents. For I have trouble deciding who they are, the parents, as the young ones run freely from compartment to compartment, having lengthy conversations with strangers who indulge them, who regard them with avuncular fondness and even pride. They are taller, more confident, from a steady diet of decent food and daily praise: a new Chinese nation in the making.

Beijing was always a military and administrative centre. It began as a garrison town for the Yan, a forgotten dynasty, who used it in the fourth century A.D. to launch punitive attacks against the skirmishing northern nomads. The worst of these were the Khitans, a Mongolian people who eventually rose to regional power in A.D. 950. Eventually the Khitan horsemen breached the Great Wall and made it their own capital under the name Janjing, the Swallow City. By 1215 the Khitan's nomadic rivals, the Jurchen from Manchuria, were calling it Zhongdu, Central Capital, just long enough for Genghis Khan to conquer them and make it his stepping stone for a concerted attack on the settled Han states to the south. It was from here that Genghis's grandson, Kublai Khan, ruled all of China when Marco Polo – supposedly – travelled through Asia in the 1270s.

Today, like many days in midsummer, Beijing is clouded over, but the clouds have no definition whatsoever. We're in the middle of a flat plain that acts like an expressway for the dust storms of the Gobi Desert. Beijing, like Moscow, is essentially a political entity whose fortunes grow and shrink with its leadership's abilities. It is less a city than an instrument of strategic necessity. Successive ring-roads, broad avenues, a subway system, even a shadow-city composed of a network of bomb shelters – forty-six kilometres' worth of passageways and all completely underground – mirror the land-use planning of the ex-Soviet capital. A fifth ring-road is to be completed for the 2008 Olympics, along with other massive transformations that will demonstrate the power of the government to implement history.

While all states and most citizens have experienced war, the critical distinction between the real urban centres such as Istanbul and Rome and these administrative war centres depends on the proximity of a threatening frontier. The cities of the West are primarily riverine and organic, depending for their growth on the fortunes of trade and manufacture. Perhaps Belgrade, which faced the Turks, and Madrid and Castile in Spain, which confronted the advancing Moors, had something of this militant Asian dedication. In North America, the frontier retreated on the ground, and capitals such as Washington and Ottawa now straddle their cultural fault-lines (Mason-Dixon, French Canada). Our only equivalent to Beijing and Moscow is the rarefied secret city of the Strategic Air Command and its successor programs (wherever these might lie hidden), networks whose power also derives from its near-invisibility and continuous self-transformation. The walls will be breached, over time.

Even in Beijing, the evidence of immigrant Muslims is noticeable. There are men strolling about the streets in their distinctive white skull-caps, and restaurants serving "Muslim" dishes, that is, seasoned lamb, no pork. Not only are ethnic Han encouraged to settle in Tien Shan, Chinese Turkestan but, according to my businessman friend Gui from the train, there are no official barriers to Muslims seeking work here in the Interior. This policy encourages their dispersal and dilution. The real perceived threat – this also according to my recent acquaintances on the train – is not another nomadic society, but World Islam. And this too is not a new threat, for Chinese Emperors had been seeking a strategic western border since the eighth century B.C., and finally reached it when they were repulsed by an Arab army at the Battle of Talas in A.D. 751. This Muslim world (a gross oversimplification, of course) has never been so beleaguered as now. The Russians consider Uzbekistan's southern border to be their border, and today supply Kyrgyzstan with troops to help flush out the Tajik rebels and their drug-dealer financiers, while the Chinese have poured billions into ensuring the Muslims' marginalization and containment across the whole of their western flank.

"Why don't you ask me the question all the Westerners ask me?" Gui demanded. "Ask me if the Uighurs want to be free, to have their own republic!"

"Okay. I ask," I responded, not sure where this was going. We were still on the train, the last hour before the central station. He was getting overwrought. Already Gui had excited the interest of the Rail Security, as the men in the charcoal-grey uniforms and checkerboard caps finally proved to be. They made him sit by their laptop computers in the dining car while they ran a thorough check on his papers. Not to keep him away from me, the contagious Westerner, no. To ensure my security as a foreigner against the schemes of this possible felon. But Gui checked out okay, so they left us alone to continue our seditious talk.

"If I tell you the truth, my government considers it treason! I go to jail for so long, I forget my name!"

He may have been right, the Chinese government went to extraordinary lengths to depict its authority as benign and progressive. A front-page photo in the *China Daily* showed a half-dozen new graduates of Lhasa, the capital of Tibet Autonomous Region. These were the first locally educated students with master's degrees in Tibetan language and history, but the caption neglected to mention what was so evident from the photo.

All the graduates were Chinese.

Chapter 26

Nocturnal Brightness: The Gods of Cloud, Rain, Wind, and Thunder

The distinction between nomad and settled peoples may be entirely specious. I am wandering around Beijing's ritual precincts, in the company of two twenty-one-year-old art students who have attached themselves to me in order to practise their entirely adequate English and sell me some watercolour pictures. The Forbidden City, Tiananmen Square, the Temple of Heaven. After three years of university here in the capital, Annie and Kelly are knowledgeable and even opinionated, loudly preferring above all the extensive gardens of ginkgo and cedar around the dark-blue vaulted domes of the Temple of Heaven, where the cool breezes run down the corridors of thousand-year-old trees, and twisted faces hide in the black bark, watching us pass.

A legion of animal grotesques smirks and grins and howls from every corner of these ancient grounds. Bulgy-eyed dragons cling to the rooftops, stone cows (or maybe they're dogs) sit tight in their granite pens, little copper stag-deer prance on the waterspouts. A great comic elephant seems to be farting huzzahs. Great Imperial lions play with a stone globe in their paws like a soccer ball.

"Oh, I like this dragon!" I reach for my camera, following the deep lines carved from the eyes down to the slack tail, where the etchings dribble off like the uppermost reaches of a mountain stream. You can see at a glance from this beastly largesse who the Emperor really was, dressed in his forty pounds of silk and gold robes: the Great Conjuror, Lord Protector of the Mystic Flesh, Conductor of the Celestial Train of Heaven, Witness to the High Animal Zodiac, and Summons Server to the Nocturnal Brightness and the Gods of Cloud, Wind, Rain, and Thunder. The whole place is wriggly with creatures born of a Han imagination that was always restless, effervescent, and endlessly fertile.

"That's not a dragon." Kelly shakes her head.

"Oh? What is it then?"

"Some other kind of creature. A dragon is very specific in Chinese culture."

She studies the sculpture critically, and behind her I can see another thousand creatures painted on the gables, housed within the temples and sub-temples – phoenixes, birds of heaven, bulls, serpents – all inviting the same degree of study, scholarship, connoisseurship. It pulverizes the individual ego, this stuff, attacks it like a fever-dream. We have our Proust, Joyce, and Tolstoy. Three fat, torturous novels, and perhaps the prolific Greek culture, for our milestones (or millstones). But what do you need to dip below the surface of Chinese culture? Twenty years of intense application? And then what?

The art students show me their work in a second-floor studio off Tiananmen Square, telling me it's their first public exhibition. Anna has done four large ink brushworks on the theme of Bamboo: *Bamboo in Morning Dew*, *Bamboo Growing Stout*, *Bamboo and Old Rock*, and *Bamboo in Wind*.

"See how the bamboo resists the wind?" Kelly explains. "How it clings to life, no matter how strong the breeze?"

For a moment I can actually see the wind, which of course is the real personality in the work. It's achingly beautiful, and she's twenty-one.

It's the ineffable, the subject of all Chinese art. I can feel the gravity of the Middle Kingdom pulling me in deep like a stray dog, see myself twenty years from now, tugging at my wispy grey beard, clumping up the stairs in wooden clogs to a tiny flat on Dhung Phut Street, a flat crammed with purloined scrolls and rice-paper scraps of intelligence, the neighbourhood kids calling out, "Hey! Master Big Nose!" My fingers gnarled and stained with ink, mumbling to myself over the arcana of the day's researches, dribbling black tea down my stained, ancient shirt (or, in my excitement at the discovery of a novel dedicatory jade-poem, drinking ink straight from the pot without noticing). The shirt that once proudly said Eddie Bauer, and now sports a complex blotch which from a certain distance looks like a Feng-Shui Winged Leopard of the Ninth Dynasty, Second Grade. That's connoisseurship. Worse than opium, this addiction. The centre of Middle of the Universe (as the Chinese traditionally refer to their country) – the Forbidden Palace, original vacation home of Genghis Khan – is only about four miles away from my hotel room, where I sit, writing this as midnight approaches. The table tilts away, the floor bends easterly while I watch. Everything is sliding off in the direction of the Ninety-Nine-Knobbed Door of Heaven.

But we resist, don't we? Snarl like pale ghost-dogs as the silken loop of Civilization grazes our necks. The West began with a wild experiment,

the Renaissance, a big pair of scissors that said let's start all over again. Cut the cord. Oh, we pretend to look back to the Greeks, they were always our excuse for this love of a bright clean future, their statues stripped naked of their original paint and furnished with the fig leaf of conjecture. Does size really matter? Should Mao be criticized for attempting the same thing with his Cultural Revolution?

The three of us go to a restaurant by Tiananmen Square. Schezuan. Anna is dieting, she barely pokes at her plate. Kelly, the skinny one, is happy when I tell her that I hate wasting food, that the two of us must eat up every scrap.

"My parents suffered like all Chinese in the Great Leap Forward, 1958 to 1961. No food anywhere. Bad times, it began with bad relationship with Russia. Almost had big war."

"That's interesting. America almost had big war with Russia too, in 1961. The world almost ended in 1961: we had to hide under our desks. I was a small boy in school, waiting for the atom bomb to drop."

The students are amazed by this story, and shake their heads in wonder. I am suddenly convinced that we had a very narrow escape in those years. Something big was afoot, a cloud that later settled down into the happy, wild 1960s and 1970s, but for a while there, we were on the brink. The Missile Crisis had wider implications than little Cuba, a worldwide tectonic shudder and scary as hell, in retrospect. Let's hope this panic was caused by only a few drunken four-star generals, emboldened by their success with Sputnik and taking it as a sign from Karl, and not some natural epiphenomenon that springs spontaneously from the disturbed soil of mechanized agriculture. Or, in China's case, the retribution of earth's jealous gods, who never got proper propitiation in those terrible years.

After lunch we visit the Museum of Chinese History off Tiananmen Square. I am keen to see the new exhibit on Inner Mongolia, and I am not disappointed. Fantastic pieces have been perfectly preserved by the dry sub-Gobi climate, and their sophistication reveals that the Khitan, the nomadic people who founded the Liao Dynasty around A.D. 1000, and their successors, the Jurchen, were something more than pastoral tres-passers, forever on the chase for Chinese loot. They had their own stuff too, distinctive and just as impressive as the Han Chinese.

Among the recently excavated new finds were an elaborate cast-bronze wine-cooler, weighing at least 250 pounds (i.e., not portable); a bodysuit of a thousand grey jade tiles tied together with gold wire, including a special jade box for the prince's genitals; a razor-sharp, nine-hundred-year-old sword without a trace of rust, forged from a special alloy yet to be analyzed; and oversized bronze masks with the big noses of Venetian festival masques. Is this where our Punch and Judy originated? With the Jurchen nomads? Were Pinocchio's wanderings a late version of some Gobi tribe's moral tale? (Become a man, or become a horse.) These "nomads" had a civilization, as did the Manchus in the northeast who eventually replaced the Mongols, to create the longest of all the Chinese foreign dynasties, the Qing.

So where are their cities today? Crushed in the dust of a billion hooves. Even the Mongols had their cities; Karakorum, a site in the south of modern Mongolia today, was one such, until it was destroyed by vengeful Qing armies in the 1600s. The archaeological evidence is compelling that Mongols began as agriculturists, and then developed a herding culture fairly late in the historical day, which might explain their taboos against eating greens and fish, and digging up the soil: to prevent cultural backsliding. According to my friend Victor Ostapchuk, the nomadic specialist, effective pastoralism is one of those all-or-nothing activities, a path requiring absolute commitment once undertaken. Even Genghis Khan could not rule at his ease after taking northern China in 1215; he was obliged to remain in a *ger*-tent erected adjacent to the great stone-and-brick palaces of Beijing. Nomads had to be ready to *move*, not defend. It was not that the nomads failed to understand cities. It was that they thought they had something infinitely superior, a new Eurasian dynamic they had learned to harness, and which carried them everywhere like the wind, a continental force that even Genghis could ride but not resist.

At the Starbucks on Gond Ti Avenue, an American Peace Corps volunteer corrects my impression that the Chinese concern with foreigners' big noses is xenophobic fancy.

"No, they consider big noses quite beautiful!" Beth Kramer laughs and takes a happy hit of her black Daily Blend. "When I'm working, they always tell me, 'Oh, you're so lucky to have such a beautiful big nose.'"

"Well, if your nose is beautiful, then mine is truly gorgeous," I respond.

Beth is twenty-four, with ash-blonde hair and perfect dairy skin, an American dream-girl. She's in China setting up an environmental-awareness program in Shantung, where they found the legions of marching clay-soldiers. She's from a small town in Nebraska. (Heart be still.)

"It's a lot of work, and we only had a few weeks to learn everything. Sometimes it's really frustrating, but I like it overall, and I'm not ready to go back to reality yet."

My voracious eyes take in her every detail. Beth has sewn a collection of fancy buttons on to her canvas bag – in a pretty pattern, she's patient, and handy. Creative too. The bag kills me, never mind her green eyes. I reflect on how stupid the guys probably still are, around her age, and how stupid I was at that age. Now she's telling me about the kids in her provincial village. The halo over her head gets brighter. Guiltily, I try to remember what my own wife looks like.

It's not so much that I forget her face. What I really miss are the convoluted and highly ornamented rhapsodies of our domestic controversies, some of which are so inventive they can go on for three days. Just like the lush fertility rituals of the Purple Court, now that I think about it.

PART THREE

White

Life as a Horse

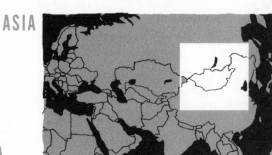

ASIA

MONGOLIA, CHINA & RUSSIA

RUSSIA

Novosibrirsk

Irkutsk

Lake Baikal

Kazakhstan

ULAN BATOR

Karakorum

MONGOLIA

Urumchi

GOBI DESERT

Great Wall

BEIJING

Lop Nur

East
China
Sea

Yellow River

CHINA

Chapter 27

Midnight Border Crossing

S ix o'clock, two more hours to the Mongolian border.

Doesn't that sound romantic? Edgy? A real Cold War–thriller line? Right out of *The Manchurian Candidate*? Let's say it again, le Carré fans. Six o'clock, two more hours to the Mexican border. No, no, no! I got it wrong that time.

Let me have another go at it! Please!

Mongolian border, *Mongo-li-an!* And their money is Tauregs or some damn thing, not pesos. A million to the George W. dollar, so with a 60-per-cent inflation rate, there will be even more of the little paper crawlers tomorrow.

The train is strangely quiet; I can't figure out why. It's shabby, a creaky grandfather to the Beijing trains. There must be forty or more foreigners here tonight, mostly Australian women who have come off a long year teaching bad English to the Japanese, judging from their pasty expressions and general incoherence. It's the largest number of foreigners I've seen in one place in Central Asia. But the Chinese passengers who constitute the remaining 80 per cent keep invisible, sticking close to their compartments, leaving the corridors empty. They go to the washroom with their heads down, as if they are being shipped off to labour camps. Maybe they are, for

why else would they be going to Ulan Bator except to trade whatever it is they've got in those big cardboard boxes of theirs? One fellow tried to store his stock in my empty first-class cabin (not sumptuous unless you are a sheep, which I am starting to smell like from a thick residue of old mutton dinners, a smell that clings to the faded Depression-era upholstery).

"What you have got? Guns, drugs?" I took the offensive.

"No, no!" He backs away. The lady conductor, whom I saw getting a gratuity from the man's female associate earlier, smiles at me hopefully, but I am in no mood to be accommodating.

The last time I did this, I glibly talked a customs officer out of inspecting the bag of two teenage girls coming back to my hometown from a Jamaican holiday, who almost certainly had weed in their purses. Seven years for importing, strict liability.

The rain that has followed us since the Great Wall in Senchun has let up, and a fat rainbow struts its stuff on the eastern horizon and refuses to let me take its picture, mysteriously disappearing into grey mist each time I zoom in on it. I put my camera down, and there it is again, grinning like a psychedelic Cheshire Cat. *Gone*, baby! We're still in China, but you wouldn't know it; the evening sun slants down on a gentle, undulating plain, criss-crossed with rabid little brown rivulets. Chocolate waterfalls mark the edges of succinct cliffs, the grass is unseasonably wet and juicy for

July. Herds of white sheep, a hundred or more at a whack, spill out of the loose groves of poplar trees for the sake of artistic contrast. Their owners stand about like road signs in the middle distance, too far away for me to say exactly who they might be.

And in the distance, or rather, *in the distance* of the distance, are the little sub-groups of conventional landscape decoration: low rim of dark hills, *standard*; stony tooth ridges, *optional*; rocks, multiple scale, *take your pick*. I believe this matte, cropped sludge is classified as desert steppe; or it would be if the weather stayed true to norm and didn't suddenly reverse itself after long centuries of simple desiccation. The sheep look unseasonably smug and, as their pasture does not remind me of anything, I must rely on their good judgment. It appears our rail line drops to a single track in places. What happens in case of derailment on the solo stretch? There are a few roads, meandering nowhere, and suddenly no trees. The most interesting thing, apart from the sheep, is the sky, filled on this Saturday evening with clouds that graze the seamless blue. Big brothers to the herds below.

What else can I tell you about? My soup? My soup at dinner was awful, inedible, some horrible peanut oil floating on top. Five yuan, I could have bought a cold Coke for that. Okay, the soup story wasn't so interesting. You're right. But neither am I, right now.

Oh look, a horse.

Teeny-weeny, in that distance again.

Distance distance distance.

The big-headed kind the Mongols used to ride.

Probably a direct descendant, a roan with a black mane.

Real sand now pokes out of the ground, long spurts and piles. Beady little sparkles flash from the passing terrain. This was a sea-basin sixty million years ago. The evidence of a great pounding oceanic surf is everywhere, rippled beds of red till and gritty pancake-pools. A trucking road follows the rail track a mile to the east, and a line of medium-sized vehicles heads south, dutifully keeping a quarter-mile between themselves. A dry seabed, as I said. That was then, this now. Space, empty. Space is one thing these people have lots of, space.

And beyond that, more space.

◇

It's Saturday night, but it sure doesn't feel like it. More like Sunday in Heaven, with everyone off playing golf, no roughs, and the holes-in-one a hundred miles apart. Little bouquets of white sheep, tails swap their butts, the superior cloud works court each other with the amatory nuzzles of old lovers. On the whole I'd rather be at home, reading this book and sipping a freshly brewed cappuccino, than writing it up in this sticky little compartment, with Chinese customs officers in a variety of pastel uniforms asking after my nationality for the third and fourth time.

Say, you wouldn't mind trading places with me for a few hours, would you? You would? Really? Great! Here, you just sit right here, right on this comfy brown velveteen bench. Don't mind the odour, it grows on you. There's still a half-cup of sweet tea on the table; I'll just nip off for a bit, maybe pop into your kitchen, root through your fridge. If you don't mind…

All right, if you get bored, there's a book in the bag.

War and Peace. Go ahead, Miroslava is trying to marry off the Prince.

I'll be back in a few hours.

Ah, that's better, I'm back. And how did you make out?

No! Really?

What? You sat in the customs shed for more than three hours? That's disgraceful! And this was only the Chinese side? The Magnolian was even worse? How terrible! And the train kept jerking back and forth, you were thrown onto the floor, and didn't get any sleep until 3:00 a.m. ?

I know, I know, but they plan it that way! An old Soviet trick, these midnight checkpoints. The train deliberately pulls in at midnight so they can hold the upper hand. Psychological, right? While you sit there in your underwear, powerless as they bark at you with their hysterical gutterisms. I know, it's not a real language at all. It's comes from the noise ox-cart's make, mixed with canary chirps. Most of it doesn't mean anything.

Me? Great. Sorry about drinking your last few bottles of Mexican beer, but I had to wash down that cold roast beef with something. Your wife? What about her? That red mark on her neck? What can I say, you really ought to pay more attention to her, she's still got a few good miles left on her, you know … Oh, don't be like that, we traded places, remember? It's just a *hickey*, for God's sake! My good man, it's not the end of the world! And remember, we're in Genghis Khan territory now. Recall what he said: "The best thing in life is to take another man's horse, and embrace his women." I'm just going with the flow here, except you don't have a horse, do you? So I took your car instead.

What's this? You've made some comments in my notebook?

Not comments?

You've been *writing*?

Wait a minute, let me see that notebook.

> It feels like a confessional tonight. The large Magnolian lady, chief officer in the black cap and high heels, stands over me and watches for signs of moral weakness as I point out my little bags, for what else could I be bringing to this empty land that would survive its immaterial power? Already the world shrinks away and disappears, only the bare texts of its boundaries remains.
> Earth, sky, a half-moon. And our two breaths: mine, laboured, rough, as I struggle with the bags; and hers – even, controlled, and smelling authoritatively of raw garlic.

You bastard! What the hell do you think you're doing?

I'm writing this book, *me*! You go back to your comfortable La-Z-Boy!

Yes, get out of here right now! Out! Now!

And it's Mongolia, not Magnolia, you, you . . . *tourist*, you!

That's it! *Good*bye.

Can you believe it?

"The bare texts of its boundaries."

The nerve!

Chapter 28

The Bare Text of Its Boundaries

There's a hawk or a falcon sitting on every second telephone pole outside the train, sometimes two birds to a pole. I've counted fifty raptors in less than six minutes of *clacketing* along, how many more are strung on these lines spanning infinity? Are there that many voles and mice in this green year? No, its the vagary of the landscape. No trees. The birds of prey have no other place to perch. The choice otherwise is to hunch down in the short grass or fly. So where do they nest in this treeless savannah?

A family of black-headed cranes pokes through a wet patch from this morning's downpour, the two young ones running ahead, as eager for the kill as their stooping parents. Another hawk with a great hooked bill, white chevrons on its mushroom-toned body, watches them with great interest. A little falcon, all spotty and dusted over with dry mustard powder, dive-bombs the insects stirred up by our passage.

We are running three hours late; Ulan Bator is still three hours away, a retreating mirage. The perfection of these peaceful hills and absolute clarity of the air mocks us with the unyielding distance yet to be travelled.

In the next cabin the two-year-old boy is getting restless. His mother has promised him, in a variety of languages, that he will soon see his grandparents. They have run out of food for him; it's been over thirty hours now. The mother maintains the city-style of a gangly Asian teenager: bare midriff, pop-group teeny-top, and skin-tight pink jeans. She keeps dishing up little spats with her sleepy husband, a swarthy European who repeatedly locks the cabin door on her, intentionally or not. I figure he's Italian or something, for last night he kept calling his son to look at *la luna* in the high-pitched whine of the failing marriage-partner.

It's during one of these lockouts that I begin speaking to her, and she tells me in decent English that she is Mongolian, age twenty-five, and her husband is a Latino, from Guatemala.

Her name is Saruul.

"Guatemala? And Mongolia? How did you meet? A raft in the middle of the Atlantic?"

"No, worse. At a party. I thought he was handsome then –"

At this point, hearing her speak English to another man, the husband slides the door open and peers out into the train corridor.

"But that was then, before we married. Is it two years later?" she sighs. "Yes, exactly two years later." Her eyes flash. "He works in America, L.A. So we commute."

"Commute where?"

"To Mongolia. I have a job here, managing my father's company. The flight is twelve, thirteen hours. But my job is seasonal."

"What do you do?"

"I manage my father's slaughterhouse. Last year we processed three thousand horses and six thousand cattle, and we have a hog farm as well. Meat for Russia."

"So what job does your husband do in America?"

"Oh, he has just a regular job," she tightens her lips. "Nothing special."

Now she glanced at him as if to say, Go away, you're bothering me; and surprisingly he took the little boy and strolled off down the car without another word.

"I'm not happy these days," she admitted. "Maybe 50 per cent of the time. When I'm working, I'm okay."

She looked more than ready to tell me how bad her marriage was, in great detail, but I could already picture their crappy walk-up apartment in East L.A., a black velvet Ricky Martin swaying his hips over the easy-credit sofabed, and cats screeching over the garbage cans every night, to the punctuation of random gunshots when the local clubs let out at 4 a.m.

No, it was more politic to stick to business and steer away from another episode of *My Dud Spouse.*

"So you don't sell any meat to China?"

"Nobody sells anything to China, you must buy their product or nothing. I couldn't even bring my Japanese fax-copier for my business in transit through China; I had to send it around through Moscow to get it into my country. They still have communism, so they have central planning, export controls, no real markets."

She was talking like a seasoned World Bank executive. I could see why her father put her in charge of the company.

"So what is the relationship of Mongolia to Russia and China?"

"Hamburger," she replied instantly. "Between two super-power buns. Well at least one, Russia I'm not so sure of. They take six months to pay, for canned horsemeat! But we have to sell to them. We can't get health clearance for the European Union market yet."

"So, Saruul, what do you feel about Mongolia's history?"

"The worst thing that happened to us was the Manchus, spreading their Buddhism."

"Why? In my country Buddhism is considered cool, you know. Trendy."

"I know that. It's the same in the States," she snapped. But she was not mad at me. "The Chinese encouraged it, to make us quiet and obedient. It was entirely political, this religion. Our true religion was and will always be Shamanism. That's who we are, really."

She looked defiantly at the passing scene outside.

"In the history of the West, some people say exactly the same thing. That Christian Statism was used by the kings around A.D. 1000 to control the people."

"We are only three million now. Once we ruled the world." Her eyes lit up. Her little boy was racing down the corridor towards her, a solid, independent little fellow, who now tried to climb the train windows on his own, to peer out at the rushing territory of his ancestors.

"What's his name?" I wanted to know for the record.

"Daniel," she smiled proudly. "He's an American citizen."

A cluster of runty Mongolian horses cropped at the edge of the next little way-station we passed. The boy spotted them and cried out to them, a greeting in some language only he and the horses appeared to understand.

Ulan Bator proves to be a collection of rancid four-storey apartment buildings; a few neo-Baroque edifices – mainly a cheesecake Opera House and the former Communist Party headquarters; and packs of Mongolian teenagers roaming the streets in Korean knockoffs of Gap and Reebok. Punk-lite, with tattoos displaying the curious, culturally indigenous *soyombo*, the composite symbol of Mongolian nationhood dating to the fourteenth century. It's an arrowhead under a rectangle under a yin-yang symbol under another rectangle and arrowhead under a crescent moon under a solar disk – all surmounted by a three-tongued flame. My guide, Amarbayar, son of the late Tsendbayar, has only one name, like all

Mongolians. He's twenty-five, a history graduate of Ulan Bator University, who will be heading off to study in London in the fall. Maybe, when I return in five years, he'll be a deputy minister or something. If you saw him in the street, you'd think he was a tall Korean, except darker, handsome after the manner of the film actor Fat-Young. Our driver, Byambaa, is what one thinks of as Mongolian (if one thinks of it at all) – short legs, walks like a sailor, burnt brown, with a permanent squint from a life spent in the continent's shadeless outdoors. I pointed out to them that the lunar crescent and solar disk in the *soyombo* were symbols of an ancient pagan cult extending as far west as Yemen and Ethiopia.

"Yes, well. There are three periods in Mongolian history," Amar begins, dutifully translating for the driver's friend, Batjargal the engineer, another man who is eager to tell me what the real story is, never mind the foreigner's guidebooks and his antic theories of cultural transmission. Batjargal wanted me to know this, the correct story:

"In the first period we Mongolians were tall and strong. We knew who we were, and we were proud. A great people, with handsome men and beautiful women.

"In the second period, we lost our blood. We grew short, no longer a good-looking people. We mixed our blood with foreigners from all over. We became poor.

"In the third period, our time today, we are searching for new ideas. We have many educated young people, and everything is changing quickly. Now, no young person wants to live in the countryside, or be a herdsmen any more."

I asked them what these periods meant exactly. A Mongolian version of The Fall in three acts? Or an actual State-mandated dogma? Neither, it seemed.

"The second period began in the 1950s, and ended in the late 1970s," Batjargal replied carefully. "Our worst time."

The three men turned as one, to see if I understood this dissertation. They were talking about the postwar Russian immigration to their country. These Slavs were the uninvited foreigners who had diluted their pure blood.

"What does Batjargal do for a living?" I asked Amar. The engineer was born in the 1950s, and graduated from Irkutsk Polytechnical in Siberia, and his career spanned this hapless period. I could see from his clothes that, despite his education, he was facing rough times.

"Drives truck, sometimes."

Some hours later we were obliged to pick up groceries in a Korean-owned department store, in anticipation of our three-day trip to Karakorum, the home of Genghis Khan and the current site of a large Buddhist monastery. Not many food stores on the way. I was stocking up on water and soft drinks, for the trip would take us to the uncertain edge of the Gobi Desert. The daily temperature was already hitting thirty-five degrees Celsius, and we were travelling in a place where you were ostentatiously on your own, as the local infrastructure famously supported snakes and lizards and perfectly preserved dinosaur bones, not casual visitors. Half my main pack was now loaded with drinkable liquids, and a big jar of German dill pickles. While not Russian, they at least promised a late-night vinegary treat to rinse the day's dust from my mouth. I remarked to Amar that the cashiers in this store were all tall and shapely.

"Oh, I think they're normal," he replied.

"Normal? What's normal?" I kidded him.

"See that one, over there? She's Japanese. Not so tall? And look how she walks, her legs are short. How do you say, like a bow?"

"Bow-legged?"

"Yes," He suddenly became agreeable in the possession of this handy word. "Bow-legged. But our Mongolian women are tall, with straight legs. Not bow-legged."

So there you have it, the answer to the original two-centimetre question, as posed in Ukraine by Dr. Arkadi Ovarcharenko some months ago. It was a Japanese trait, this bandy-legged business; and if not Japanese, it emanated from the east of wherever this discussion of racial integrity was taking place. Can three million people do the job of running a country the size of France?

Not without identifying who they are, first.

Chapter 29

Karakorum

After a night at the *ger* camp just outside Ulan Bator – this a kind of enclosed, suburban resort village, consisting of a dozen or so big round tents with real wooden beds, electrically powered, filled with secretive, cloistered Japanese tour groups, a confetti sprinkle of hale, trekky Europeans, and a shrill coterie of hard-drinking Australian schoolteachers straight off the Beijing train. These last, in my considered opinion (as an international roué of long standing), might consider dropping that third Pyrex tumbler of Genghis Khan Extra Smooth Vodka for an extra long run out on the steppe, instead. There's a certain muttonish desperation to their dogged determination to "party" far past the age of thirty, especially in front of twenty or so other campers of diverse nationalities, who will undoubtedly remember the lonely blue besotted flag long after they've forgotten the sodden red faces. For people who teach conversational English, their conversational skills are abysmal. ("What'ja call this tent-thingy again? A gurt?") They're embarrassing to be around. I would try to go elsewhere, but our camp is fatally dark at its outer perimeters and there's no bloody way to escape them. They commandeer the crackling camp bonfire and begin pulling out their bottles from every pocket and flap.

"Believe 'ow cheap the grog is here?"

"What'ja pay, Annette?"

"Three dollars got me four pints. No, five!"

"Forgot my bloody glass, oh well. Just 'ave to chug it."

"Who needs a glass. We're on holiday!"

I have not seen Australians travelling in such a tight group for fifteen years. They have either regressed, or the rest of us have moved on, far beyond this sour old game of chain-smoking, excessive drinking, and fatuously arid barfly conversations. ("Might go for a ride tomorrow, if I'm not too hung over." "*That'll* be the day!") They appear to be locked in a time-warp, a self-destructive defiance that predates the digitalized, self-help enlightenment of the 1990s. Not cool. Of course there are sophisticated and sober Aussies out there somewhere, they just didn't make it to Mongolia this summer.

After a late-night colloquy in my tent with Dave, an American medical student, and his Italian-American girlfriend, I am inclined to the latter view; namely that we have left Down Under far behind in its irredeemably solipsistic limbo. While living next to the U.S. leviathan has its costs, steep and shaky ones, the constant stimulation keeps us other former colonialists fit, dancing away on our beavering little toes. We can't *afford* to get slagged every night. Oz has no such dance partner. Or as a red-faced engineer from

Adelaide had told me on the train from Beijing, "We've got only one problem, now that we finally pulled the plug on all those welfare types. How to keep the bastards from coming over here, in their junks or what have you."

He looked at me suspiciously, as if I too might have been one of them. It was this *here* of his, of course, that said it all. We were actually in deepest southern Mongolia when he said it, but for him the Oz nation was a castle-keep, boiling its rampart oils deep within the armoured hearts of its real citizens, wherever they might be at the moment. Their job is to stay impervious, wherever they are, out in the world. I give them ten years, tops, before they begin to turn on each other.

The American doctor, Dave Williams, on the other hand, was one of those Yankee patented inventions of the twenty-first century, the hipster brainiac. He had a scraggly beard straight out of the Allen Ginsberg School of Hair Design, a blue Maori tattoo encircling his right thigh, and a penchant for farout travelling. He had come to my *ger* tent to talk about the Big Picture, and I tried my best to accommodate him.

"So. The Alien," he begins, setting down the vodka bottle on the low table in the middle of the *ger*. He means to continue our interrupted conversation from the tour bus earlier that day. "What do you think it means? The green guy with the big head?"

"It's the Theatre of Extinction, Darwin's Dilemma," I begin, musing aloud. "Is Evolution the same as Election? But who gets to leave with the Technical Rapture, and who stays behind, still human? The Alien is both promise and threat. If the brainy little guy transcends us with his tiny mouth, it's because his *brain* does all the consuming."

"That's intellectual. What about on the social level?"

"Roswell, 1951 or 1952. The Birth of the New Order. With *National Inquirer* space-kidnappers, it's always the genitals that get transplanted, right?"

"Nietzsche's *Übermensch*, seated on a flying saucer," Dave agreed.

"Yeah, but the secret concern is always this *untermensch* – and the rest of us, left behind. What do you think?"

"Well," Dave pulled at his beard, "I read Nietzsche, Whitehead, Heidegger. Also Plotinus. And their ideas fit with Niels Bohr's. I mean, Einstein was great, but nobody really understands the significance of quantum mechanics yet. Popping in and out of existence, no straight lines to anywhere. Reality isn't what it used to be."

He poured another shot.

"I agree." I nodded vigorously. "We've barely assimilated Darwin and Freud."

Midnight in the Garden of Big Ideas. We were now going fully at it. The vodka bottle is still intact despite the frequent little shots between rounds of intellectual mayhem. I went for my favourite bugbear:

"So, Dave, what about evolution? Is it consciousness-based, not mechanical blind chance? Random speciation seems to me a tautology. Is the 'other' kind willed into existence? As a paradigm for self-imposed genetic manipulation?"

"You're talking about sympatric speciation," Dave replied evenly.

"Aren't you the sharp one." You can see why I dig the guy.

"Cool. But it's not purely idealist. The females contain the other end of a physical feedback loop, one that alerts itself to the possibilities in the males. Big peacock tails not only display surplus male energy, but there's a 'peacock-tail' factor within the female herself, one that is probably linked to other, less-visible characteristics, to which these traits are usually paired."

At this point I look over to see how Graham, the British world-traveller stretched recumbent on an adjacent *ger* bed, is taking this.

"You okay, Graham?"

"Fine, this is interesting. Better than late-night radio."

On my left, Amar the guide is sitting up on his bed, watching us word-lessly. Dave knocks back another shot. His eyes are cherry red. They're both cool. Dave's chic Euro girlfriend, Chiara, sits at the other end of the table – keeping up with the drinks and watching him with a tender, early-Renaissance adoration.

"What about the interface of biology and cybernetics?" I began a new round.

"That's where it's at," Dave replies, and continues his riff heavy on the fractals and Karl Jaspers. At twenty-three, he's enrolled in the University of Alabama Medical School, after completing a double degree in science and philosophy. He has come to Mongolia on his own, to check out their national health system, taping local throat singers after attending horrible surgeries, the whole weird show. American Polymath, with a hot New York *bambina* at his side.

Had I been his age, we might have been at each other's throats, competing like hell with one eye on the babe, looking for that stark male truth in a coffee-house victory. Now it was a new, and perhaps final, century – we needed each other. Wasn't this the reason for travelling in the first place? To find out where you belong?

Here we were, at the loneliest margins of the known world, both reaching out to feel for ourselves the jagged edges of the planetary picture, talking past midnight in a tent in Mongolia. A speck on a dark plain. Surrounded by the *whrr-flutter* of giant nocturnal insects.

After a day and a half of rough driving, we came to Karakorum, hard by the Gobi Desert.

"How do you say it? Washboard road?" Amar commented wryly.

"Washboard? More like washout road!"

Bamp-boomp! Ba-ba-ba-bong!

We careened over another series of head-bopping gouges and deep pits. You could lose five years of your life in one of these sinister black holes.

According to the Mongols' historical accounts, Karakorum was the twenty-third capital city of Genghis Khan, the nomad who never stayed long in one place, as befitted a successful conqueror. On the grounds of the Mongols' capital there now stood a Buddhist temple complex surrounded by a rectangle of high, whitewashed walls: Erdene Zuu Monastery, with its ritualistically significant, 108 stupa-style ornaments. Three hundred metres to the east of this enclosure, a joint German-Mongolian team was busy excavating the ruined palace of Ogedei Khan, son of Genghis. A successful warrior in his own right, it was young Ogedei who had made the fatal attack on Kiev in 1241, swooping down on a dark winter night when everyone was huddled in their huts, trapped like herd animals between the fire and the ice. Clever lad!

It was about noon when Driver-man stopped at the front gates of the temple to let Amar and me out of the car. The Gobi sun beat down on us like a hammer, and we quickly dashed for the shade of the bronze-studded portal.

"*BANG!*"

Loud curses.

Driver-man stopped the car again and furiously got out. From nowhere a largish stone had smashed into our windshield, dead centre to where I had just been sitting. I looked to Am.

"Maybe bad luck? Something doesn't like me?"

My side of the windshield was now a network of glittery silver fractures. The day's journey back to the city would be seen through an imperfect diamond the size of a television set.

"No, no! Good luck!" Amar insisted. "You were already out of the car, inside the protection of the temple." He pointed to the bronze gate.

I took a deep breath. Did demons always lurk around such holy places? They certainly did, if their designers were to be believed, for the practice of placing gargoyles and temple lions was universal, and supposedly efficacious. Whatever it was, the stone-throwing ghoul missed me.

The Erdene Zuu Monastery was said to contain the stones left from the destruction of Karakorum by the much-vilified Manchus, as part of their seventeenth-century campaigns in Mongolia. A number of tourists, mostly French, were blindly dodging in and out of the various sub-chapels and prayer-alcoves of the temple complex, wandering through narrow interiors that, despite the oil lamps, remained Stygian dark after the bright glare of the courtyard. One could see almost nothing of their grimly exotic tankas, the Buddhist scroll paintings, or the gilded bronzes of Wrathful Tara, one of twenty-one manifestations of the Goddess of Perfection. A panoply of goddesses, merciful or frightful, presided over a Yam-Yum, the entwined double sculpture representing cosmic sexual congress. Wooden prayer wheels creaked painfully, adding to the confusion. Donation boxes sat primly at every exit. In light of my recent deliverance, I hastened to pull out some currency and made a contribution, then entered the main palace, where a score of red-clad apprentice monks were chanting tunelessly over their bowls of millet mush. Or so I supposed. Their daily meal, in any case.

"What's that stuff they're eating?" I asked Amar in the spirit of attentive documentation.

"I think airag."

"Airag? The fermented horse-milk?"

"Yes." He turned to speak to a young monk who was glaring at him. "He says to take off our baseball caps," Amar translated sheepishly.

"I thought you knew the custom."

"I was never here before."

"Oh."

I watched Amar watch the other pilgrims, the widows and mothers and old farmers, who bent to kiss the scrolls in the cabinets, then lit more lamps filled with rendered oil under the wrathful or the peaceful deities, depending on their inclination. The French tourists appeared to want nothing so much in the world than to join wholeheartedly in these mystical festivities. They were constrained to sit on the narrow banquettes, nodding fervently in time to the wooden rhythm of the lunch-hour chant. The boys in the robes were about fourteen, and they turned and gawked as each new specimen of the European miscellany stumbled into their prayer chamber over an unlit transom. Their customary way of tripping up the demons, no doubt.

I decided to study these visitors, an odd bunch. Among the first to limp in during our monastic sojourn was a theatrically skinny woman in a little red dress, her sleeves artfully torn off and left ragged at the shoulders, while her female companion sported the unshaved, hirsute limbs of the fabled yeti. Statements, so many statements. Another woman's legs had been scorched red by the Gobi sun, while her ankles and feet remained pure white. She'd obviously been wearing thick socks outside. Now she joined her equally expressive companions in rocking back and forth, a two-toned fan ready to roll into Nirvana too. That was it. A couple of red-beaked Brits, a lone-wolf German or two, in clunky hiking shoes. Nobody who looked like Peter Matthiessen, Brad Pitt, or Mel Gibson. And me, sitting disgruntled in the dim corner, thinking back to the hand-painted devil-puppets of Dewson Baptist Sunday school, those interminable Greek Orthodox masses at St. Vladimir's, the desperately earnest, Protestant-flavoured YMCA summer camps, the comically squeaky Anglican sermons, whatever. My highly variegated religious upbringing. They only succeeded in cancelling each other out, all these factions. I was frankly just as bored with this production too.

"You okay?" Amar asked, sensing something was amiss, from the way my leg tapped to a beat that failed to correspond to the hungry boys' monotonous chanting.

"You watch, if you like. I go."

"I come too." He got up.

We walked out into the potent glare. The overwhelming Gobi sun was doing its best to detonate our heads and scramble our brains all over the yard like rotten cantaloupes.

"You want a drink?" I croaked.

"Yeah, okay."

"Coke or Sprite? Or, as the Buddhists put it, Coke, Sprite."

Amar looked at me.

"Soda-pop wisdom," I said cheerfully, glad to be out of the clutches of Lakshi, the demon goddess of negativity.

"*Hmm*," he grunted.

What if religion was simply an international brand?

Where was true wisdom to be found, then?

One of the German steppenwolves, prowling off by himself in the glare of the distant courtyard, caught my attention. When I reached him, he was taking a photo of a remarkably personable raven, poising seductively for him atop a crumbling temple gable.

"Light okay?" I inquired politely. "A bit harsh, no?"

"I've seen worse!" He laughed. I was delighted to learn that his name was Wolfgang.

He said his wife, Eva, was part of the team working on the hilltop excavation, so we hiked there together, just in time to see one of the Mongolian diggers fall on his ass and roll down the hill with his bucket of earth following close behind and hitting him hard on the head with a resounding *thunk!* at the bottom. I thought it was joke, but there was blood.

"How's your project going?" I asked Eva, who was red-brown and flushed from the heat, but jolly enough otherwise.

"Well, you can see for yourself."

The local digger slowly got up and waggled his head.

"What have you found so far? I promise I won't steal your secrets."

"No, no. Be my guest. Steal the whole thing, please!" She jerked her thumb at the squared-off terraces. "At this point I really don't care."

"It's Ogedei, you think?"

"Yes, see that line there?" She pointed to a faint hump that ringed the site. "That was their 'fortified' wall. Being Ogedei, of course, he didn't need fortifications."

We stared off into the summer haze for a moment, the grasshoppers under our feet crunching away as if they were going to eat the whole planet alive by noon tomorrow. I decided to stroll around the site, watching for more slapstick from the local workers, fellows who had probably never used a shovel before in their lives. Mongolians had a general cultural prohibition against digging up the ground, a taboo that turned them into a crew of fumbling Charlie Chaplins on this job.

"No photos!" A kid yelled out from the largest mound, two storeys or so.

German accent.

Und here ve go again, I thought.

"Oh? Why not?"

"Because my mother said so!"

It was Eva and Wolfgang's man-cub, protecting the family den from foreign interlopers. What was it with the Germans and their Third World tombs? What exactly were they looking for, out here among the fly swarms and horse droppings?

"We don't like this," Amar muttered to me as we walked away.

"Foreigners coming to dig up the tombs?"

"Anybody digging up these places. It's not respectful. These are our sacred places, not a place for making theories."

This was a college-educated Mongolian speaking – the new generation, not some herdsman who mumbled rude enchantments to the new moon (although maybe Amar did that too).

We got in the heat-stuffy car and headed off for lunch in a *ger* camp set twenty kilometres back in the blue-hazy hills. *Mongon Mod*, "Silver Tree," was much like the other *ger* camps, a dozen or so round, white-felt tents, surrounded by a gaily painted wooden fence and advertised with a huge wooden steppe-wagon set up at the pennant-draped entrance. The ten-year-old tourist industry had already created its own strict iconography. Inside the restaurant-tent, a uniformed waiter brought us heated towelettes, handing them to us in metal clamps with an air of fastidiousness that might have brought credit to a Parisian sommelier.

The stocky, gimlet-eyed proprietor watched the proceedings from a nearby table. He was bare-chested and heavily tanned. A gold chain, bearing some sort of leather scroll or fetish charm, hung from his broad neck. He was what they call in Papua New Guinea a Big Pella.

We were the only guests.

"What's his name?" I turned to Amar, who was examining his moist towelette with unfeigned interest. A few guttural words were exchanged between the two tables, volcanoes ready to blow in unison.

"He says his name is Batsugar."

"Batsugar? That's a hard one to forget."

At least it wasn't Dogvinegar or Catmustard, I reasoned.

"He says if you are Canadian writer, maybe you can ask archaeologists to come to his hotel and dig. He has many things on his land, old things."

"When did he say all that?"

"Just now. He says these tombs are Bronze Age."

I glanced over at Batsugar, who was clearly waiting for some kind of reply to this fusillade of information. I knew the Mongolian language was economical and efficient, but these exchanges of compressed data were like the timed code-bursts computers sent each other.

"Tell him I would like to see these tombs," I nodded.

Batsugar smiled broadly. He'd noticed me playing nervously with the two cameras secured to my belt, and did not need the translation. After a lunch of Hungarian goulash (which I would henceforth recognize as a Hunnish nomad takeout dish) and sweet watermelon, we strode through the campground, followed at a respectful distance by the entire kitchen staff – two pretty girls, the cook, and the waiter, all in starched white uniforms. Batsugar stroked his resonant belly and pointed to a weedy plot immediately between two tourist tents.

The tomb.

A hoard of fifty or sixty pieces of jagged granite has been used to describe a square, which I paced off at exactly ten feet on all sides. I stood in the middle of the patch and gazed around, trying to imagine why this site had been chosen – long before 1000 B.C. too, if Batsugar was correct when he said the museum director from Ulan Bator had identified it as Bronze Age. I walked the plot, absorbing its layout. Amar, Driver-man, and the kitchen staff heeded my every move in absolute stillness, awaiting my word.

What could I say? A bunch of rocks stuck in hard-packed earth? I glanced down at my feet again, and suddenly, as my eyes grew accustomed to the bright afternoon light, the faint colours of the stones resolved themselves into a distinct pattern. The square was clearly divided into three parts by colour. The chunks of granite on one side were red, the second black, and the third, quartz white. I squinted up at the sun. Sure enough, the black side faced south and west, the red, east, and the white, to the cool, true north.

"It's like Lenin's tomb in Moscow." I pointed to the red and black granite. "Same colours, same materials. Everything."

Amar nodded thoughtfully and conveyed these sentiments to the onlookers. It transpired that the modern Mongolian national politician Sukhbaatar had also been interred in just such a tomb, back in Ulan Bator's main public square. We proceeded to two other sites, a few hundred metres from the first. The nearer one was formed of a collection of roundish stones, which made up a rectangle about ten feet by twenty. Batsugar claimed it was a mass grave, an entire clan from the early Iron Age, and that a probe would have to be drilled at least five metres deep to get a control bearing. The phrase came out in English; he had obviously done his research. I could imagine him a few years hence, welcoming hordes of tourists into his casino, The Golden Skull-Cup, with its daily live floor shows re-enacting Genghis's selection of bed partners from the female "captives" in the audience, while a chorus of throatsingers worked their ungulate charms off in the background. The third site was *outside* the fence, as Amar took pains to remind me repeatedly, throughout the day.

"*Hun*," was all Batsugar said as he peered down at a small, rocky plot, which for some subtle reason exited my interest far more than the others. Hun might have meant anything, any one of the dozen migratory Turkic tribes, or the historical Huns of the fourth century A.D., Attila's hordes who gave their name to Hungary. We stood in silent contemplation of the mystery contained within. The kitchen staff sensed something too . . .

"I don't like this idea," Amar grumbled as we drove back to our own camp in the austere heat of a Mongolian summer's afternoon.

"What idea?"

I kept my eyes on the potholes, guessing how long my spine would take these floundering wrenches and tongue-biting snaps before giving out.

"He doesn't own these tombs. One was outside his fence, but he acts like they are all his."

"You think they should be left alone? No archaeologists? No tourists?"

"Yes. No digging."

"And Genghis Khan's tomb? Suppose they found that? They should not dig it up?"

"Yes, but they will never find it."

"And what does Driver-man think?"

I turned to Byambaa, who was squinting into the oncoming road and its craters, like a slaughterhouse worker on the shift line. Next!

A grunt.

"He thinks the same thing as me."

"I see." I closed my eyes, let my hand flop out the car window to catch a bit of road breeze, happy until a flying grasshopper hit my palm hard with a dull *smack*.

"You have good day so far?" Amar was always solicitous.

"Yeah. I'm just a bit tired. Those Japanese were really yelling last night. I thought the Aussies were going to be bad, but they all conked out."

"Yes, the Japanese were very excited. Laughing and crying."

"Why? The Empress had a baby boy or something?"

"No, they see the stars for the first time."

I opened my eyes at this and turned to the back seat.

"Say again, please."

"The Japanese tourists? They never saw stars at night before. When they see them last night, in Mongolian sky, they laugh and cry. The guide-men, they got presents from the Japanese, for showing them this."

Now I understood why Amar had taken such pains to point out the nearly full moon to the Australians earlier that week. "It becomes round like this once a month," he had told them, quite unabashedly, as their eyes grew large with silent indignation that this young man should be claiming Celestial Heaven for his small nation's exclusive domain.

Chapter 30

So What Is Your National Pride?

"So what is your national pride?" Amar asked me as we drove across the grassy plain in the afternoon to visit the Gobi nomads. Amar and Driver-man turned as one to hear the answer.

"I don't know. What is *your* national pride?"

I watched a herd of hardy Mongol horses graze along the skyline, and I kept thinking of Dr. Zubar's pronouncement, back in Kiev, that the pastoral life was a big dead end. But surely it was a dead end only when it finally died, and failed to produce offspring?

"First, Genghis Khan. Second, our clean and beautiful country. We are proud as Mongolians for these things."

"Okay, I see . . . Well, one is, we have a beaver, very industrious animal, two —"

"Beaver, what is that?"

"It lives in the water and eats trees."

"A fish?"

"No, like a rat, only bigger."

"I see . . ."

A guttural transmission fires off between the guide in back seat and driver in front. Driver-man thinks this is rich, he shoots me a quick look of jubilant hilarity just as he hits another pothole. Foreigners!

"And the other national pride?"

"We invent this idea called multiculturalism. Everyone can come to our country, wear their own hats from the old country, and still be Canadian at the same time."

Amar and Driver-man waited, clearly expecting more than this.

"We also have these big waterfalls," I offered, getting flustered. "Niagara, it's called."

They appeared to like this idea better, nodded, and left me to my own thoughts.

My thoughts were that the world was an older place than we liked to imagine. This business of opening tombs, for instance. They were rarely if ever "lost," as I could plainly see from this flattened countryside; the local plains were visibly littered with them. Wasn't the practice of this archaeology an effort to distance ourselves from their function and meaning? To obscure our own roots by cutting them off at will? And at whose will? On whose authority?

The Mongolians, like other pastoral peoples, held to a tripartite universe, a blue upper heaven, a red middle earth, and the black underworld. What business did we have, fooling around with their latter realm, a dimension we would all visit soon enough? Our fate was to enjoy and suffer this middle world, a place of blood-letting and frantic coupling and defecating and vomiting and fighting and snoozing, the grand buffet that the great Mongolian artist Balduugiyn Sarav depicted in *A Day in Mongolia* back in Ulan Bator's main museum, a cosmic vision of intricate and unsparing human detail. Dozens of local artists had taken their cue from this anecdotal masterpiece, and painted their own versions of picaresque reality. Anyway, the citizens of this country could easily spot the covetous gleam in the excavators' eyes. How this translated itself into the hijacking of the national legacy for various personal and political agendas was the real issue, never mind Batsugar and his dreams of fat custom.

What about all that tomb loot shipped off to Moscow and Beijing?

"Where are you going after Mongolia?" Amar broke into my thoughts. "Driver-man wants to know."

"Uh, Siberia, then Moscow, and back to Kiev." I wondered idly if they had any idea where these places actually were.

"*Arck*, Kiev!" Driver-man grunted agreeably, a toothy grin of recognition.

Of course *they* knew the place. They had sacked it eight hundred years ago. They probably still remembered every pothole and dried horse turd on the trail to Eastern Europe too.

"Do you know, *Moscow* is a Mongol world, not Russian?" Amar spoke up, confirming my suspicions.

"Really? What does it mean? A hundred thousand heads? White-skinned women-coral?" I was overtired, I could see the *gers* of the Gobi nomads dotting the lower slopes of the upcoming hill, and I was not up to the prospect of another afternoon tea with stone-hard sheep's cheese and a bowl or five of fermented horse-milk.

"A river like this."

Am undulated his palm in the air.

"Meander?"

"Yes. Meander."

"Interesting. What about the Great Wall?"

"We call it the White Wall."

"Because it's the *north* wall of China?"

"I don't know."

"What about this thing around your neck, the Buddhist thing?" It was called a *dozghe* in Tibet, the Cosmic Thunderbolt – a double-headed iron symbol – but Amar's version included a lunar blade identical to the Mongol arrowhead I'd seen back in the Chersonessus museum in Crimea.

"We call it a *char-koltz*. This means 'ant' in our language."

"The insect?"

"Yes, because it has three parts like an ant for protection."

"Does it work?"

"I don't know. We will see."

Amar was off to study in London in a few weeks. As we pulled into the nomads' homestead I wondered what adjustments he would have to make, in his transition from the ultimate country boy to an uptown city dude. All in one go too. I could see him at a swanky club party, in a black silk shirt and kid-leather boots. The modelling agencies would love him.

The nomads' camp was littered with horse dung and heaps of broken twigs, not much different from my Uncle Mike's failing chicken farm, *circa* 1961. Replace the collapsing wooden outbuildings with canvas *gers*, but keep the cowshit, the bluebottle flies, and this air of profound rural stupor that so enraged Lenin that he attempted to erase it with ideological sorcery and mass murder. In Mongolia, his successors kept to the same program, killing the monks and collectivizing the manure in an attempt to rationalize their total mental fatigue.

A collection of motorcycles and four-wheel jeeps at the *ger* ranch added nothing to the bucolic gloss of my struggling imagination; the local herdsman greeted us wearing a denim workshirt and a Yankees baseball cap, and offered us a seat inside the main tent. As I bent to enter, I noticed two pink tourists sitting outside, on little plastic stools set in the middle of the smelly stockyard in the late-afternoon sun, enjoying the small slice of shade created by a tent overhang.

It was cool inside the owner's *ger*. The interior was ornately decorated with orange-and-red Chinoise furniture like our elaborate tourist camp.

"He buy it like this," Amar translated my questions. "It costs maybe $25,000."

This seemed a phenomenal amount, but then this tent was the man's main digs, with four real beds for the family. The owner told us he had "all five," the full Mongolian complement of sheep, goats, cows, horses, and camels, and that he worked eighteen hours a day. Every day, and right through the winter too. They never named their horses.

"And no name for their camels, either?"

"No, never."

I tried to frame a question, about how they identified individual horses in working conversation, but it was beyond my linguistic ability. The airag, the fermented horse-milk I'd consumed (two bowls), wasn't bad at all, and I quickly became tipsy, ready to attack the White Wall with one more bowl. I staggered out of the tent after accepting an invitation to look at the horses, and noticed that the other two tourists were still firmly planted in their trodden-down manure field, doggedly contemplating the horses, the horse droppings, and the horse flies feasting on the horse droppings. What had they paid for this authentic experience of theirs? I had already met Crystal, a Swedish woman who recounted how she got "sick from both ends" as a result of a homestay like this, and who was obliged to subsist on Coca-Cola for the rest of her tour. Were they similarly indisposed?

The tourists, and now there were three, all red-eyed and still tanked from the night before, consisted of two Australian women and an embittered middle-aged Briton who spoke of Europe's coming end with evident relish. Neither the distance of his journey, nor the novelty of his fertilized surroundings, relieved him of his spiteful vision of a civilization in its last death throes.

"It's over, we're finished. Lost control."

His bloodshot eyes glared at the horizon, where something always waited, depending on your eye colour.

I turned to the other woman, a sharp-nosed blonde in expensive "trekking" shoes. She had the whole kit – utility belt, canvas sub-baggies, drip-dry hat – and here she was, trekking, after a fashion, through the dung field. Her name was Laura, and she worked as a media buyer in London. She'd emigrated from Oz only six years ago, somewhat of a surprise since her accent had already achieved that clippy bite of Sloane Square, with only a few false notes of nasal-grate squeaking through at the end. Laura was just as anxious as the bitter Briton to talk about her homeland's prospects, and these were not good.

"The Australians must do something! They must face up to Asia, and deal with it, instead of wimpishly burying their heads in the sand. *Which* they are particularly good at."

Laura shot a look at the Briton, presumably including him in this Whingers of the World category.

"They used to be bolder, the Aussies? Are you saying now they're defensive, insular?"

"What do you expect? An island continent, nothing to stimulate them? They almost elected a party called One Nation to form the government. Very right wing!"

"So this reaction is happening all over?"

"Yes, except in London. London's cool. I love it there."

She was openly proud of her hasty exit from Sheila-Land, something I had never encountered before in Aussies. They usually adored themselves. But her new accent proved the point; it chipped at each word, every consonant pronounced dead on, as if the Sydney drawl had been surgically removed by a professional voice coach. Australia was no longer cool, at least in the media world, where such things infinitely mattered. I turned to the other woman, Wanda, with the messy hair and limp posture of post-prandial exhaustion. Wanda said she and her husband were ex-Marxists, and they didn't like where Oz was going either.

"Ex-Marxist? What does that mean? You wanted to collectivize the kangaroos?

The airag was still working its furtive magic on me, but her alcohol level didn't think my alcohol level was too funny.

"We have *serious* problems at home. Internment camps for illegals. Stress."

"But what about your Australian directors, actors? Those unique leather boots with the pull-tabs? There was once a real kick coming out of the country, am I right? Is it all dead now?"

Her face grew red, the descending sun was slowly setting it on fire.

"Yeah, yeah, Peter Weir and all that. Sure." She sipped at her drink. A clear liquid but not water. "But on the whole, Australians don't trust intel-lectuals. They don't read; they've had it easy. Now they wake up and see where the real world has gone to."

"But we used to really dig Australian culture." I tried to make my point as the two women watched me with an apathy bordering on premature senility. "It seemed like a way, a path, to some kind of national identity. Now I'm getting nothing but negativity."

"That's 'cause it is," Wanda said, downing her drink at one go, bored with the question already. She studied the black car I had arrived in, an ambivalent squint that coupled class resentment with an apparent lust for its air conditioning.

"Pretty toff, that. Riding around out here in a black Merc."

"*Merc?* Oh, right."

Good old boy me, I knew *Merc* for Mercury.

"So how can you *write*, if you get driven around in *that*?"

I stared at her. The proof that communism is a psychological virus, and not a historical consequence of Russian society, was sitting right before me, blowsy-drunk in the dried mud of horse-faced Asia. Drunker than eco-trekkers usually get at four in the afternoon, but then the surliness in her voice was unmistakeable.

"Well, you know what Lenin said," I replied cheerfully. "'I don't care whether the kulak is black or white, as long as he catches the bullets.'"

As far as I could tell, she didn't get the allusion.

So here it is, folks, you heard it here first: Despite the recent Olympics and having a whole unsullied continent to play in, Australia has tanked. Fallen into a miasma of resentment and small-mindedness from which parties like One Nation are only the beginning of a downward spiral into historical oblivion. I once believed Australia was the teenage America, full of promise and punky attitude; I didn't realize it was a *flavour*, and a flavour going stale for lack of refrigeration, of authentic coolness. Yeah, I used to think Australia was cool, before I realized that countries were like that pretty girl back in Grade Nine, whose precocious charms evaporated by graduation day, leaving a strangely dull suburban slacker pushing a grocery cart.

So I say, Watch out, Mongolia. Choose your dance partner carefully, and put on your best shoes. Stay alert, for nations come and go, and the times are always dangerous for those who go slinking off into a dull stupor under the midday sun, far too soon.

I try to convey all this to Amar, as we sit drinking a Heineken back at our tourist *ger* camp, watching the full moon rise over a mountain shaped precisely like Cheops's pyramid.

However, Amar is more interested in other things.

"Do you think they will come," he says, looking back over his shoulder.

"The rich Liechtenstein girls? Of *course* they will come." I sip on my beer.

I can see he wants more than this, for the two girls are beautiful and he's twenty-five.

"A Mongolian *prince*?" I go on, encouraging him. "And his crazy *writer* friend? . . . But do you understand what I am saying about Switzerland?"

"Yes, neutral country, banking laws. Never attacked, all the citizens have guns and a real people's army." He rattled it off, today's little talk.

"Yes, Amar. Listen. I want you to study these *successful* countries in London. And if you meet a Swiss or Dutch, talk to them, right? And learn everything you can from them, okay?"

"I will," he promises.

"Good." I take a breath.

I can't help trying to tell him everything I can think of, here in the Gobi, on our last day before we leave. *London! London!* I want him to become at least a deputy minister, maybe more. His father died last year, and I have tried to say what his father would have said to him, only weeks before his big trip to the new capital of the world.

"And here they come."

The two women are dazzlingly pretty, and although pretty isn't the drug it used to be for me, still it manages to get my heartbeat going. Amar, of course, is stricken. The full moon, the cool, sweet desert air filled with thyme and the French perfume of two girls, young women who have landed here in the middle of nowhere from Planet Dior. They join us, under the moon.

I'm happy, and I'm happy for him too.

"So is Amar your guide, or what?" Laura, the taller, buxom one, asks me.

"Amar? Not really." I toy with my drink and look at him with secret pride. "No. Actually, we're related."

Chapter 31

Twenty-One Taras, or, *I Married a Mongolian Train-Trader*

Zanabazar, the great seventeenth-century Mongolian polymath –
accomplished sculptor, Prince of the Realm, astute politician,
Buddhist teacher, and beloved son – is the most human of his remote
nation's many heroes. For a country of three million, Mongolia has produced more than its share of world conquerors, men and women in
whom self-reliance and a dexterous practicality are the chief and distinguishing virtues. Genghis is more the mythical father figure, but his high-
powered karma has come back to haunt his descendants. First came the
three centuries of Qing despotism, which ended only in 1911; then a few
decades of Bolshevik bloodshed followed, which for some reason the
average Mongolian doesn't seem to mind nearly as much as the previous
Chinese carnage, although with a current life expectancy of fifty-five,
there can be few who actually remember anything of either period at this
late date.

But there's a third wave full of karmic juice, and it's got no name or
human face at its surging peaks: it's the effluvia of the modern world, commerce, competition, world markets. A locally produced guidebook,
Mongolia for Visitors, puts it all into perspective:

Mongolia's strict banking laws were introduced soon after democracy began in 1992. These laws have proved effective, keeping the national inflation rate to a relatively low 50% per year.

At the Khar Zakh, the Black Market, the main shopping bazaar back in the capital of Ulan Bator, three guys try to rob me at once, a squeeze-play grotesquely signalled by their rolled-up newspapers and predatory eyes – a clumsy pretence, as if they were really devout fans of editorials on the sewage system. Rank amateurs. I yell at them to step back, and the nearest robber yells back at me, still grabbing at my bag. As I wrest it away, I can see the crowd around us is getting ugly too, just as eager for my tourist blood.

He's right to act defensive-aggressive, my scabby-faced little bandit, for if I had him in my power, I'd surely beat him unconscious, maybe even kill him. As the Buddhist monk said publicly a few months back, it's okay to kill the September 11 terrorists, because it would put them out of the misery of their bad karma; but what surprises me is not my own murderous instincts, which I am always free to own up to ("Feel like murder, don't feel like murder," as the Buddha might have shrugged). No, it's the crowd's eagerness and evident complicity in the attempted robbery. These gangs *work* the market. Their routine is practised and theatrical, and the fact that it is publicly countenanced (a group of four overweight cops stands a dozen paces away, strangely removed from the scene) implies that Ulan Bator is an entirely different country from the honeyed Mongolia of sweet pastures and broomswept tourist *gers*. Out there on the range, the little nomad communities sanction all conduct, to the point where hospitality is internalized and implicit in every social relationship. But the city, that's the world.

After this adventure, Crystal the Swedish student tells me that twice the day before some other bad young men in town roughly seized her by the arm and threatened to drag her off with them. She is glad of our company, and now sticks close to us.

Not only Crystal but every traveller I met in Mongolia agreed that Beijing was great. The nation-state that provides public security for its citizens is irresistibly powerful, and draws others to it, a lesson that is reinforced by the stories of a South Korean industrialist with whom I share a sleeper cabin, on the night train to Siberia later that week.

Brendan Oh tells me he is seventy-two, and shows me his passport to prove it, a U.S. passport, the proud blue eagle and everything. He lives in L.A. now, Beverly Hills. Vigorous, intelligent, and mysteriously informed, he owns factories in Siberia and Mongolia. I waste no time in sitting down with him, pumping him for nuggets of wisdom, both eastern and western versions.

"I have five hundred employees in Russia," he tells me. "Lumber, planks. We ship to China, twenty boxcars a month, another eight to ten to Korea. Plus I own a department-store complex, two hundred different shops inside. Now I am researching Mongolian mud treatment. I've got an order for one hundred thousand units of mud treatment already, two years of scientific research. I spend fifty thousand dollars just for analysis."

I am dazzled. We are heading off into the Siberian wilds in a rickety old border trader's train, to the town of Irkutsk by Lake Baikal. Just before we chugged off, swarms of large-rumped Mongolian women boarded the train, running through the cars at the hoarse direction of a big-chested guy, and spent every second until the train left frantically packing and repacking their smuggled wares. Crappy velveteen blankets, stiff frilly bras, baggy Chinese jeans. Cheapster ware. Lacklustre acrylic dresses that nobody in newly chic China would buy, let alone wear.

"Oh, they sell it to the Russians," Brendan hardly blinks as a big-butted woman in tight red short-shorts slides a counterfeit Adidas gym bag, stuffed with extra-large nylon panties, under his luggage. "No customs, they save 20 per cent value-added tax and 25 per cent clothing tax. Regular importers can't compete with them."

I watch as our grey-uniformed Mongolian conductress helps one of the smugglers push an overstuffed satchel deep into the uppermost reaches of our cabin.

"The bribe is about ten dollars," Brendan nonchalantly explains. "The only problem is on the Russian side. Sometimes the Russians kick them. Wait until tomorrow. You will see."

"I can hardly wait."

Ms. Giga-Butt looks at my pillow speculatively. I grit my teeth and walk out into the corridor to get away from the acid vapours of chemical sizing emitted by her unwrapped bags.

"Only way to deal with it is to get mad as hell," a young Dutch guys tells me, smouldering away in the breezy standing room between the rolling cars. "We had four days of them from Moscow on the train. Pure hell."

"Was this in the guidebook?" I wonder aloud. Is this the famous Trans-Siberian Railway? Or some third-rate alternative they've fobbed off on us?

The handful of foreigner passengers, four or five backpackers, are equally disgusted and unhappy, and we still have thirty hours to go – which apparently includes a ten-hour customs inspection at the Russian border, beginning at midnight. It's not a train, it's a box sitting in the woods. And no washrooms either. They're locked tight.

"Tomorrow maybe you use the toilet at 4:30 a.m. They lock it at 5:00, and so no chance to use the toilet again until maybe noon, or later," Brendan warns me. "I make this trip many times. I know the 'drill.' Have another orange. Want some noodle soup? Korean. It's okay."

"No thanks." I sit back against the sticky vinyl backrest. "So tell me, Brendan. The world of business, politics, the Big Picture. What's going on these days?"

"Ah!" He likes my questions, and I love him for liking them. He peels a tangerine, placing the pieces in a neat little pile. Unlike the Chinese trains, there is no garbage bin, only the open window, and ejected things hurtle past your face when you least expect it.

"It's like this: I was born in 1929. South Korea was completely destroyed in the Korean War. Nothing left. So we must build from the beginning. All new, choose the best, no old thing. Now it's Japan first, then Korea, Taiwan, Singapore."

"And the U.S. ?"

"They still strong, but watch out. China is now super-power – no, *hyper*-power. Arab world, Japan, even Russia – America can control. But not China. After Olympics in 2008, China steps up, U.S. can do nothing. Maybe they take Taiwan, maybe not. But they choose, not America."

"And the atomic bomb, 1945? Some say the U.S. should not have dropped it on Hiroshima."

"Of course innocent people die, but otherwise war goes on for three more years. Lots of Americans die, for Japan never surrenders. Japanese very smart; they invade Korea, rule for thirty-two years, make everyone learn Japanese, forget Korean. Put all the boys in the Japanese Army, make all the girls over sixteen years sleep-workers for the Army. Must take twenty soldiers a day, agree or be killed. That's why Stalin deport Koreans to Uzbekistan, they are 'army-Japanese' now. I even had a Japanese name!"

The night unfolded exactly as Brendan Oh had predicted: a ten-hour wait for customs that began in the stickiness of the witching hour, no food on the train, nothing to see out the window but a mean little suburb that grew more squalid with the dawn.

I step out of the railcar, determined to relieve myself, even if I must tread on someone's wretched bean garden. There is no train. It's just our solitary sleeper car, sitting all by itself on a side-track in the middle of a grotty railyard. We've been moved off, like containerized freight that might keep a few more days before it goes bad. Welcome to the Siberian Express. What's the milk run like? A two-man handcart and half a bottle of vodka?

After customs clearance at the Russian border, Brendan takes his two briefcases and exits. "I take a taxi, always. I get home three hours before the train."

He leaves, and I have the cabin to myself. Something hard is sticking into my shoulder. A wired bra has been stuffed under my sheet. I hold it out into the corridor and another big-assed trader-woman snatches it away without a word.

"Gee, I thought it was a gift."

Maybe I'd like them better if it weren't such junk. Maybe it's all a matter of taste. Like the svelte Liechtenstein woman said to us, shopping can be *so* educational. Of course she rejected us, me and my Mongolian protégé both, and Amar understood this, and why. We were obviously skint, a Canadian writer and Mongolian student. Come back and see her when we were successful, famous, and dripping in Euros; which of course we would, but with other women at our sides. Companions always and assuredly more beautiful and younger than she, for women who made such conditional challenges inevitably outbargained themselves in the end, and the race was already decided by the time they were ready to close a deal.

So whom should Amar marry? It's the only important question, here in this heat-addled compartment, where I amuse myself by killing as many of

its inexhaustible supply of border flies as I can, flattening them two at once
with my cap. Can I get three? I am merciless in my vengeance, and relentless in my execution of justice. Shall he marry heterogeneously, like the
bridegroom whom the city-slick Londoner on our train tells me about, a
Mongolian guy who married a Ghanian-Corsican?

"Mongolian, and Ghanian-Corsican? What's that, cool difference?"
I asked pointedly.

"No, it was attraction at first sight," the Londoner replied stiffly.

"Were you there?"

"No, he *told* me it was."

"Attraction? What the hell is that?" I mused alone, tart and grim.

The Londoner moved away from the obsessing stranger, who was now
staring at the birch trees popping out of the empty hills like so much
microwaved popcorn let loose. Yes, my eyes were red and I was heat-crazed,
rationing my bottled water to hasty little gulps each time I got dizzy. Not
good company, I know. But still: Who should Amar marry?

The Mongolian women were extraordinarily beautiful, the most
beautiful in Asia. Tall, leggy, clear-skinned; if he could find a true princess
among them, a woman who was not shy of life and didn't drag him down
into a compromising smudge pot of domesticity, then okay. A foreign
princess, of course. But where was such a one to be found, in this dumb-
struck age of uptalking mall-queens?

The great Zanabazar had already studied the question of the ideal female
back in the seventeenth century. His gilt-bronze sculptures, the celebrated
grouping, *Twenty-One Taras*, were now gathered in lots of five and six under
halogen lights at the Museum of Zanabazar in Ulan Bator. Green Tara, White
Tara, Wrathful Tara; each perfect, lotus-seated goddess (said to be based on a
real Mongolian beauty whom the artist knew well at sixteen) held a different
mudra, or iconic posture. The mudra of Wrathful Tara consisted of the
char-koltz, the Reality-Cutting-Knife, in the right hand, and an empty bowl
of zero, in the left. Fill the void with Enlightenment. Ah, Tara. Her perfect
toes curl out from the lotus bloom to caress the phenomenal world.

Maybe that's how to find a wife, Amar. Study the *Twenty-One Taras*.
Study diligently the enlightenment the great Zanabazar received, as to the
nature of the Perfect in woman.

Chapter 32

Baikal

Suddenly the train is empty, the border traders have all departed, the birds of summer swing loose and easy from the sky. We are rolling through a vast countryside of broad rivers, shimmering lakes, distant hills. Startled, a grey heron flaps its wings as the train rushes through its marsh, dropping a load of white scat to gain more altitude. The villages of Siberia are rocketing by at a hundred kilometres an hour, fenced in with green and grey pickets, and the sun-brown children hang off them by the dozens, bare-legged and smiling, their shockingly white hair ignited by the late-summer glow. It's August and it feels like home, like Canada in late summer, with this surprising gift of new mountains, wrapped in luminous purple gauze.

What space! What freedom to roam!

My watch says it's after 8 p.m. The sun is still high, but the distant range is growing feeble, fading in the chalky light and returning to its ancestral shadows. We're headed northeast, no longer in Asia. Siberia, green, watered, unconditional, is a continent unto itself. And in the middle, a vast lake.

Baikal. Thirty million years old.

It stares up at space, unblinking, cold, lucid, brilliant.

The eye of an unconquered god. Time's favourite child.

The dwarf rumbles to the edge of the village, bouncing over the ruts, kills his motorbike, and slides off. He struts across the wooden plank-path, bangs through the ramshackle gate, and enters the enclosure, skipping around a rowdy patch of rhubarb bigger than he is, even with his oversized handmade leather boots. He trips on a loose board, stumbles and nearly falls, furiously swings his arms counter-clockwise to regain his balance, then hops up to the creaking porch of the cottage.

A large stone oven greets him, baking warmly away in the narrow kitchen; the small bath-hut, or *banya*, at the edge of the enclosed yard is also smouldering, but weakly. It will need more firewood soon. The tiny cow barn is already stacked with chopped logs, the outhouse is clean, re-dolent with fresh pine boards installed only last week. Everything is spare, orderly. His mother, Olga, points to dinner sitting on the pine table. She flits about the yard as bright as a tropical bird, with her preternaturally red hair and blue eyes. No English, she must demonstrate with her raw hands how to use the wooden bucket to wash ourselves in the morning. Boreal finches chirp overhead, peering down at these newcomers sitting by their backpacks in the sun, staring with wonder at all this primitive pageantry.

A cow moans, bloated with new milk. Clover, dill, cattle droppings, pine needles – and above all, the cold enormity of blind water down the hill, strangely opaque in all its forms. Perpetual mist, rolling fogs, chilling breezes, and this shifting blue light. The lucid refractions continually sweep across the nearby forest like open cataracts, spilling over the hillsides and flushing the shadows away from the ferny understoreys. It's gelid, this chill, ulterior light. Lunar, and impossible to escape. We sip our black tea and keep our thoughts to ourselves.

Fox-Girl shows up just before noon with the fleeting success of the morning sun, which has lazily mounted the wooden walls of our tourist quarters, and now triumphantly warms the cabbages and pea-flowers of Olga's little garden plot. Our wiry guide takes no notice of our collective interest in the little village and its odd inhabitants: the boy on the large bicycle who maddens the stray dogs into making hopeless charges after him; the half-witted woman in the bronze patent-leather coat, who slumps unmoving beside the rustic carved church; and the handsome neighbour, who takes his seat on Olga's sunny bench, then coolly rolls out his Russian cigarette, holding it between forefinger and thumb, billowing out smoke as pungent as a Halloween bonfire, silently giving himself over to his daily rite with the complete and insouciant abandon of a twenty-first-century Cossack. I want to take his picture, but Fox-Girl is anxious to get going. Her sharp little nose twitches, her pale-green eyes are already reading the light of the path we must take into the native wood.

We trudge down the rutted road. The muddy village dogs leave us alone.

We climb all afternoon. Livid beech trees grow thick on the hills and the dark hills grow thick around the endless water, paling unevenly at their edges. If we need flatness, we can hike down to the lake; or at least we can until it churns itself into a violent wrath, which it will do as soon as the wind changes, white froth on a black frown. As if on cue, a dull rumble announces the approach of another fierce-eyed storm. It's rolling off a distant lake arm, arising from the improbable depths of that shivering silver expanse to the west. But headed where, exactly?

Even here, in this indulgent copse of birch and poplars, with the late-afternoon sun stroking our faces, and Fox-Girl smiling at last, we pad along carefully, circumspectly. We are approaching our goal, the summit of a local landmark, an outcrop of volcanic gneiss named for a murdered Polish exile. Oh yes, it's hard to believe, standing here in the tender sunshine, the northern lake seducing us with its charms, summer's airy promise and these cream-puff continental clouds, that this land is drenched in blood. Old blood, foreign blood. Every year it's the elk hunters' lazy tracker-dogs who manage to dig up the bones of the forgotten dead, despoiled from their pretty meadows, maybe that wet fern-marsh over there. This afternoon's peace is deeper than the primitive peace of the Buryatia's sky-god Omo, more potent than the bucolic peace of a nearly pristine nature. (A small smokestack in the distance, a mite in the vastness.)

No, it's the peace of the graveyard of History itself. Genghis Khan, it is said, was a Siberian, born of this same local Buryatia tribe, animist fire-worshippers who held Baikal's southern shores from ancient times; and if he was, then his grave almost certainly lies here too, one tomb of many hidden among these poplar and birch sheaves, alone under stars that scatter themselves between the raised arms of victorious Heaven.

"They had to use a much stronger rail gauge here, for the Circum-Baikal," Fox-Girl squints, bends, and snatches up a loose iron spike, rusty with age. She holds it up, a talisman.

"The most expensive railway ever built."

The dead weight of the forged spike speaks of the lives of the men who ended here. Now we walk slowly along the deserted grassy track, curious as to what else we might find among the forgotten litter. A Swiss, a Briton, a Japanese, and a Canadian, led by a Russian sprite with the quick, nervous gestures and small, sharp teeth of a forest carnivore.

"We will have our picnic there, by the tunnel. We can see Shaman Rock from the shore."

Boiled eggs, homegrown tomatoes, crusty sandwiches of farmer's cheese, and cold water hauled from the central depths of the lake. We laze in silence; we've walked more than two hours. There are no flies. The water is still perfectly calm, what we see of it. And how far is that? Ten miles? A few hundred yards? Impossible to tell; the boiling mists it generates are all part of it too.

"What is Shaman Rock, exactly?" someone asks.

We can see it in the distance, an odd pyramidal apex of white stone, thrusting out of the water at the mouth of the Omo River. Local scientists claim it's the peak of a massive underwater structure, one that bears no resemblance to anything else on earth. But they say that about a lot of things; and the wild light reflecting off the rock is mystery enough right now.

Fox-Girl is not easily distracted. She stares fixedly at the pinnacle, studying the problem as if it's a wily mouse that must be stalked with absolute conviction.

"The story is that Baikal, the Father of the River, threw this stone at his daughter, to stop her from running off with her lover."

She nods to herself, and pushes her sun-bleached bangs off her pale, elfin face. It's her own story too. She left her remote Siberian home three hundred kilometres north to come here to this southern shore, for a boy. Now she's not sure if it's the boy she wanted, or the lake.

The light devours us, mesmerizes the afternoon trees, causes a sharp breeze to stir the beach grasses. The sedge begins to sing, a long, thin, reedy whistle.

Let's go, she says. We pack our lunch things and clamber back up the stony ridge.

Is the search for Genghis's final tomb a trivial gesture, an impulse to reverse the flow of history? To find something that can only deny what is humanly possible? Why break the earth apart if we can already read its signs? And the signs are all around us, for we are already living in a tomb. Every moment is fatal, ablaze with our own understanding. We are its witnesses, if we choose.

"What did the Germans tell you?" Fox-Girl wants to know.

She's twenty-two and untamed and wants to know everything: my conversation with strangers the night before; the type of film I'm using; the state of these odd, six-inch red lichens poking out of the hillside like tumescent polyps. All of it.

She's reading *The White Canvas*, written in the 1930s.

The author died in a camp, unpublished.

"We were standing in front of the big pink castle, the one that the New Russian is building above the village," I recounted. "And the German couple said it's back to that, the two-class system. The rich in their wired hilltop castles, the poor scraping in their huts, down below. 'That's the future,' they said, pointing to the gangster's big pink house. That it was coming to that in Germany, and the rest of the world too."

Fox-Girl considers this, chewing on the prospect. A picture forms in the middle distance of her green eyes. The Swiss woman becomes alarmed at the notion, sharply sucks in her breath. Me, I don't care. I know we've all survived our history, and that it was always the same history. It will eventually collect itself and flow into a thousand new places beyond the next bend.

Now we struggle through whispering larches to mount the big round hill, and survey how far we've come this long afternoon, amazed at how different it all looks now, for the lake has changed its colour once again. Now the breeze lifts itself over the broken stone skirt of the beach, growing stronger, and flails away at the sugary aspens crowning the high ridge over our heads. Below our feet, hand-crushed gravel, rudely smashed by *zeks*, the Soviet convict-prisoners. Fishbones, vodka bottles, purple loosestrife, rusty buckles, a used condom, it's all here. Our ancestors knew what they were, and where they are now. So what is our task?

"What about Dostoevsky?" I confront the Fox-Girl.

Alone of the Russians I have met, she gives me a thumbs-up.

"The best. *They* don't like him, of course, because they think we are born blank," she murmurs, speaking of Soviet philosophy.

"That's the difference," I say. "We have therapy to help us adjust to reality. Psychiatry."

I look at the Swiss woman, who nods carefully.

"Pah!" Fox-Girl snorts.

It's clear she doesn't believe in psychiatry either.

"Look at this." She bends over a patch of tiny orange-red flowers. "You make a tea from this leaf, flower. It's good for the heart."

"Heart? In what way?"

"All ways," she says with a sigh.

At the edge of the shore, a shimmering. The light changes again, for its own sake. Everywhere we step, a keen edge opens like a new blade. We march along, oblivious to the patterns, dreaming with the lake of pure chance, of a new start to everything, a pure white canvas greater than any sky.

Chapter 33

About the Dress They Sold the Cow For

S ummer's end. On the way home. I am unwinding for a few days in the
western Ukraine capital of Lviv, a Central European city of one million
souls – like Prague except smaller, a Baroque valentine left intact by the
German and Russian troops through the Second World War. Taking breakfast with dawn's favourite screechy birds in the Hotel Dniester, I spot four
Germans sitting down at the next table. Early risers too.

I'm still on Siberian time, what's their excuse? I have been travelling
long enough to spot computer-bagging industrialists when I see them,
even through one squinty red eye. From the way they absently sip at their
orange juice, receiving the pointless little obsequities of the inept waiters
without acknowledgement, they are clearly at the end of some trade
mission. The giant heads on Easter Island must have watched their worshippers dither away just before their oceanic apocalypse in much the same
abstracted fashion.

You've seen those pictures in *National Geographic*? Where the man in
the white suit stands perfectly still in the marketplace, and all around
him the busy hawkers flow like rose-coloured trout water, turned into
streaks of jelly by the magic of time-lapse photography? It's a trick that
illustrates the ineluctable difference between the Big Time and the brown

masses. One of the four Germans is a blonde, swanky gentlewoman, Bridget from Nuremburg, and because she is thirty and splendidly attired and smiles brightly at me (taking my dishevelled appearance for the sure sign of the seasoned adventurer), I abandon my reluctance to get burned again by Teuton-ivy, especially at this ungodly hour. So I venture a remark.

"Beautiful morning, isn't it?"

Bridget tells me she is the company's IT specialist.

"You've got some investment in Ukraine?" I anticipate. "But it's not going well?"

I have read the latest business reports. Ukraine's economy is moribund, hampered by a poor banking system, shallow liquidity, a cumbersome barter-system with Russia. Anybody who could leave was already abroad, working in Italy, Spain, or Portugal, EEC hotspots where they could do better than the thirty dollars a month the average local worker earned, here, on the wrong side of the Euro-denominated border.

"No. On the contrary, we have good prospects."

She smiled. Flawless teeth, laser-cleaned and everything

It was wonderful, this brute assurance of the New Century's upper classes.

"Really?"

"We have four thousand workers, and the plant will be our biggest in the world. We make car parts. Electronic, of course."

"Of course," I nodded, and stupidly wondered aloud how such workers could afford electronic car parts for their twenty-five-year-old Ladas, on thirty dollars a month? Or was it the other way around? The meanness of these economic numbers charged these perfectly preserved Renaissance and Baroque buildings outside the hotel grounds with an air of antique desperation, if not outright menace. Sure, it's one thing to tour a "living museum," choking with dying marble angels and comic-fierce lions; it's quite another to survive in a town that is achingly picturesque and nothing else. The charms of limping daily over broken cobblestones soon wear thin. The locals were clearly tired, worn out, anemic as the ghosts of Kafka. And the Germans were out again in force, this time as the vanguard of the new world-culture.

Cut-throat efficiency, and no competition.

"Well, of course our production is for export," Bridget explains, observing me closely to see if I get her implication.

"Ah. Cheap wages." I nod, watching the four dopey waiters standing ready, at our exclusive beck and call. "Good workers?"

"Yes, the local women are quite dextrous. They must be, to do the hand-wiring." She demonstrates a bit of technical business with her fingers. "Quite reliable too. They know how to work and show up on time, usually."

"So you hire mostly women for your factory?"

"Yes, almost exclusively."

"I see. No men?"

"They're not as reliable."

Four thousand jobs, all for women. That's four thousand husbands, four thousand partners, four thousand boyfriends who will never learn the semi-skilled techniques needed at the fulcrum of our digital age. Discarded men who must continue to drive their crappy trucks, and take whatever grunt-labour comes. How do these hiring practices skew the dynamics of a culturally backward society like Ukraine's? Of course, the millworkers of the early Industrial Age in Britain and America were all women too.

And that's the point. What's changed since the days of Dickens and Dreiser?

Later that afternoon, having dined on a big tankard of 1715 Ale, a floppy Wiener schnitzel, beet borscht with sour cream, salad, and a cappuccino (all of which cost me exactly four dollars), I talk to a Bulgarian entrepreneur who is also busy setting up a manufacturing plant in Lviv. Anton hailed from Sofia. At fifty-six he is well built, looking younger despite his admitted penchant for loose women, hard drink, and long workweeks going seven days, flat out. Like most of his class he has a keen eye for pulchritude in all its forms, the Nuremburg IT specialist included.

"I set up paper plants, all over here, in Russia, Uzbekistan, Ukraine. Everybody wants paper. The government wants to own the paper that goes into their money, people with e-mails print them out all the time, and the Tetra Pak is preferred to the plastic bottle."

He smiled happily.

"You must be very strong. What's the best place to do business here, what's the worst?"

"No such thing. It depends only on making the necessary contact with the right level of people in any country. Everybody is born, dreams, suffers. Only the level of understanding that we reach is different. You must connect with those people, people who share the same level with you." He closed his eyes.

I waited while he sipped his "health-cocktail" of apple juice and white wine.

"But Moscow? Those bald men in bulletproof Mercedeses? The over-dressed women?" I pressed him anxiously. "How can you do business there?"

"By going to St. Petersburg instead!" he grinned. "In Moscow, there are not many real businessmen. They play a stupid game. Ego, brutality. I am more important than you. As they wish." Anton dismissed them all with an airy wave, and downed his drink as he watched the café's one pretty wait-ress move awkwardly between the narrow tables with a connoisseur's indulgent pleasure.

"And the women of Russia? Who do they dress for? To catch a man, or for other women? They seem, so, uh, distant to me."

"*Cold*, you mean, and you are right." His grey eyes sparkled. The white wine must have been good, he signalled for more. "They dress this way also, a game of power. To show other women, I am better than you. It has nothing to do with love, romance, the imagination. They are hard like the men, maybe even worse."

He smiled at the waitress, who smiled back. It was impossible not to admire this man; like Brendan Oh, the Korean lumber baron, Anton was playing high stakes far beyond the limits of personal necessity. It was a great game too, like tennis or chess, and I mourned the lost wisdom that this man, like so many other entrepreneurs, working alone out here on the lost margins of the provisional world, would carry off with them into the next world.

When the last deal had closed, and the final handshake had been given.

Was it Ukraine's role to be Europe's designated Mexico, left in a condition of semi-permanent want as an industrial dumping ground for over-produced lines of cheap cosmetics and a pool of raw labour? Then what about the persistent friction between settled and nomadic states? Did it still apply? Or was there an obscure intentionality to this division – a concrete

and sovereign substructure to the political play of the Old World? Did the apparent bedlam of the region's history mask an implacable order that will always resist individual human effort?

It's too awful, this smell of its new future. Same fire, strange smoke.

At the airport in Lviv, I met two women, one American, the other Canadian, who both spoke to me of the conditions of life at the margins. They had each recently travelled this hinterland between the settled West and the freebooting East. Urgently, and with great conviction, they poured out their souls to me in quick succession. Just as I was leaving the empty corridors of the continent too, as if it were their last chance to get their stories out, before the door slammed shut again, perhaps forever.

Carmen was a Canadian visiting from Winnipeg. She had married "late in life," to a young man from Lviv. She was anxious to share her impressions of the country beyond the fences of its seedy international airport.

"Well, of course, coming to a foreign culture like this is always difficult. But my husband, Vlad, wanted to see his parents again. So we came."

She patted her damp forehead, and checked the clock high on the wall of the airless waiting room. Our flight was now officially a half-hour late.

"So how was it, seeing where your husband grew up?"

"Well, I'm not sure that he *is* grown up."

She looked over at Vlad. He was pacing by the gate, a good-looking guy with a full waxed moustache, the kind favoured by baseball pitchers and successful TV mortgage brokers.

"He's younger than I."

She blushed and studied the tourist poster under the clock.

"And his family, they liked you too?"

"I don't know, they spoke in Ukrainian all the time, with Vladimir translating. So who knows what they were saying? But I guess it's the same for him in Canada. We went camping across Canada, right after we got married, and when we were in the national parks, I couldn't get him to understand that we have wild animals like bears. That he had to be careful. The concept of nature is foreign to him."

Vladimir had caught the tail end of this conversation, for he sat down and immediately said something like, "Yes, of course I do. I *love* fishing."

"Fishing. Yes." His wife nodded glumly.

"How long have you two been married?" I inquired brightly.

"Two years. We met at a ballroom dance club. In Winnipeg."

"Ballroom dance club?" I couldn't help looking at Vladimir's robust killer-moustache. It seemed to wink knowingly right back at me. "You mean like the rhumba? The foxtrot? I didn't think they still had those places."

"The samba," she sighed and blinked again. A nice, scrubbed woman. Red-haired, mixed Irish-English, some Gimli Norwegian undoubtedly thrown in for good measure. Unmarried, working hard, in a half-congealed frosty city of a million women just like her, and maybe one or two men who could put their pants on unaided. It was chancy if not tragic.

Vladimir said something else about their flight being delayed, and she ignored him.

"That poster?" She nodded towards the picture of the two customs officers, a man and a woman in blue uniforms, with that eager-to-please grin of ersatz flight attendants. The caption was in English: *Ukraine Welcomes You.*

"It's not true. That poster's a big lie. They hassle you at Immigration and again when you leave. They charge you ridiculous prices for terrible hotels.

They ignore you in the shops and serve everybody else behind you because you're a foreigner. They charge you three times more for train tickets and sometimes five times more for museums. The police stop you all the time and ask to see the registration of the car. I didn't realize how great we have it in North America until this trip."

She took a deep breath. She'd got it off her chest at last, to a stranger. Now she rolled her eyes as Vladimir regarded her, through the hazy afterburn of her critique of his homeland.

"You know," he looked up at the ceiling and squeezed his thick eyelashes in concentration. A heroic pose. You could see why Carmen had originally fallen for him. A good neck, wide shoulders, narrow hips. He knew his moves, the meaningful gesture. "It's like this."

We waited.

"We have a saying in our country: All people must go through three things in life."

"Yes?" I prodded. His wife chewed the top of her lip.

"We must go through fire, water, and . . . glory."

"Uh-huh. That's interesting," Carmen interjected and turned to me. "So what did *you* think of Ukraine?"

"Just a minute," I replied, wanting to hear what Vladimir's folk-saying was saying, exactly. "What's this fire, water, glory?"

"Ah." He sighed meaningfully. "Fire is conflict, fighting. Water is, you know, how do you say it? It falls, it is on the ground."

"Okay, whatever. What's glory?"

"Glory? Is like red metal they use in pipes."

"Copper?" I looked again at Carmen, whose red hair perhaps had something to do with this increasingly obscure allegory.

"Yes, copper." He went on: "Suppose you win a lottery, two point two million dollars, and then you do not want to be with your old friends. That is glory. It is old saying in my country."

I glanced sharply over at his wife without further pretence at discourse. She shook her head impatiently. It was clear she did not comprehend her husband of two years either.

◆

The second woman approached me outside the transit lounge, immediately after the first left.

She was bright-eyed and eager.

"I heard your conversation. So you're a writer, huh?"

"I try to be, we'll see. It's always a chancy business. And I'm so wrecked I don't know what the hell I've got. If anything."

It was true. I was toad-tired.

I looked down at my chest, studying my black shirt. It was matted with improbable food stains and salty discolourations, a body map of the dusty continent. I looked like hell. It was no wonder that the customs officers had obliged me to go through all my bags, then suddenly and anti-climatically left me alone, to repack my crusty socks and wads of now-meaningless scribbled notes. They also confiscated two pairs of scissors that had survived Chinese security, a million miles ago. Now I couldn't trim my beard in the airplane washroom, now I was obliged to stare at my gnarly face in the mirror, and splash tepid tapwater on it.

"We can sit together on the plane," she offered. "Unless you really want to be alone."

"Uh…" I watched the people in my allotted row shuffle forward, bushy-browed old Slavs with angry eyes, exuding the collective aroma of garlic and cheap rye whisky. "Okay."

She began moving passengers around in the plane while I stood there, rocking on my heels, still on Siberian time and dreaming of great flashes of blue ripping through the improbable features of my fellow travellers.

"So, I'm a photographer," she began as soon as we were settled and took off. "Vera."

The seats she'd arranged were good, the air conditioning worked. She'd even got the brawny Polish steward to bring me an iced glass of black-currant juice.

"Vera." I raised my glass as the plane hit some minor turbulence. Another blotch added to the map of Asia on my chest. "So, here were are. You're what, Ukrainian-American?"

"Exactly. From Rochester. I work for Kodak." She showed me a picture of myself in the LED of her digital camera. There I was, suddenly back in the airport, frowning at Vladimir's moustache.

"Ah, a photojournalist." I was slowly warming to her, but what was this insistent pursuit of my attention? Usually I picked the people I wanted to talk to; now the roles were reversed.

Vera had to tell me everything, all about her travels. She'd also been to Kathmandu and had lost her hotel in a cloud of ganja too. She knew her pixels and the problems of narrative structure. More, it seemed my clothes and careless attitude were the hallmarks of a fellow artist, so she happily showed me how she took photos on the sly, her camera's shutter as silent as a baby's sigh.

"I took pictures of church interiors, village garbage heaps, the contents of people's closets, washing their dirty hands under the cold pump, everything you're not supposed to."

She was panting, keen with excitement.

I recognized that zest, the joy of the huntress at the height of the chase.

"You're pretty good-looking," I said thoughtfully, not caring any more for convention, and studying her features like a sculptor. "Actually, you are quite beautiful."

"I'm forty-six."

"Really. I thought you were, like, thirty-five."

"Thanks, that's my husband's age. When we got to Ukraine, people came up to me and said, 'We'd heard you were an old rich witch, who had married one of our people, *nash ludy*. But you're young and pretty!' They marvelled."

"So it's a gossipy country?"

"Gossipy? It's the old world! Villages with no stores, donkey-carts to go off to town! Gossip, and undying memories. That's what makes it so terrible, and so fascinating. I took hundreds of pictures, and wrote down all the dreadful stories. It was great!"

"What kind of stories?"

"Well, I found out about my grandmother. She was my grandfather's second wife? They had three children, the youngest was a daughter. One day the neighbour heard awful screams. She had chopped up her daughter with an axe, then swallowed a bottle of lye. It took her three days to die."

"That was your grandmother?"

"Yes. Some versions say the daughter wanted to die, she was pregnant, and her mother accommodated her."

"Whew. Everybody's got stories like that, in their family. My father said his grandmother was tied to a pole and left to die in the field, raving, because they were terrified she had typhus, or some fever-thing, and that's how they 'treated' them in those days."

I took a deep breath. Vera seemed charmed by this account.

"See? These stories? The real thing! Raw life! What runs through us all, no holds barred, all exposed. The rest? Everything else? It's all surface, the apparent social order everybody wants, clings to with all their might. The ideal, that gossip separates us from like a rusty knife. Such bitter tragedies."

She smiled, exultant, and fingered the chrome buttons on her camera as she turned and surveyed our fellow passengers, slumped and dozing away. Me, I was never so awake as now.

"This is like what I just heard," I intoned. "Fire, water, glory."

"Glory, yes. I'll give you an example of that. In the Carpathian village I just visited, all the young girls graduating from the high school compete with each other to get the best store-bought dresses. It's a big deal; *everything* in fact. And I found out that this one family was so desperate to put on a good show, a social performance, and not let the usual ugly gossip destroy their daughter's reputation, that they sold their only cow to get money for the right dress."

"It seems like some cruel fairy tale," I ventured uneasily.

"It *is* a cruel fairy tale. Even their high heels cut their feet, make them bleed. Just like The Red Shoes. But they don't really care. Not as long as they can get to the dance."

We were passing over Poland now, or maybe it was Eastern Germany, and perhaps the sky only looked brighter because we were flying into the welcoming arms of the midday sun. Below us lay the snug farms and brisk roads of Central Europe, the logarithms of human desire offered up on blackboards and efficiently solved in years past. Everything was etched clearly in this northern light. Here was the place where the past ended, where the future was conceived, studied, and cultivated like a fruit. Museums and laboratories, the twin distilleries of the Western soul.

At the end, Central Asia seemed to me a large and vast box-store, empty of real purpose and resolve. Not a place so much as a condition, a material and even spiritual bargain-basement vacancy. A yawning gulf into which various peoples had fallen, and over the centuries conspired to survive in a kind of flamboyant, restless limbo. But their survival had come at cost. It had left them without a true history, without the protection and power of civic passion, something always more potent than their purloined monuments and colourful fruit markets. Moscow, Paris, Berlin – these were true cities, products of an electric will, many times destroyed and many times rebuilt anew. Their foundations lay not in the hilltop tombs of alleged founders, but in the collective insistence of their own people, hell-bent on reconstructing a fresh vision after each calamity.

The towns of Central Asia, on the other hand, remained furtive, provisional, concocted in stealth and kept under shrouds. Like the headless prince of Samarkand, they always went hiding off below. No amount of gold booty, no collection of kidnapped scribes or foreign planning engineers, would ever make them flourish otherwise. Perhaps we should consider the whole of the continent as one giant tomb, one we should leave undisturbed forever. For what archaeologist can ever claim his art has reached the pinnacle of perfection?

A hundred years ago the German grocer and amateur archaeologist Heinrich Schliemann jolted the world with an aggressive dispatch of Troy's buried loot; now he was vilified by official Turkish plaques that described him as a shoddy technician and vandal. What will scientists of our ever-more immaculate future say about our own primitive techniques, of the losses we will inevitably wreak? It seemed to me that ancient Asia's job was to stay where it was, buried under its weedy mounds forever. The winds blowing over its grassy steppes will keep blowing; the sun will rise over the great plain tomorrow, and the day after that too. Its annals teach us a simple truth. That of the four elements – air, fire, water, and earth – it's the wind that reigns supreme. Nothing stands in its path for long. We all bend, and fall like grass.

Epilogue: The Joke

"You like to hear Soviet-era joke?" the Bulgarian asked me.

"Okay, sure."

"Good. Man goes out drinking with his friends, gets drunk. Midnight comes, now must go home. But which way? Comes to dark apartment building. Key fits, must be his. Goes to apartment. Key fits, must be his. Goes into bedroom, takes off clothes, gets into bed beside woman. Key fits, must be his!

"In morning, man wakes up. What's this? Strange woman in bed! 'What are you doing in my apartment!' he shouts at lady. 'What are you doing in my bed!' she shouts back."

"Ha! So everything interchangeable in Soviet era? People mass-produced, too?"

"No, wait. Now neighbours angry, bang at apartment door. 'Boris! Natasha! Why you fight like this every morning?'"

"Ah, so it *was* the right apartment after all!"

"No, no, this is real joke! – Must be his, yes? – Key fits? But nothing else, so who *really* knows?"

Acknowledgements

The author wishes to express his profound gratitude to at least two hundred people, including the lady train conductor, or *deravana*, in Ukraine, who put her hand sympathetically on his shoulder one night and said, "It's not so bad. By next year, you'll barely remember her face."

In particular, many thanks to the following: in Canada, designer Steve Wilson, editor Pat Kennedy, publisher Douglas Gibson, nomadic specialist Victor Ostapchuk, and especially art historian Daria Darewych; in the U.S.A., Christine Laptuta; in Ukraine, Dana and Arkadi Ovarchenko, Myron and Rada Spolsky, and Taissa Bushnell; in Uzbekistan, Larissa and Timur Bagirova; in Kyrgyzstan, Slava Degtjarjov, Farida Kuzmenko, Marcus Bensmann of Nadmistenburo Zentral Asia, and especially Svetlana Fedina of Ak-Sai Travel in Bishkek; in Chinese Turkestan, Lin-Pao and Lui Guiqing; in Mongolia, Amarbayar Tsendbayar; and in Siberia, the Fox-Girl herself, Anastasia Vedernikova.

Thanks always to Rosi Zirger, who continues to let me get away with it; Giselle Piper, the rock; my brother, Vernon Frolick, who did everything but write the damn thing (or maybe he did, while I snored away on that endless night train to Ulan Bator); and Jasmine, Sigfrid, Adam, and Isabel. I also wish to acknowledge the financial support of the Ontario Arts Council, which in the end saved me from selling the family cow.

And finally, thanks to the band Allrise, whose album *Blues* helped me get through a few hard places with harder names.

Some Classic Works for Further Reading

Ukraine and Russia

Derevych, Daria, ed. *Spirit of Ukraine: 500 Years of Painting*. Winnipeg: Winnipeg
Art Gallery, 1991.

Dmytryshyn, Basil. *Medieval Russia: A Sourcebook, 900–1700*. New York: Holt
Rinehart, 1967.

Zenkovsky, Serge A., ed. *Medieval Russia's Epics, Chronicles and Tales*. New York:
Dutton, 1963.

Uzbekistan, Kyrgyzstan, and Chinese Turkestan

Blunt, Wilfrid. *The Golden Road to Samarkand*. London: Hamish Hamilton, 1973.

Le Strange, Guy. *The Lands of the Eastern Caliphate*. London: Frank Cass & Co., 1966.

Mogowan, Robin. *Fabled Cities of Central Asia*. New York: Abbeville Press, 1989.

Rolle, Renate. *The World of the Scythians*. Munich: Verlag C.J. Bucher, 1980.

Schafer, Edward H. *The Golden Peaches of Samarkand: A Study of T'ang Exotics*.
Berkeley: University of California Press, 1963.

Mongolia

Anon, Trans. *The Secret History of the Mongols*.

Lister, R.P. *The Secret History of Genghis Khan*. London: Peter Davies, 1969.

Maclean, Fitzroy. *To Caucauses, The End of All the Earth*. London: Jonathan
Cape, 1976.

Morgan, David. *The Mongols*. Cambridge, Mass.: Basil Blackwell, 1986.

Spuler, Bertold. *History of the Mongols: Based on Eastern and Western Accounts of
the Thirteenth and Fourteenth Centuries*. New York: Dorset Press, 1968.

About
the Author

Photo by Lucy Gray.

KATHERINE MCNAMARA is the editor
and publisher of Archipelago (www.archipelago.org), an on-line literary
journal. Her poems and nonfiction have been published in anthologies,
journals, and reviews. She lives in Charlottesville, Virginia.